Acclaim for

Sister Souljah's

No Disrespect

"This is a kinder, gentler Souljah. . . . She talks about
love, about respect, about strong families and strong
communities and 'why the movement isn't moving.'
. . . Souljah has swapped her fiery rhetoric for a stab at
healing the world."   —*Arizona Star*

"Sister Souljah's message of responsibility and self-
reliance is worthwhile for young African-Americans."
                                        —*St. Petersburg Times*

"The book—a candid page-turner full of personal
revelations and searing analysis—reveals Souljah to be
a complex, educated woman. . . . Souljah is not driven
by hatred, as her detractors have implied, but by
love—particularly a deep and abiding love for black
people."   —*Atlanta Journal*

Sister Souljah

No Disrespect

Sister Souljah was born in 1964 in New York City. She attended Cornell University's advanced placement summer program and Spain's University of Salamanca study-abroad program. She later majored in American history and African studies at Rutgers University. Her travels and lectures have taken her all over America, Europe, and Africa. In the mid-1980s, she founded, in cooperation with the United Church of Christ, the African Youth Survival Camp, located in Enfield, North Carolina, for children of homeless families. In 1992, her rap album, *360 Degrees of Power*, and video, "Slavery's Back in Effect," catapulted her to national attention. She lives in New York with her husband and son. This is her first book.

No Disrespect

Sister Souljah

No Disrespect

Vintage Books

A Division of Random House, Inc.

New York

First Vintage Books Edition, February 1996

Copyright © 1994 by Sister Souljah

All rights reserved under International and Pan-American Copyright
Conventions. Published in the United States by Vintage Books,
a division of Random House, Inc., New York, and simultaneously
in Canada by Random House of Canada Limited, Toronto.
Originally published in hardcover by Times Books,
a division of Random House, Inc.,
New York, in 1994.

The Library of Congress has cataloged the Times Books edition as
follows:

Souljah, Sister.
No disrespect / Sister Souljah. — 1st ed.
p. cm.
ISBN 0-8129-2483-5
1. Afro-American girls—Life skills guides. 2. Souljah, Sister.
I. Title.
E185.86.S67 1995
306.8'08996073—dc20 94-32161

Vintage ISBN: 0-679-76708-8

Manufactured in the United States of America

30 29 28 27 26 25 24 23 22 21

To a new era of understanding and action,

rooted in honest, open, and sometimes painful

talk between people

Contents

A Note to My Readers

I never said I was an angel. Nor am I innocent or holy like
the Virgin Mary. What I am is natural and serious and as sensitive as an open nerve on an ice cube. I'm a young black sister with an unselfish heart who overdosed on love long ago.
My closest friends consider me soft-spoken. Others say I have
a deadly tongue. And while it's true that I have a spicy attitude like most of the ghetto girls I know, I back it up with a
quick, precise, and knowledgeable mind. My memory runs
way back and I'm inclined to remind people of the things
they'd most like to forget.

Most brothers and sisters born into the confusion of
North America who emerge into positions of leadership do
so less because we're saints in the purported European sense,
and more because we have an intense ability to feel in the
African sense. We feel not only for ourselves, but for the
entire African family. We feel our people's pain, their tor-
ment, their joy, and their happiness. We feel the spirit of our
ancestors who challenge us to be more than what white society gives us as standards and limitations. So everything I
believe is said to be extreme. Yet none of my critics can deny

that conditions for African people in America and throughout the world are extreme.

No matter how backward and negative the mainstream view and image of black people, I feel compelled to reshape that image and to explore our many positive angles— because I love my own people. Perhaps this is because I've been blessed with spiritual African eyes at a time when most Africans have had their eyes poked out. I see the beauty and talent in my people in all areas of life. Our potential is infinite. I humbly thank God for this vision, because I've seen African people, young and old, overlook themselves for the span of a lifetime. I've seen beautiful, original, deep tar men, whose appearance and spirit resonate with and represent the power of God, feel small in the presence of frail, pale spiritual midgets. I've seen big-eyed hyperactive black children sit side by side in classrooms with white children who felt superior because they had a greater ability to sit still. Meanwhile, African children have a greater amount of energy that, if loved and shaped, could have led this European world out of its cold, twisted, and bellicose behavior.

So, like most ghetto girls who haven't yet been turned into money-hungry heartless bitches by a godless money-centered world, I have a problem: I love hard. Maybe too hard. Or maybe it's too hard for a people without structure—structure in the sense of knowing what African womanhood is. What does it mean? What is it supposed to do to you and for you? How do you judge a man, an African man? Then again, what is an African man? What are the criteria? What is a man supposed to do? What is his relationship to his family? What *is* a family? Is it a group of people who watch television together? Or is it a group of people who are allowed to yell at and ridicule one another, wake up the next morning, and pretend that it never happened? Is a family supposed to have a function in society? But hell, who knows what "society" is? Is society a group of people who go to work all day for pennies just so they can eat and be healthy enough to go to work tomorrow? While we neglect and sometimes even refuse to talk about all of these obvious but crucial issues, young black women and men wander around in stupidity and ignorance—glorified stupidity all dressed up in Nike sportswear and sneakers. The result: When uninformed young African males and females grow up, we become uninformed black adults who engage in relationships in which love is war.

At the root of our confusion is a condition and mentality we all have passed down to us. It is a mentality that functions with or without our permission, on both a conscious and subconscious level. We don't discuss this problem though. It is a problem rooted in a forbidden topic.

The forbidden topic is, *shh,* slavery and the behavioral, mental, spiritual, and money problems it created. You know, the little episode in history that lasted only five and a half centuries, which means only five hundred and fifty years. Which represents only twenty-two generations of black folk. Sisters sold away from sisters, brothers sold away from brothers, wives separated from husbands, many of them raped by white men who denied fathering racially mixed babies. The African languages were illegal to speak. Reading was illegal to learn. Writing was illegal, too. African gods were illegal to worship. African ceremonies were illegal to perform. African beliefs and values were life-threatening to practice. Blacks were not paid for their work. Fighting against these conditions verbally, physically, or legally could be punished by death. Loving one another meant a long life of unending pain and grief. African unity was shattered, as was the capacity for collective organization.

This is why, even today, most black folks find it hard to stick together. Even the ones who yell "African unity" the loudest find it difficult to rid themselves of an acquired inner self-hatred. This goes hand in hand with a deep-seated jealousy of one another. Almost all African folk in America find slavery a hard thing to discuss. Many avoid the subject and insist that that was then, now is now. They seem to believe that we are not still feeling its overwhelming effects, that racism is not still a powerful system and force in our lives. But, of course, slavery's consequences still affect us. That is why, to this very minute, we have such difficulty relating to one another. It is why there is a shortage today of strong, viable black men in America.

Before slavery, we as African people had understanding and answers for most of life's basic questions. Our lives, beliefs, values, and rules were deeply rooted and clearly understood and respected by our communities. We celebrated life and encouraged and loved one another. We had strong families, schools, organizations, and nations. We governed ourselves and had well-functioning economies, conducted trade, enjoyed sports, and took part in meaningful entertainment. We lived side by side with other Africans who spoke many languages and honored various traditions.

We were not without problems, of course, but we managed to work them out among ourselves.

During and after slavery, most of us Africans were stripped of the knowledge to answer even the simple questions of life. A lot of the blacks we call "educated" are so European in their ideas, approaches, and actions that they can no longer talk to their own people. Their proposed solutions to our problems are not accepted because they are alien to our adapted culture and traditions. A few of our people make a serious attempt to live a true African lifestyle, but often become so different from what blacks have been taught is "normal" that the majority of our people still cannot understand them, what they are saying, or what they are proposing we do to handle the most basic issues of life like relationships, finance, community. On the other hand, many of our people have no desire to learn the African way because the African way has been misunderstood, misrepresented, and poorly packaged by both black and white people in America. Our old African way of life is not therefore considered a successful, meaningful, or profitable way of living. Our balanced and positive African way of thinking and living therefore was pressured, beaten, raped, murdered, and legislated out of the majority of us and banished from memory.

But Harriet Tubman was different. She was a bad black soldier who remembered one of the most basic African beliefs, that "I" means "we." That if one is not safe, all are not safe. That if life is not fair and balanced, tragedy will fall on all our houses. She must have had African spiritual eyes because after she "got free," she went back to get everybody else. She could have just chilled in the North, built a white house with a white picket fence, got a light-skinned husband and died with her fingertips in a jar of skin-lightening cream. But she didn't. She marched her big black ass back through the woods a thousand miles, half in the dark, and went back and got her African brothers and sisters. And she didn't just extend a warm hand and a warm smile. She didn't tell them the dream of integration and milk and honey on the other side. She knocked on the door of slave cabins in the middle of the night with her gun cocked and said, "It's time for us to go." And, when the scared, whipped, and psychologically emasculated black men and women shook with fear refusing to go, she understood their state of mind and still put her gun to their heads and said, "Either you come with me tonight, or you die right here tonight. It's freedom or death." *Ooooh,* but was this love, or was it violence? Was this democracy or the radical ravings of an egotistical terrorist? Should the slaves have had the right to vote on the matter or should they have yielded to force?

It is with this kind of spirit and that kind of love that I live my life and offer this book, which deals with the African man and woman in America and our ability to relate to and love one another in healthy life-giving relationships. I am especially concerned with the African female in America, the ghetto girl whom nobody ever tells the definition of womanhood, or manhood for that matter. So she slips in and out of relationships, getting chopped up psychologically, spiritually, and sometimes even physically. She has been taught very little about what structure and family really means. Learning as she goes through each experience, her life is a collage of mistakes, scars, and smiles. Maybe when she's twenty-eight or so, and I mean just maybe, she figures out what being a woman really means. But she won't tell anybody 'cause nobody told her. Like a worn-out shoe, she throws on the polish and won't ever admit to the dumb shit she did because it's far too embarrassing. She can't believe she was so stupid. So she quietly hides the abortions, the stab wounds, and lies about the men she's "had." She puts a Band-Aid over the broken pieces of her heart, puts Revlon on everything else, and faces the world like perfume on shit with a fake smile and a false sense of security.

But Souljah won't hide. I won't hide because the Bible says to whom much is given, much is expected, and I already told you I was blessed with spiritual eyes. To hide would be too costly. The cycles of pain that come to young women and men from not knowing would simply continue as usual. Plus, I finally figured out what takes many people a lifetime to discover. I figured out: To love myself, to understand my value and my power, to please God, I must add to the good in the world and not the evil. This understanding makes me willing to handle the embarrassment of telling on myself. By exposing my experiences and the experiences of many of the people around me, I hope and pray that many African men and women will gain an understanding of love and life, that they will have a chance to save themselves the pain of ignorance. I hope they will be able to avoid making the same mistakes—especially our youth, who are our most precious souls. By showing you myself and my friends who come from various backgrounds, privileged and underprivileged, I'm letting parents see the real lives that their children must prepare for.

Too many parents have no idea what their daughters are doing and little concern for what their sons are doing. Too many parents assume that if a youth does well in school he or she also does well in relationships. Too many parents keep secrets, unaware that silence teaches children nothing. Too many parents avoid looking at the way they have raised their children to fail, to be destined to repeat the same old mistakes.

This is a work of nonfiction. All of the stories in this book are based on reality. Conversations held years ago are freely re-created. Their essence is as true as human memory will permit. The names as well as certain details have been changed to protect the innocent and the guilty and to avoid embarrassing anyone other than myself. I have taken some liberties with chronology, and have not hesitated in a few instances to combine into one character several aspects of different people in my life. The important thing is not who these people are, but the circumstances that each person deals with. Although these chapters are often explicit, graphic, scary, and sexual, it is critical for parents, sisters, brothers, teachers, counselors, public and urban policy developers, preachers, and politicians to know that I have written the truth about today's relationships. This is what we're up against.

Anyway, I have no apologies. At least not to any of you. Only to God. I intend no disrespect.

No Disrespect

one

Mother

In the projects, somebody can call your mother a one-legged whore who does nasty tricks for men for five dollars and she will still be the most important and influential person in your childhood. She is the only one a child can depend on for survival and to interpret life. She is the only one who will put together some type of dinner by any means necessary. Even for children who grow to hate their mothers, their hatred will be the strongest love they know. In the projects, rather than right being right and wrong being wrong, momma is right and whatever she says is wrong, is wrong.

But aren't all mothers everywhere the central figure in the eyes of a child? Mostly the answer is yes. But for children in the projects the answer is even more so. The difference is the "extreme complication of circumstance." The reason: Most children in the projects don't have a father to speak of. In the projects, the prospects and opportunity provided through education are almost nothing, since no real effort is made to educate people properly or culturally. In the projects, the escapes and outlets created by money are eliminated because there is no "intelligent finance"—only haphazard consumerism. In the projects, the creativity and will to survive and to overcome horrible circumstances is usually destroyed because there are no "freedom spaces" where a child can go to think and expand the mind. In the projects, there are often no trees, no flowers, no understanding of agriculture, and no more than makeshift playgrounds.

Of course, against the odds, there are a few people who make it. What about them? And what is meant by "making it"? Usually, they are the people who managed to escape down a slim corridor of chance through the strength of their mothers—mothers who were able by piecemeal work, faith, prayer, or prostitution to control or barter their lives in exchange for the partial freedom of their babies.

But physically escaping the projects is not one-fourth of the battle anyway. It's breaking the cycles of spiritual, emotional, intellectual, mental, and cultural death that even a brief stay in the projects can mean. It is struggling to understand basic concepts—like who you are as an African male or female. What is a family and how is it formed solidly before the penis and vagina cause reckless destruction to life and organization? What is a thought? What is a mind? How do we teach a mind to think when so many have become comfortable with not thinking? What is the relationship between your talents and skills and business? How and where do you get information when no information seems available? And most of all, how do you not end up consciously, or subconsciously, a whore, literally or figuratively a whore like your momma?

Now, don't be alarmed by the word "whore." It can be applied to anyone who engages in an activity that they don't believe in, that they don't gain from, don't want to participate in, feel violated by, but are forced to do by the limitations of their own mind, the limitations of society, or both in order to survive. A whore can use the mind, body, or spirit as a source of small or large income.

I was born in the Bronx, the second child of my mother and father's marriage. My father was a hardworking man and always had a great love for people. He was generous almost to the point of irresponsibility. After listening to any neighbor's sad story, he might find himself giving away half of his paycheck with no concern or expectation of ever getting his money back. He believed in family but resisted his own father's definition of what it should be. His father had two wives and two sets of children for his own pleasure and didn't ask anybody's permission or acceptance. My father didn't want to repeat the suffering, pain, anger, and lack of parental guidance that he grew up with. But my father drew his understanding of what it meant to have a family from television. He wanted to be a man's man. He believed that it was solely the man's responsibility to bring home the bacon and rule the household. He believed that the woman must work hard at being beautiful; that she make her husband as comfortable as a king in his own castle; that she perfect her skills of housecleaning and cooking and have a lot of babies. After all, he figured, she had all day to correct any flaws in her appearance. Most of all, he demanded that she be fully dependent upon him. No driving, traveling alone, taking classes. No need to think too hard or waste time worrying her pretty little head with survival or business, matters that were properly the province of the man. He must be the source of her money, love, sex, and strength, and the center of her existence. My father was six foot five inches tall, brown-skinned, and had a handsome baby face.

My mother was the exact personification of my father's dreams. In fact, one might think that they had spent their childhoods watching the same white American television programs. She was unquestionably the most physically and facially beautiful woman in any room she entered. Her skin was rich brown and flawless. Her eyes were almond shaped and seductively situated. She was an excellent cook and fully prepared to serve her man. Indeed, she was an enthusiastic and willing student for my father's philosophy of dependency because she herself had been abandoned by her father. A West Indian black man, her father had left when she was only nine months old. He returned eight years later to get some pussy from her mother in exchange for taking the "family" out for a rare, good restaurant meal. After they all burped, he was never to be heard from again. So my mother grew up with no direction. After she'd been deserted, her mother had to work so hard just to survive that she had no time to share what little knowledge she had about women, men, and life. Therefore, my mother was comforted by the notion of my father wanting to fully possess her.

So she fell right into place. She had three children by my father. She stayed home all day keeping house, watching soap operas, exercising with Jack LaLanne, preparing meals and waiting for her hardworking husband to return home after conquering the world.

But this apparent paradise soon collapsed. My father was discovered by on-the-job physicians to have the disease that is called epilepsy. He was immediately fired from his long-time job as a truck driver. His employer said that the possible "blackouts" that can accompany the disease were too dangerous for the trucking industry to risk. After losing his job, my father became deeply depressed. He had never liked the idea of his family receiving "benefits or entitlements." He went on job interview after job interview only to discover that a black man has a hard and sometimes impossible task of finding and keeping a job. A sick black man has even less of a chance. My father's conviction of what a man must be and do quickly collided with the reality of his unemployment and was further complicated by his having a socially and economically unacceptable disease. Soon his mental health began to erode. Through it all, he kept my mother from working, believing that, were she to do so, it would be a direct insult to his manhood. He grieved severely as benefits ran out and he could no longer provide for his wife and family. My mother, just twenty-two years old and utterly dependent on him, became frightened by his unraveling self-esteem and what seemed like senseless ramblings. She fled to the projects with her three children. She had no money, no high school diploma, and few skills. She was, however, unmistakably beautiful, and she would use her looks if she thought she had to. She divorced my father. He, however, did win the right to see us on the weekends when he was not out "bugging."

One weekend when I was about four years old, my father came to take my brother and me to the park. It was so far away that we would have to take the subway. On the train he talked endlessly about how we were not to trust anybody. He told us that we lived in the projects now and we would have to be a lot smarter than we were required to be before. We, of course, were normal children and were simply excited to see him and were eager to get on the swings. He rambled on while we blotted his words out. When we got to the park we went wild playing on everything in sight. Then, my father called me over and asked me if I wanted to get on the slide. I happily and anxiously said, "Yes, Daddy." I climbed to the top of the slide and said, "Daddy, I'm gonna come down backwards, you catch me, okay?" He said, "Come on, baby, come to Daddy!" With my full force and weight, I zoomed down the slide and came crashing onto the ground, causing my head to bleed. I started crying and screaming and asked my father: "Daddy, why didn't you catch me?" He smiled at me, doctored my wound, and simply said, "I told you not to trust anybody."

My father's visits became irregular. He went from representing one we loved, who disciplined and instructed us, to being something of a loved and favorite clown arriving on intermittent weekends with guilt-filled eyes and broken dreams, filling us up with endless chocolate bars, Superfly movies, hot dogs, and toys. On the last evening that I was to see him for a while, he arrived with a picture of a crying clown. He told us to hang it on our wall, and when we looked at it, we should think of him, because that's "who I am."

The projects were an endless maze in which a wrong turn could result in a little bleeding, a "casual rape," a critical beatdown, or even death. It seemed the frustration level of each person was based on how many years they had been trapped within those concrete walls. The longer they had lived in the projects, the higher their frustration, and the colder their attitude. We soon learned why. The first thing we had to acquaint ourselves with was the environment: tall brown buildings, unofficial garbage dumps, no parks, roaches, rats, and mice. There were hundreds of mothers and thousands of children. There was rarely any conversation about fathers because between the two buildings in the immediate area where we lived, there were only five families that had a father living in the house. Yet and still, there were men. Men on the corners. Men on benches. Men in the lobbies and men in the parking lots fixing broken-down cars. But these men seemed like "rentals." They spent a certain amount of time in several different apartments doing everything they could to make it seem like they were not there to stay or even to be a permanent part of a family. They had distant relationships with the children of whichever woman they were screwing, never being called "Daddy" or "Father." Usually children called them by their first name—names like "Rob" or "Ted," or in the best of cases "Uncle Rob" or "Uncle Ted." These men's limited engagements with their children's mothers were never taken seriously on a conscious level by the children. This was fine, of course, because that way the children openly showed their disrespect and disinterest in any of his rules or regulations, and the man got to do what he wanted to do anyway: get the pussy, maybe a little cash, and don't have to say shit to the little bastards that weren't his anyway. These men were rentals; like rent-a-cars they were temporary, expensive to keep, and likely to break down anytime, anywhere. They were rentals because they really belonged to someone else. In fact, most of these men had children of their own elsewhere in the ghetto. But they had long since fled that responsibility. The common thing was that these men were unemployed and spent most of their time standing around talking to one another, decorating the neighborhood.

When my mother moved in, there was talk among these men. She was considered the finest piece of ass they had seen in a "good long while." They wondered where she came from and what fool had turned her loose. They were shocked that she had three children, something they learned by watching her walk with us hand in hand, in and out of stores and welfare agencies. They said she looked like she was only sixteen years old with her booming body and tight little pussy. Soon a wager was set on who would fuck her first. When we walked down the street they would call out to her, "Hey, baby, give me some of that jelly!" But my mother was what the women in the projects called "stuck up." This simply meant that she hadn't been around long enough to lose her pride, that her spirit was not yet broken. It meant that she didn't sit around gossiping with them and telling all her business. She wasn't smoking reefer or shooting drugs and she wasn't giving up pussy. The impact of my mother's ways could be felt by the men in the area, who were used to getting "same-day service." It caused them to increase the bet and made the prize seem that much sweeter.

The women in the projects were peculiar. The attention my mother got from the fools made them hate her. They said, "Who does she think she is? You on welfare just like us, bitch! Think you too damn good?" These women had fully accepted the lifestyle and conditions of the projects. They accepted men as rentals. They gave up their "stuff" freely with few expectations or demands. When one of them got her teeth knocked out by the man she was temporarily screwing, she would run and tell the other women in the building. They would tell her why she deserved the ass whooping and then one of them would start screwing the same man. The conversations among these women ranged from the new outfit with matching shoes they'd put on layaway at the department store to who had a weave, whose hair was real, who was the father of so-and-so's baby, and what new entertainer they wanted to "git wit." The deepest the conversations ever seemed to get was whether or not welfare had cheated one of them out of money that month or how they had gotten over in their check for ten or fifty dollars.

You can imagine the children of these mothers. We learned young that people were considered worthless. Kids fought that image by dressing up. Clothes were the only things that seemed accessible on a dead-end budget. No one owned cars or houses or bank accounts. Any extra money went toward buying leather, suede, sneakers, expensive denim outfits, and second-rate jewelry sold to us as fourteen- and eighteen-karat gold. The mind-set was day-to-day; no one planned for or expected anything in the future. Children quickly learned that the projects were divided into camps. There were the good kids whose mothers feared for their lives and kept them locked in or on a highly supervised schedule. There were the kids whose mothers were absolutely crazy; as a result they raised themselves in the environment and beat up and preyed on the good kids for basic survival. Then there were the average kids who knew the rules, grew a hard exterior, didn't want to fight, but would if they had to. Sometimes they won and sometimes they lost, but they knew a good fight was better than being a permanent victim. They played hard and had street laws of loyalty. They didn't like cops, took no great interest in school, and didn't think long-range about careers, business, or growing old.

We also had to adjust to the welfare system and its bureaucrats. They wanted to know everything, and I mean *everything.* Not just your address and Social Security number and birthdate. They would ask my mother if she had a boyfriend. And if she did, did he give her any money so they could deduct it from the extremely small amount of money they were giving her each month. They wanted to know if she received any gifts from men or from her family. If, for example, she received a toaster as a gift, she had to report it to the agency so they could deduct its value from her welfare check. The welfare agency would authorize a social worker to roam freely through your apartment to report any "findings." Findings could include men, extra toys, new furniture, et cetera. Everything was organized to make it clear that they as the government were your parents and you, as "dependents," were children. The welfare workers acted as though they were paying your monthly benefits out of their own pockets. They became indignant if you asked questions about your case or if you challenged any of the information they were giving to you.

The services were designed to make us feel inferior. For instance, some days we had to stand on line starting at eight o'clock in the morning (òr until they got ready to open) until four or five in the afternoon, merely to receive two blocks of cheese, butter, and two big steel cans of peanut butter. When you finally got up to the front desk you would be asked a whole new round of personal questions in front of what seemed like scores of other people. (There were no private offices.) The welfare worker would talk loudly, to embarrass you. If you responded softly, as though you wanted some privacy or confidentiality, she would broadcast your responses by repeating them loudly. For medical services you had to spin the roulette wheel and wait for a clinic appointment. You arrived at 8:00 A.M. to stand on line, even though you had an appointment, and it was best to plan to spend your entire day in the clinic.

The basic assumption of welfare was that since you were on it, you of course had time to stand on lines, wait in lobbies, and stay at home waiting for social workers, simply because you obviously had nothing else to do. Self-improvement in the welfare system at this time was unknown. For instance, if you were on welfare and you found a job, you had to immediately report it to the welfare department or risk prosecution as a welfare fraud. If you were foolish enough to go the honest route, the welfare agency would take away your rent subsidy and raise the rent to full market value. They would cancel your Medicaid so your children no longer qualified for subsidized health services. They would cut your food stamps in half and slash your monthly benefit check.

This strikes some people as fair, since you are now employed and ought to be able to pay your own way. Here's the catch. If you are on welfare and you get a job, usually it is minimum-wage employment with no benefits. Therefore, when you report your new job to the agency and they cut and scale down your benefits, you now earn less money from your job than you would have if you had simply stayed home doing nothing. So, to make ends meet, you have to quit your job. Or, say you get a decent job with a decent wage above the minimum. You report it to welfare and one of your children gets a common illness like chicken pox. The private medical fees will still cost more than the decent wage you earn. So, in fear of medical bills and wanting to protect those services for your children, you quit your job to regain Medicaid.

Or say you decide you've met a good man. You would like to get married and try again at having a family. You must report it to welfare and they will cancel everything because you are not allowed to be married and receive welfare benefits. This policy perversely encourages single-mother households, as women are asked to choose between their man and the financial survival of their children. It destroys any impulse of self-improvement. It is a system designed to fail.

It was not long before my older brother and I learned the rules of our new life in the projects: We must stick together at all times. We must all go downstairs together and all come back upstairs together. No matter how much fun we were having with our friends, we were not to lose track of our youngest sister or we would be beaten. If anybody put their hands on us we were to all jump in and beat them senseless. If one of us got beaten up and the other one did not help, we would all be beaten when we got home. When we were sent to the corner candy store (where everybody around bought their overpriced groceries), we were to take the money, hold it tightly and securely. If we were to lose the money or have it taken from us, we would all be beaten. We were to talk to no strangers. We were not to get into anyone's car or even approach the window. No visiting any friend's apartment without permission. We were to stay off the roof and out of the cellar. We were not allowed to play in "the dumps" (a local toxic waste dump the neighborhood children used for a playground). We were not to let anyone put their hands on our "private parts." If they tried to, we were to tell Mommy immediately. We were not to sit on anyone's lap, not even Daddy's. We were never to tell anyone our personal business no matter who they were. If anybody called the house we were to say, "My mother is not available right now," as opposed to "She's not home." We were not to tell anyone where she was or when she would return. Just take a message and hang up the phone. When the welfare lady comes, no talking. Show good manners, stay in your room, and if she comes in, answer no questions. If anybody tried to trick us, we were to say, "I don't know, you'll have to ask my mommy." It became obvious to us that we were living in a war zone.

My mother thought church would be a DMZ, and she made sure we attended every Sunday. I found it confusing. While it did challenge me to think about many things that I would not have ordinarily thought about, the teachings just never added up. We went to a nondenominational Christian church. I was told that nondenominational meant that everyone was welcome and that titles like Baptist, Catholic, or Methodist were not important—just the universal belief in God. There was no dress code. The church was "come as you are or as you please." We were told that God loved us no matter what we wore. My great-grandmother was the pastor. My great-grandfather was dead. Nobody grieved too much for him, however, because they said that he gave my great-grandmother fourteen children and left her to raise them alone while he was out romancing the young skirts. He ended up in a mental institution and many people said he got what he deserved. My great-aunts and uncles were all in either their mid-thirties or their forties and were the deacons and deaconesses. (There were also people from the surrounding Bronx community.) Most of them were either having marital problems or divorced. Most of them were having serious problems raising their children and keeping them healthy and alive.

I remember that one male cousin died of an overdose of heroin. Another was locked up for rape. Yet another was shot in the head and murdered because of a drug deal gone sour. (His father buried him in a five-hundred-dollar suit with hundred-dollar bills clutched in his hand.) I had several female cousins who were single mothers, each of their children having different fathers. I had an aunt who, after a brutal marriage, sent her children off to college and moved in with her "woman," never to return to the life of heterosexuality. Most of the other women in the family were physically attractive and were surviving financially by keeping a steady flow of boyfriends as a source of cash.

Even though these problems affected most everyone in the congregation, we never discussed any of these things in church. Nor did we talk about the definition of family and how to keep one together, the cause of difficult times in the world, racial problems, or how to develop one's mind intellectually and spiritually to overcome these difficulties. Instead, we were told simple generalities. We were read scriptures that seemed to have little to do with life in modern times. If anything went wrong, it was because of "the devil," or because you were listening to the voice of the devil. But I wanted to know just who the devil was. How does the devil get his power and maintain it so well? How do we recognize him? How do we recognize his work? How do we tell the difference between good and evil? What is the criteria?

We were told that there was no need to be angry about anything or with anybody because God loved us and he unselfishly gave his only son, Jesus, to the world. God forgives, so too must we not be angry; we must be a forgiving people. We were told that Jesus was nailed to the cross and he wasn't angry, so why should we complain about our "little bit of suffering"? We were taught to "Do unto others as you wish others would do unto you." This made us peaceful. But when we were peaceful, we were still the targets of violence. In answer to that violence, we were taught that "two wrongs don't make a right." So we were encouraged to give love and accept hate and bad treatment in return. To seal the argument we were told that Jesus turned the other cheek while fighting evil and injustice. We were urged to count our blessings and look toward the bright side of things.

So instead of banding together and discussing and developing a plan to save the broken lives and spirits of the shattered families in the congregation, we got together at the big houses of a couple of wealthy uncles who had "succeeded," and there we celebrated family, life, birthdays, et cetera. At these "celebrations," however, there were alcoholic drinks, there were reefer sets for the get-high crews of aunts and uncles, card games and gambling—you name it. You got to meet the new female interests of the men and the new male interests of the women. One year my uncle brought a white girl as his date. She wore a see-through dress and no panties and screwed whichever uncle paid her attention at the time. Everyone's children ran around the house and played in the backyard.

I saw the difference between what adults said and what they did. My confusion grew, and church became more of a ceremony or empty performance than something that could be taken seriously. Nevertheless, I began a private relationship with God. I said my prayers every morning and every night. I thanked God for life and for seeing a new day, something my great-grandmother had taught me to do. I also had deep discussions with God about all of the emotions I felt. The most overwhelming one was fear. I explained to him that living in the projects was scary to me and that each and every day I feared for the life of my mother. I told how much I hated the men on the corner with their sexual comments and fantasies. I talked to God about the drug problem and how it seemed like every other person was shooting heroin into their arms. The drugs stole their minds, robbed their physical beauty, denied them their future. I said how I knew that the fruit drinks made for children at block parties and public events were being spiked to get more drug addicts and boost drug sales. I confided that I feared that one of the junkies would enter my room at night and inject me with some heroin and make me go crazy. That's why I slept on top of my arms even though it gave me cramps. We discussed my nightmares that shook me awake. Above all, I told God how much I loved my mother, brother, and my little sister and asked Him to protect them from "the bad men." I prayed for strength, survival, protection, and life, and for better times. In exchange for my prayers being answered, I offered God my faith and obedience, and promised to be good and work hard always in His name.

Soon one of these men from the corner was in my house. His name was Tyrone, Ty for short. He was considered the "slickest nigga" around. Since we all lived in a constant state of fear, I sensed my mother felt more security in the fact that he had "the juice" around the neighborhood. He told the drug addicts to skip our apartment when they were out robbing houses. He put the word out on the streets that he was "fucking" my mother so don't nobody mess with "his shit." My mother could now walk down the street and none of the men would say anything disrespectful for fear that Ty would punish them.

Like most men around the way, he usually came by in the evening. Even though he had no job, he ran his schedule like he had one. He felt extra large about conquering my mother's booty, since it had been on the block so long and no other guy got to "tax" it. The scary thing to me, however, was that he wore a green army coat. I had come to fear all men in green army coats, and when I'd see them in the building I'd run. If one of them came into our apartment, I'd scream.

One night he came while I was still awake. My mother asked him to take off the coat and leave it in the front closet, explaining that her daughter was "oversensitive" and had a "complex" about army coats. He agreed to take it off that night but added that the first time would be the last time. He told my mother he would have to have a talk with me. Before I went to bed he called me into the living room to ask me why I screamed when I saw green army coats. I said, "Because everybody I see wearing them is crazy." He said, "How do you know they crazy?" I said, "'Cause of what they be doing." He laughed and said, "What they be doing?" "Talking to themselves, singing real loud when nobody's listening, nodding out and falling down, or just looking crazy like they gonna hurt somebody." "Why do they do that?" he asked. "I don't know," I said. "Don't tell me you don't know why. That's too easy." By now my eyes were filled up with tears. I looked him back in the face with a blank stare. He said, "All right, I'll tell you what. You can go back to your room and you think about why they do the things they do. The next time you see me, I want you to tell me your answer. Life ain't got no rewards for people who don't know how to think. Not even little girls." I dropped my head and turned away, whispering good night to my mother.

Two days later Tyrone came to visit my mother again. He called me out of my room as soon as he arrived. He kept his army coat on and when I saw it I took a deep breath and started to back down the hallway. "Come here!" he said. I looked at my mother wide-eyed as she stood helplessly behind him. I searched her eyes for support. She looked sympathetic, but she made it clear with her eyes that she was no longer in charge. He repeated himself. "Come here." I inched toward him slowly. "Here, touch my sleeve." I looked at my mother because she had already told me no touching. She nodded, as if to say "Yes, go ahead." I touched it. He said, "This is a coat, only a coat. It's green and it's made out of material. It has no arms, no legs, and it cannot hurt you. Do you understand?" "Yes," I replied, almost in a whisper. "Now, what's the answer to my question?" he asked. "Because they don't say their prayers." He laughed, and said, "What?" I felt betrayed by his laughter, but I explained, "The men in the green army coats act crazy because they don't say their prayers." He said, "Who told you that?" I replied, "Nobody." He said, "Well, where did you get it from?" I said, "Mommy said if you say your prayers, God will protect you. But if you don't say them, you could lose your way and go crazy." "When did she tell you that?" he asked. "When we lived at the other house," I said softly.

"Here, step into my office." He pointed toward the kitchen and pulled out a chair. I sat down. "The black men in the army coats are men who came home from the Vietnam War." I didn't know what he was talking about. He went on to explain that there had been a war in a faraway place. The black men I saw in the green coats had fought in the war. They had seen a lot of ugly things like blood and death. He said they had killed other men, women, and children. They didn't want to do it, but they were ordered to do it, otherwise they would be put in jail or even killed. He said that the people in charge of America had sent these black men to go fight for them. It was against the law for them to refuse to go. He said the people in charge were white punks who sent strong black men to go and fight their battles. He compared the people in charge to the "punks around the way who talk a lot of shit and can't back it up when it's time to throw down. So they run and get somebody else to fight their battles for them." He said the black men in the green army coats fought hard for the "white government punks" and some of them had even lost their legs, arms, and lives. When the ones who made it out returned, the white punks who were in charge, but always hated them anyway, wouldn't give them jobs, pay them money or respect.

"So," he said, "some of them are crazy because they killed other human beings in Vietnam. Some of them are crazy because they couldn't find jobs to support their own selves or family when they got home. Some of them went crazy because they saw their own friends get killed. Some of them are crazy because they on drugs." He then looked me in the eye and said, "But no matter how crazy they are, always remember the black team is your team. That's all you have to work with. That doesn't mean you can always trust the black team. But better than being scared of the people on your own team is being smart. Smart people," he said, "can always outslick the dumb ones and stay alive." He added that if you were dumb and didn't know how to think, you would always be beaten up and picked on by the big dumb guys.

Then, he said, he wanted to make a deal with me. "Go and get your brother." I went and got my brother. We stood in front of Tyrone. He said he would give me and my brother $1.50 per week if we both learned how to think and be smart 'cause he don't like being around no dummies. He said everyday we had to try to read the first three pages of the New York *Daily News,* plus two comic strips, "Beetle Bailey" and "Blondie." Then on Wednesday nights, he would give us a puzzle to solve. If we could solve the puzzles, or "brain teasers," then on Fridays we would get paid. If we couldn't solve the puzzles it meant that we still didn't know how to think so we wouldn't get a dime. We both smiled, accepted the deal, and ran to our rooms.

For the next six or seven months, I was as happy when Tyrone came over as my mother was. So was my brother. Ty taught him how to "outslick" the bully Dario, who lived downstairs from us and always took little kids' money. He taught him how to fight, how to walk, and how not to look like a "sucker." Some of the fear that gripped us slipped away. There were things that confused me, though, about Tyrone. He seemed like a good person but some nights I would wake up real late and hear my mother screaming. She wouldn't be saying words I could understand, just making noises. Sometimes I would hear her laugh. But then sometimes it sounded like she was crying. A few times I'd hear his voice cry out, too. I didn't want to think that he was hurting her because I didn't like thinking that way about him. But my love for my mother was more important to me. Finally, after listening to their noises, I got out of my bed, went to my mother's closed door, and knocked. "Mommy, are you okay?" She would say, "Yes, I'm fine. Go back to bed." After I did this every night for about a week, my mother became very aggravated with me and soon she said, "Get back in that bed and don't get up or knock on my door again!" So I stopped getting up but I would still listen to the noises that confused me.

One night things were different. I heard banging on the front door and Tyrone screaming, "Come on, Peaches, open the door, open the door." My mother, who I could tell was standing inside our apartment on the other side of the door, was crying. "No!" she screamed, "you're high! I have children in here. You stay out there." Tyrone refused to leave. He banged on the door all night till early the next morning. I lay in my bed paralyzed with fear and decided that night that whatever this thing called "love" that Mommy and Daddy, and then Tyrone and Mommy, had, I was not going to have. I mean I would always love my mother and my family but not no man-woman love. It was all too painful and I don't like no pain.

If we were using musical instruments to describe what went on for the next few months, we would need the entire orchestra. We would use flutes to define the happy times when me and my brother were learning and laughing or when Tyrone took us all to the movies. We would use big bass drums to describe Tyrone's "mind attacks" and fits of anger when he would wake up screaming because Mommy said sometimes he forgot that the Vietnam War was over. We would use saxophones to signify our pain and tears as we cried over broken promises and strange behavior. We'd really need an electric guitar to play as Tyrone tiptoed around our apartment stealing the money my mother had saved to go Christmas shopping. Pianos to play soft music as me, my brother, sister, and mother sat under the empty Christmas tree on Christmas day. The bass violins to give you the sound of our hearts dropping when Tyrone would appear after long disappearances. A clarinet to play as he snaked his way back into all of our hearts.

And, while the projects enveloped us and our home life confused us, our Italian-, Irish-, German-, and Jewish-born schoolteachers who lived nowhere near our neighborhoods filled us up with Kool-Aid and chocolate-chip cookies, singing "B–I–N–G–O–and Bingo was his name–O!" While the sugar raced through our bloodstreams, a classroom full of black children bounced off the walls and ceilings. The teachers shouted over our voices, "Why don't you all just sit down and keep still?" When we finally calmed down, Mrs. Pelitary or Mrs.

Greenwall would read us a story about Cinderella, or tell us how George Washington never told a lie.

One day my mother announced that she was pregnant and not about to get an abortion like the other "tramps" in the building. After all, how could they feel life in the belly and voluntarily snatch its breath away? My brother and sister and I went through all the stages of the pregnancy along with my mother. Tyrone, however, checked in and checked out. By the fifth month, rumors spread around the neighborhood that Ty was now "fucking" Miss Lucy. She was the new light-skinned cutie on the seventh floor. My mother paced around the apartment mumbling about how she wasn't gonna put up with Vietnam flashbacks, malaria, breakdowns, lying, stealing, and now Miss Lucy upstairs. Later that night she broke up with Tyrone or, should I say, through his actions he broke up with her. Whatever the case, while my mother cried in the living room, I cried in the bedroom because when he left her, he left me and her pain was mine, too.

Word flew around the neighborhood that Ty and Peaches were through after almost two years. And even though my mother was pregnant, men still found her desirable. We therefore were to meet a few more men from the neighborhood, but we had learned not to take them seriously. They were just rentals, passing through. As my mother brought life into the world, a baby girl, the projects spit up death. Yolanda, the woman upstairs, stabbed her man in the heart several times and killed him. Everyone said he came home drunk all the time and would beat her ass good. Well, this time she wasn't going for it so she fought back in a defense that ended in murder. I tried to understand the murder of somebody I knew personally. I tried to picture it in my head. Night after night I'd see my version of the scene and it all made me feel sick and empty. So I'd talk to God about death and what it meant and why it happened. The people around me seemed not to mind, though. Or if they did they didn't show it. Yolanda was out of jail in a jiffy and walking around smiling and partying like nothing happened. A month or two later, a friend of mine named Cedric stabbed and killed another little boy over a kick ball. Cedric was seven years old.

Around this time, my mother started dating a policeman from the area. He was six-feet-tall and about 190 pounds. He was the new "chief of security." At night they would talk about how bad the neighborhood was getting and how we needed to get out of the projects. But he was in the middle of a divorce and had no money. It wasn't long before word was out on the street that "Slick Tyrone had gotten played out by a cop." In answer to the gossip, Tyrone put out the word that he wanted his baby and was coming to get it. The cop, who people called Big Joe, then made it clear to everyone in the neighborhood that he was licensed to carry a gun and wouldn't hesitate to use it. He told my mother privately, however, that he was smart enough to know that "niggas are crazy" ('cause he himself was a "crazy nigga"), so he planned to get my mother out of the projects after what had been a wild five years for us.

In June, at the end of third grade, a U-Haul truck arrived at my school. My mother appeared at my classroom and grabbed my arm. She had my brother and two sisters with her. She stuffed us in the truck. I cried and said my books and stuff were still inside my school desk and where are we going anyway. She said, "Shut up! No questions today."

We ended up at my grandmother's house in Teaneck, New Jersey, where she lived with her second husband, a longshoreman. My grandmother was not pleased to have the house that she spent her life working to put a down payment on invaded by her single daughter and four rowdy children. She let my mother know that this was "temporary housing," very temporary. So my mother shifted us back and forth between Big Joe's apartment in New York and my grandmother's house. When my mother tried to transfer to the welfare department in Bergen County, it was more than difficult. The policy was that if people had extended families or lived with relatives, their families should take care of them. This policy ignored the fact that while my grandmother was a member of the "new black middle class," she was living from paycheck to paycheck and had very little money in the bank. Not only was she not capable of supporting or supplementing the income of my mother and her four children, she was interested in receiving money for rent and the additional utility expenses.

Teaneck was different. There were blacks who owned houses. There were trees, grass, parks, smiling faces. The fear that had gripped my heart every day for five years in the projects began to slowly ebb. But there were also attitudes in Teaneck. I remember my mother sent me to the store for some milk for the baby and gave me some food stamps. When I arrived at the counter to pay the white cashier, I handed her the food coupons and she screwed up her old wrinkled face and said, "What is this?" I stood silent for ten seconds, not even understanding what she was really asking since I had always bought food with the stamps.

Then I said, "They food stamps!" She reached beneath the counter, pulled out a small silver bell, and started ringing it loudly calling for the manager. All the black people behind me started huffing and puffing and sucking their teeth. Eventually the manager came and said, "We can take these stamps but we cannot give you cash for change." "Well, you can't keep my change!" I said in my best New York style. He then handed me small square pieces of paper and plastic chips and said I could purchase food from this market with these papers and chips. They looked like play money to me. I grabbed my stuff and walked away embarrassed. When I got home, my mother said I shouldn't be embarrassed. But later on, I noticed she always sent me to the store instead of going herself.

We lived in Teaneck for the next year and a half. The strange thing was that even though our physical environment had improved, the economic and psycho-spiritual conditions of life did not. In fact, because we were surrounded by both black and white working and professional people, our impoverished condition became even more apparent to us. Because we were living in my grandmother's house, we had the opportunity to act like we were doing okay. The fact still remained, however, that the house, the neighborhood, and none of the material things belonged to us.

My mother got a job at the telephone company, working from four o'clock in the afternoon until midnight. This left the responsibility of raising my infant sister to me. I did everything from preparing bottles, changing diapers, laundry, bathing, and cooking to talking and rocking her to sleep at night. I also had to watch my other little sister, who was full of energy and mischievousness. We stopped going to church regularly because my mother said it cost too much money to cross the George Washington Bridge. Besides, we rarely had access to a car that worked. When I asked about the churches in Teaneck my mother said I had to understand that these churches were uppity and we didn't have enough clothes or money to attend them. Their attitudes were not like Great-grandma's church and they would make us feel uncomfortable and unwelcome. So I continued to say my prayers personally to God. On some weekends, Big Joe would come and pick us up and take us back to New York. We would stay in his building where we played with our black and Latino friends while Mommy and Joe stayed upstairs.

Eventually, my mother and Big Joe found a two-family house for rent in Englewood. Big Joe, however, had been laid off from the police force without pay during an internal investigation of an incident for which he was eventually cleared. Big Joe was a tyrant, and my brother and sisters all hated him. He wanted everything to revolve around him. He demanded that we automatically agree with him—not because he was right but because he was "in charge." So we plotted to get rid of him. One day we painted the toilet seat black and didn't tell him. He sat on it and got a paint ring around his butt. We laughed so hard we nearly cried. The fact of the matter, however, was that he helped to get rid of himself. He was so insecure and possessive of my mother that he didn't want her to take night courses at the local community college. But my mother, having experienced my real father, told me to never—no matter what—allow a man to interrupt your work or education. She had earned her high school diploma since her divorce. She made it clear that Big Joe had better stop nagging her about her enrollment. Suspended from the job he loved, Big Joe was reduced to driving taxis and doing odd jobs. Eventually the frustration and differences in opinions about the way things should be done led him and my mother to part ways. (We, of course, headed back to welfare since he was no longer there to pay his half of our meager existence.)

I started school in Englewood halfway into my fifth-grade year. On my first day of class I was told by the other children that where I lived on Spendel Avenue was the cheapest and lowest block in Englewood. They said I would be tested by the teachers and placed in classes based on how dumb or smart I was. They said that everybody from Spendel was dumb, so I'd probably go to special education with "the rest of them." I, as a little black child, was shocked to see little black children and little white children joining together to jump on top of me. In New York such a thing would never happen. The blacks stuck with the blacks. The Puerto Ricans stuck with the Puerto Ricans. The whites stuck with the whites. The only exception to this rule was when the Puerto Ricans and the blacks united to fight the whites. These Englewood kids, however, had no concept of color or black unity, and, for reasons that eluded me, these little black children thought that they were the same as the little white children.

It soon became obvious to me that they were not the same. Only black children filled up the special education classes. Instead of reading books they played checkers, watched television, beat each other up—all with the teacher's permission, supervision, and indifference. The term "special education" was, in fact, synonymous with the black children who were to be written off as uneducable by the time they were eleven or twelve. The intermediate classes were mostly white with only a few blacks. The top and "most intelligent" classes were almost entirely white and had no more than a handful of black students in each discipline whether it was English, science, mathematics, or history.

As this little integrated goon squad taunted me, I remained silent. I remember thinking how backward and different they were from the kids I had known in New York. Inside I was not worried about what they were saying because I knew I would be placed in the top classes in every area. Ever since I was four years old my mother had made sure I had my public library card. I knew, as any New York street kid would know, that I was more mature. I wasn't even ten yet and already I had experienced two murders, several drug overdoses, mental illness, danger, and poverty. I could cook any of two dozen different meals, meats, vegetables, salads, and desserts. I could take care of babies down to the most minute detail. I could think fast, and felt I could mentally outmaneuver most adults. I could care for an entire family while maintaining the illusion that my mother was home with us. I was articulate and prepared in math, science, reading, sport, and play. After all, this is what I had promised God I would do.

It was easy to see why the black children in Englewood were confused about who they were. What we were taught was ridiculous. No teacher gave black children any reason to take pride in their color, in their origins, in their past. Never did anyone tell us that we were a people of great antiquity whose contributions to civilization were many and profound.

The unique cause of our presence in America—slavery and racism—was not discussed. Yet I remember spending months in social studies learning about Eskimos in Alaska. In the most advanced English class, where I was placed alongside two other "blacks," we were asked to read *Siddhartha Becomes the Buddha,* an Asian play by Sri Chinmoy. We also read, of course, great poetry and essays by great Europeans and great white people in America. Great black poets and writers and statesmen were nowhere to be found. This, in a school system that was 60 percent black.

The parents of the black children were confused as well. Either they were overworked and poorly educated (thus disconnected and uninvolved in the schooling of their children), or they were black professionals interested in advancing in the white business world, assuming that to be successful they had to accept and even to celebrate white culture like their children did in the advanced classes. Even though many of these parents were homeowners and paid a good amount of tax money, they demanded nothing substantial in exchange for it. There was no movement for an African-centered curriculum. No push for racial consciousness and special programs. There was no real movement for collective political and economic power.

Instead, the black parents went merrily along as the white children received the benefits and preferential arrangements—and there were many—that were provided through the tax dollars of both black and white working people. In fact, the black parents went to great lengths to prove that they were not black and conscious, or black and hostile, or black and demanding. They attended all kinds of integrated unity festivals and candlelight unity sing-alongs. They would openly denounce and distance themselves from any black person who spoke of organizing events that were specifically black in agenda and orientation. Unless, of course, it was about the early years of Martin Luther King, Jr. and his sacred "I have a dream" speech. Any event the black parents organized they were at pains to stress that it was for E-V-E-R-Y-B-O-D-Y.

Meanwhile, many white students and their parents attended separate all-white, semi-private community gatherings, separate Hebrew schools, and Jewish community centers where black children were not allowed. Now, of course, there were no signs hanging in the windows saying, "Nigger keep out." It wasn't necessary. When they wanted to exclude you they would simply not invite you, raise admission prices beyond the reach of the average black family, or claim their gatherings were religious. If they were caught discriminating with taxpayers' dollars, they would simply turn their programs, institutions, or centers into privately owned establishments, so they could continue to discriminate without interruption, to protect their superiority, and to preserve their privileged way of life.

Now, don't get me wrong. Black teachers were tolerated as long as they toed the line, as long as they followed the established curriculum, and didn't try to get too fancy. So too were the small number of well-to-do black doctors, lawyers, architects, and real-estate brokers as long as they kept quiet. In exchange for the chance to have their own child allowed a small piece of white opportunity, they gave their cooperation and an unspoken promise not to cause any trouble or change. They made a silent agreement not to use their acquired skills to organize the unorganized and uneducated blacks. And through their silence they would help keep the undesirables unaware, uninformed, and uninvited.

The difference between myself and the suburban-bred black kids was that I was not passive or content. I had not grown up soft, naive, and unsuspecting. My mother had not hidden me from the realities of life; to do so would have meant death. I understood that there was a difference between blacks and whites in America. I understood that there was a difference between good and evil. And I understood that there was a difference between being in control and being controlled. My goal was to gain control over my life so I would not have to be like any of the people that I had ever met. I wanted to be in charge of my direction as opposed to simply reacting to whatever everyone else said and did and planned for me.

Of course, like any child, I had my strengths and weaknesses. My strength was my relationship with God and my ability to think and pray. To be able to hear the sane inner voice inside my mind. I would soon discover that this was a true blessing. So many people, young and old, had either ignored the spiritual voice inside themselves and listened instead to the fools that surrounded them, or they had responded to a voice that was not actually the voice of the God inside of themselves and therefore had been misled down a path of self-destruction. All around me I could see people casually destroying themselves by shooting drugs, smoking crack, selling sex, drinking alcohol. No longer could they hear the voice of their own conscience.

My other strength was self-love. This is a phrase that is largely overused but highly unachieved. In fact, if you asked any of the black people in the projects or the suburbs if they loved themselves, they would automatically say "Of course! Yeah! That's right! Hell yeah!" But people who love themselves do not allow themselves to be abused by others. I discovered, at a very young age, that neither black people in the projects nor in the suburbs truly loved themselves, because in varying degrees they were all cooperative victims of abuse. I decided early on that I would not ever cooperate or suffer silently while being abused. Never would I allow anyone or group of people to dominate and trounce my spirit and soul. This attitude and determination would follow me forever.

As for my weaknesses, I confess that observing my mother's relationships with men made me decide that I would simply not be bothered with the pain of male-female relationships. I had never seen the involvement "pay off" or settle with a happy ending. There seemed to be short commercials of pleasure and long-running dramas of pain, tragedy, and confusion. So I tucked all of the emotional boy-girl stuff away in the corner of my existence and became extremely involved in the education of my mind: reading, writing, raising questions, and challenging thoughts. I also became extremely competitive, which can become an ugly and selfish trait. I felt I had to be the best in everything, whether it was an academic, athletic, creative, or artistic endeavor.

I was also scarred by my New York experience. I had no belief in true friendship and would deny that it could exist. My father had taught me well. I guarded myself so well that I could cut off any person with whom I had been involved on any level if I thought they had turned against me or hurt me in even the slightest way. I would wake up the next morning, not even take

35

a breath, walk past the person, look them dead in the eye, not even blink or think twice, and act like I had never known them. In my mind and heart my "friends" were only temporary acquaintances. As a result, people said that I was cold. And it was true: I had few experiences with girls as friends or boys as boyfriends. If I was intellectually advanced, I was socially way behind. I didn't worry about it too much since I saw very little good coming out of such "friendships" anyway. Girlfriends seemed jealous and backstabbing. Boys seemed mindless, one-dimensional, and purely sexually driven. Parents seemed disconnected and uninterested, and the outside world racist and unconcerned about the hand it dealt to black people.

By the time I was fifteen I was an intellectual comedy as my strengths and weaknesses and hormones all kicked in. I knew an older girl named Dana. She was having a serious relationship with a guy named Ronnie. Everybody in school knew about it. Me and Dana hung out because she was older and I had a habit of looking for a good conversation. One day when I was at Dana's house Ronnie stopped by with his younger brother, Jay. Now, Jay was the color of caramel with big huge brown eyes that seemed to be filled with water even though he wasn't crying. He had lips like comfortable pillows and a light mustache. He was thick with a nice physique. I was very attracted to him. I felt my whole body heat up when I looked at him. I watched him from the kitchen while he talked to Ronnie and Dana in the living room. As I listened, I noticed that he had a raspy voice like one of those old masculine musicians. But I didn't say anything or mention it to Dana. Somehow she knew anyway. Maybe because I asked several questions about him over the next two weeks in what I stupidly thought was a roundabout way. Finally, Dana said that Ronnie and Jay wanted to take us out to the movies next Saturday. My insides said yes. My mind resisted. My emotions took over and I said yes, thinking it should be all right since there would be four of us in a public place.

Saturday evening came and I told my mother I was going over to Dana's house. She said okay. We met up with Ronnie and Jay at the movies. Once inside the theater Dana and Ronnie, as usual, were all over each other. But I was just meeting Jay. I felt hot but I didn't feel like expressing it. My emotions and imagination were enough for me. Just looking at this brother, admiring his body, and doing whatever I wanted to do with him in my mind was plenty. When the movie was over, Ronnie and Dana said we were going to Ronnie's house. I was horrified. I did not want to go. Dana took one look at my face and pulled me aside. She said, "You have to come to cover me. If you get home early and I don't, I'll get in trouble. If I show up at Ronnie's house late his mom will get suspicious and watch over us like a hawk." So I asked, "Where does Ronnie live?" She said about two miles from my mother's. So I said, okay, I'll stay for a little while.

When we got to Ronnie's house his mother was drunk and had one of her boyfriends over. She was entertaining him in the living room. She gave us the evil eye and told Ronnie to take his company and go upstairs to his own room. Well, my heart dropped because I had made it a rule never to go in the bedroom of any guy and now I was being ordered to do so by someone else's parent. I wanted to go home but I had no ride. I didn't want to leave or start an argument with Dana. I decided not to panic. I would do what I'd agreed to and make her keep her word to leave soon.

Now we were all in the bedroom, which Ronnie and Jay shared. Dana went and sat on Ronnie's bed and Jay gestured for me to go and sit on his. Nervously I sat. Ronnie closed the bedroom door. For the better part of ten minutes I listened to the sound of Dana's and Ronnie's tongues sliding in and out of each other's mouths. Off came Dana's coat, then her top, then her bra, and standing erect were two firm medium-size breasts. Ronnie, now shirtless himself, was running his tongue over Dana's nipples as she moaned in delight. He slipped his hand around the lamp and turned off the light.

Meanwhile, I'm sitting on Jay's bed like a snowman. My body was tilted away from Dana and Ronnie's side of the room but I could still see them out of the corners of my eyes. Deep down inside I wanted to see them because I had never seen anybody just "do it" right in front of my face. It turned me on and aroused my interest. But my guarded self was in control: My mother had always painted pregnancy as the end of the world for every woman and had even said that it was the reason why her own life had been ruined. Now Jay stood before me inspired and gleamy-eyed as though his high-powered stare could burn through my clothes. The only light in the room was the light sneaking in from the hallway outside the bedroom door.

Jay broke the silence, and whispered, "Stay there, I'll be right back." (As if I had a choice.) He quickly returned with his button-down shirt opened and two arms filled with stuff. I saw him place a towel on top of his dresser. Then I heard some paper and plastic tearing like a candy wrapper or something.

The next thing I heard was the unscrewing of a top from a jar. It sounded familiar and in two seconds I realized, sitting there in the dark, that it was a jar of Vaseline. Terror shot through my whole body and I stood up and zipped up my coat.

"What are you doing!" I said.

"You know what I'm doing," Jay said evenly.

"What's that you're opening?"

"Come on, you know what it is. Don't try to tell me some bullshit like you're a virgin or something."

My eyes opened wide and indignant and I said, "I am!"

"Yeah, right."

"I am!"

I looked toward Dana and Ronnie who were bucking wildly all over the bed. It was obvious that I wasn't going to get her out of that sensual grip. My eyes shot back toward Jay. I was filled with fear. I hadn't escaped all that I had in my life to lose it like this.

Seeing me panicking and breaking out in a sweat, Jay said, "All right, all right, just let me stick it in your ass then."

I gasped for air, ran out of the room, down the stairs through the screen door, and the entire two miles to my house. I came stumbling through my door huffing and puffing. I told my mother what had happened and how shocked I was.

She cracked up with laughter.

Like many young "hip" mothers, mine made no big ordeal out of sex itself. There were really only two rules: one, don't do anything that you don't want to do, and two, don't get pregnant. There was no instruction on how to meet a man, how to judge a man, test a man, love a man, or keep a man. There was no vision discussed or placed before a young daughter's eyes as to what the end result was supposed to be. Was it marriage? Was it family? Was any of this important anyway? In my mother's house pregnancy was just another word for doomed, and marriage was the same as failure. But sex was cool.

In school on Monday morning everybody who had found out was tripping on me. The guys were saying that I was a virgin and that I was "lame." Lame meant that you didn't even give up kisses. Kids talked about how smart I was and how I probably read encyclopedias. A boy named Scooter, who was known to be real "nasty and low down," said to me, "You know, your ass is too big and your hips are too wide to keep all that good stuff to yourself. Now I know your type. You waiting for some Prince Charming to come take you away into a palace to live happily ever after. But let me tell you a little secret. There ain't no Prince Charming. When you think you met him, he'll break your heart. So why not let me get some pussy now and I'll teach you all you need to know while you're young, so nobody will take advantage of you." I rolled my big brown eyes at him and sucked my teeth, like a New York girl with attitude would.

By the time I was sixteen years old, I had seen at least ten men come into my house in an attempt to have a relationship with my mother. Whether it ended in tears or smiles, the common denominator was that it ended. I began to see my mother not as the perfect angel that guarded me from danger and provided me with food, clothes, shelter, and survival lessons. Instead I saw her as a young and confused woman with many imperfections who married young. Like many adults, she wanted her children to do as she said and not as she did. Like many adults she didn't understand the power of her example.

As time went on, the more I saw and felt the gap between her words and deeds, the more that gap hurt me. Worse was the loss of my respect. I continued to love my mother, but the loss of respect would alter the nature of our connection, our relationship, our spiritual bond. There were many examples.

My mother had always taught me that drugs killed the mind and spirit and that we should never destroy our bodies with drugs. Then one day, while looking for typing paper, I found rolling paper and marijuana in her room. When I asked her about it, she said it was hers and so what! She shrugged her shoulders and said I was silly and oversensitive and that reefer was no big thing. But I was dead set against any kind of drugs. I found that my "friends" who smoked reefer would always say it was a cool drug. But what they never seemed to notice was that it made them extremely lazy. They were tired and had a tendency to never complete their schoolwork. Plus reefer almost always led them to try another drug for a higher high.

Now one day I came home and found my mother and sister fighting physically on the floor. When I broke it up and asked what was wrong, my mother blurted out, "She stole my reefer!" My sister yelled, "It was mine 'cause I bought a nickel bag yesterday." Each word they spoke was like a stab to my stomach; that fight would leave a permanent wound on my mind and heart. Afterward, I thought deeply about that day, and grew more and more to understand how the day-to-day pressures of being black, penniless, structureless, culturally restricted, and frustrated in America could tear away at something that was supposed to be sacred: our loved ones and our family.

Then there was the confusion in the morals we were taught. For instance, my brother was allowed to have young women go into and stay over in his bedroom. Neither my sisters nor I were allowed to do this. My mother said she didn't want us to get pregnant because our lives would be over. But why wasn't she concerned about anyone else's daughter getting pregnant? Didn't she realize that if every black mother was only worried about her particular daughter that one day her daughter would be allowed to sleep over in the home of some other unconcerned parent?

My brother was also encouraged to not "get serious with any one specific woman." Even when he found one steady girlfriend my mother urged him to be out "exploring." I asked my mother why she would encourage the breakup of a one-on-one relationship? I also asked her if she saw any connection between the way she was raising my brother to behave and the behavior of the men who had broken her heart over the past fifteen years? When I asked my mother these questions she said that I took life too seriously. She told me that even some of the men I admired—"the great black men of history"—had a "truckload of women." To me, that still did not justify encouraging the cycle that seemed to end with more fatherless children and an even more vicious cycle.

I tried to understand and balance my mother's words to me as a young woman. She cautioned me against wasting too much time on these men "who are all the same." She repeated that pregnancy would "ruin my life." She warned that marriage "never works." Yet when I would wear a button-down blouse she would tell me to unfasten the top three buttons. I resisted, saying I didn't want my breasts to show. She would say a little cleavage never hurt nobody, loosen up, it's sexy. If I wore my skirts long, she would say "put a hem in that skirt, you have pretty legs, you should show them." On holidays, my mother would insist that I "take a drink" to celebrate. I'd always say, "No thanks, I don't drink." She'd say, "You need to learn to relax, have a drink anyway." Usually I'd end up taking the glass and giving it to my brother or sister, who were more than happy to have extra. I couldn't understand why I should show cleavage, be sexy, and loosen up if I was not supposed to get pregnant. I couldn't understand why it was okay to have sex if I shouldn't get married. And I couldn't understand why I should drink alcohol if I did not want to and was raised by her to believe that drugs and alcohol would destroy me.

The summer I turned seventeen, a terrible thing occurred. I was coming home from one of my two-month-long educational trips. By this time I had won several trophies, awards, scholarships, and tuition-free conferences based on my extracurricular activities, community work, academic achievement, and the skillful running of my mouth. I gained the opportunity to travel around the country experiencing all kinds of educational events. These events were almost always for white youth. But, by hounding my guidance counselors, reading the newspapers every day, participating in the board of education meetings, and writing for the school newspaper, I found out about all of the hidden benefits and made sure that they were available to me and known to other students in the school. That summer I had gone to Washington, D.C. Now I was on my way back home.

I flew into John F. Kennedy Airport. I went to the luggage carousel and picked up my heavy suitcases, which were always filled with books because I could not afford clothes. I went through the exit gate. There were hundreds of people gathered waiting for their friends and relatives to come out. My family was supposed to pick me up. I heard a man calling my name. I looked up and saw a white man. He looked Italian. I didn't think he could possibly be talking to me. I kept walking. As I walked he came toward me from the opposite direction, placed himself directly in my line of view again, and called my name. I kept walking. Then I saw my brother. I smiled happily and headed toward him. As I walked toward my brother the white man did, too. Then he placed his hand on my brother's shoulder as though they were lifelong buddies and said hi to me, gesturing as if to help me with my luggage.

I rolled my eyes at him and asked my brother, "Who is this guy?" He laughed and said, "This is my boss, Tony. He's gonna give us a ride to the house." I skeptically said okay, since my big brother was there.

When we got to the house I was happy to see my mother and family. I had been gone for the entire summer. There was a lot to tell—the people I'd met, liked and didn't like, the places I'd been, the things I'd learned. My mother seemed genuinely happy for me, as though she was grateful in her heart that my life would be different than hers had been.

While I was talking to my mother, brother, and sisters, the white guy was sitting on our couch looking rather comfortable, familiar, and relaxed as if he had no plans of leaving. After a while, he even had the nerve to try to involve himself in our family discussion. I turned around and said: "Who asked you anything?" He said he was "just commenting." I said, "Well, I look after my mother's interest." He got up from the couch and said, "I am your mother's interest."

The heat and anger began to rise up from my ankles to my neck. I searched the eyes of my brother and sisters around the table. My sisters got up quickly one by one. My mother slid into the kitchen. My brother refused to connect with my eyes as he turned to Tony and said, "Come on, man, we gotta finish the roof at the Genesee Avenue address." Tony got up, and together they left.

The next day, early in the morning, Tony was back, ringing our bell. I opened the door and said as nasty as I could, "What!" I put my body in position to block his entry. He said, "Yeah, can you ask Peaches to come downstairs?" I said, "For what?" He said, "Look . . ." I interrupted, "My brother works for you? Well, I'll get him. But as far as I know my mother doesn't work for you!"

By this time my mother was standing behind me in her robe. She said, "I'll get it." I said, "I got it!" She said, "Move out the way." Instead of moving I slammed the door in Tony's face, leaving him on the outside and me and my mother on the inside. She said, "Why are you so rude?" I said, "Why is this white guy so bold? Who is he and what does he want with you?" She said, "He wants to talk to me." So I screamed, "For what?" She said, "Get out of the way." I said, "I hope you're not sleeping with him, because you damn sure can't be sleeping with the devil!" My mother said, "Calm down. People are people no matter what color they are." I said, "Yeah, only niggas say that! The whole world is arranged by color. The whites rule and the blacks are the ruled no matter where you go, Mommy! Don't tell me you think this asshole loves you because he doesn't. I can guarantee you that! Because they don't love, Mommy. They conquer and they possess. And I know these

45

people, Mommy. I deal with them every day. They want it all. They want everything. They want it all. They want total control. Control over your mind, your money, your body, your spirit, and eventually your soul! I deal with them, Mommy, when I have to but I'm smart enough to know who and what I'm dealing with."

My mother rolled her eyes lightly and said calmly, "Men are men. Someday you'll learn that. You talk all this stuff about black this, black that. But where were all these great black men when my children were starving and needed a roof over their heads? They're there for the fun but not for the responsibility. They don't have no money, no power and even when they do have money they ain't giving none of it to me. You were here left sitting in the dark because Con Ed turned off the gas and electric because of no money. I called Phillip. Here he's supposed to be some big-time ambassador to the United Nations, but I see all he said was 'Oh, that's a shame and I gotta go.' So we sat in the dark for almost two weeks damn near starving to death. Is that love?

"Where is your father? Where is Tyrone, Joe, Rob, Steve, Alan, Reggie, Bert, and all the rest of the black men who supposedly loved me?"

"The state of mind of all of those black men, Mommy, was created and controlled by these white people through their schools, their laws, their thievery, their enslavement, their value system, their finance system, and the evil way that they have dealt historically with our people. The whites have almost completely conquered the black man. They've driven him homeless, landless, languageless, penniless, and damn near mindless.

"Daddy wanted to love you. Circumstance destroyed him. Tyrone loved you. Circumstance and the Vietnam War destroyed him. Even Big Joe wanted to love you but white people kept him powerless for so long that when he became a cop he couldn't even handle the position. As for the others, if a black man can barely finance himself in this world, how many of them do you think can take seriously the responsibility of financing you and your four children?

"But there's one thing I know, Mommy. That white man out there does not love you! I promise you that!"

"Love don't pay the rent," she said.

"Sex for money is prostitution, Mommy."

She lowered her eyes and said, "You don't know if I love him because when you look at him all you see is white and that immediately turns you against him."

"That's what you think. But I have a spirit, Mommy, and I can feel. I can see and I can listen even when no one is talking. I've seen you in love and I know that you do not love him."

"We'll talk about it later." I sucked my teeth and went straight to my brother's room. My brother was getting dressed. When he saw me he looked as if to say he didn't want to be involved. But, of course, I pushed him anyway. "So how long have you been working for this 'roofer'?" "About a month and a half," he said flatly.

"If you work for him, why does he always want to talk to Mommy?"

"I don't know nothing about that. All I do is fix the roof, and the pay is good."

"So what's up with him? Is he tryna 'do' Mommy?"

"Look, the man has a wife and a child. He's from Paramus. He's a roofer and that's all I know about him."

"Do you think if a woman doesn't love a man and she sleeps with him for money that it's prostitution?"

"I think you should stop trying to burst people's bubble. You always think it's your job to tell people the truth. You stick a mirror in their face. A lot of people don't want to see themselves. Don't you realize that the reality is too much for a whole lot of people to handle?"

As I stood there a moment to think about what he was saying to me, he left. Afterward, I thought about the black men who turned their heads during slavery as if they didn't know the white master was raping their wife, daughter, sister, and even mother. I tried to understand what it was that gives black men the capacity to say and do nothing while they are being so obviously violated. I tried to understand if pride was dead or if this was some new definition of strength that I didn't know about. Or was it that the men who spoke up and did something were all killed by white people and I was left here on earth with only the cowards. Were they cowards or just survivors?

I went to my room and I started to write a letter to my mother. I wrote about how it had always been she who had encouraged me to study, read, and learn. But now that I had done so, she seemed to have a problem with what I had discovered. I explained my objection to her "relationship" with Tony. I spoke of the effects of slavery in destroying the family structure of our people and of our native beliefs. I told her the difference between the oppressor and the oppressed, the master and the slave. I told her about a beautiful woman in history named Sally Hemings whom I had once read a book about. She was the mistress of Thomas Jefferson. Even though he was sexing her, she was still a slave and so were the children he fathered with her and never officially claimed. I told her that white people get and take what they want all the time. They get what they can use out of it and then throw it to the curb. But that black people never got what we wanted out of the equation. That we still suffered from a slave mentality. I tried to make her understand that yes, black people did wicked things to each other, but everything in life taught us to hate ourselves and each other. That's why it was so easy for most black people to destroy one another. But who taught white people to hate black people? They taught black to hate black and still teach it. But who taught them to hate us? It could not have been us, I wrote, because most black people love and worship white people.

I closed my letter with a proposal for a solution. Believing that financial pressure made my mother see Tony, I proposed that my older brother, who was in college and had a job, take care of our middle sister. I would get a job and take care of my youngest sister. That way we would all put our money together and wouldn't need to be dependent upon any outside intruders or any men that she did not love.

She read the letter, but she did not change. It was as though body snatchers had somehow invaded her body and turned her heart cold. Life was too much and too harsh for her. Tony would end up only one of more than a handful of white men that would invade our house. I had more than several clashes—one or two of them nearing violence—with all of them. My mother described her "personality change" as being the "year she would become a real lady." When I asked her what she meant, she said, "I'll have a man with some money and some power. I'll get my nails manicured and my feet pedicured. I'll always use exquisite manners, meet all the right people, be in all the right places." She told me she was going to be a model or an actress, that she had the talent plus she was finally going to make her beauty "pay off." To me, it seemed she was trying to solve her problem by "turning white."

Still, I thanked God in my prayers for my mother, whom I had known, loved, and respected for seventeen years. I thanked God that she had the strength to save us and secure us from the projects, the danger, the hunger, and the mental devastation. I thanked God she had the intelligence to teach us to be drug-free, compassionate, level-headed, and in control. I thanked God for allowing me to know her before the world took her because some kids didn't even get seventeen good years with their mothers. But I had come to believe that the woman walking around the house posing as my mother was not my mother. She was America's creation and that did not belong to me.

two

Nathan

I was excited and hyped to be going to college. After all, college is the one place on earth that offers young people the chance to be free. By living on campus, far from home, we get the opportunity to act out all of our suppressed personality traits and hidden desires. We then become the person we've always wanted to be.

College offered me the opportunity to select my own courses, my own professors, my own direction, and to rid myself of the things I considered ridiculous. Even though I still had some constraints, I felt more like an adult—more in control. Actually, I had felt like an adult since I was a little girl. And while some people cherished their youth, I loved the idea of being able to think and decide for myself.

College would free me sexually as well, for the first time. In high school, if you were considered "intelligent, advanced, a high achiever" you could not also be considered sexy or sexual. You were dismissed as a rocket scientist, or a genius, or a complete nerd. I knew there was something wrong with this way of thinking because even though my own "friends" chose to ignore it, I had been blessed with a good amount of natural beauty. My mother said that my intelligence was what was scaring men, so they never got to admire my beauty because my mouth, my thoughts, and my assertiveness drove them away before they had the chance to get a good look or feel for who and what I was. I had decided quietly that if they were scared of me, they couldn't possibly be men. After all, weren't men supposed to be strong and weren't men supposed to be stronger than women? So in feeling good about my appearance, my body, I paid more attention to myself. I had exercised throughout the entire summer before college and used some of the money I had earned in scholarship awards to buy some new clothes.

My first day in my new college dormitory room I stood in front of my mirror, admiring my long eyelashes, my big brown eyes, broad shoulders, full titties, small waist, and baby-making hips. I knew that this body was a weapon, but I also considered it to be sacred—something that I would give and share only with one special person. Don't get me wrong. I was as "hot" as any other young woman. The only difference was that in high school, all of my sexual affairs happened inside my mind. I had steamy fantasies about certain brothers whom I considered to be strong—men who would have never thought that I'd be thinking of them in that way because I had deliberately misled them with my intelligent ways. But I had them sexually, without their permission and to my own extreme pleasure, because I truly was the only one who could feel the heat of my fantasies. But everything would change now, because at college I would be with thousands and thousands of other anonymous people and hundreds of black men to choose from. I was sure that at least one of them would like me.

Let me not forget Chuck, my high school boyfriend whom I dated for two years. But he was awkward. So awkward that even after seventeen years of being a virgin, I gave him some on my eighteenth birthday, but still considered myself to be a virgin because he didn't know what he was doing and I certainly didn't feel the way I felt when I had my fantasy affairs. Still, he was the only boy who wasn't scared of me. He was respectful, intelligent, and treated me well. But now I was in college, a virgin once removed (ha!) who nonetheless still felt obligated to be loyal to Chuck who was also far away at another school. But somehow I knew that something or someone was headed my way.

The girls who would live in my dormitory began to arrive throughout the day. Later that night, a girl, who introduced herself as Mona, moved into a room near my own. I was glad to see her because the first days of college are lonely even though you are meeting a lot of people. She came with a tall guy who I assumed was her man, but as I watched him complain about having to carry her stuff up the stairs and the stupid way that she packed and mixed things up, I knew it could only be her brother. Mona was tall, or about two inches taller than me. I was five feet, six inches, which most people considered tall for a girl. She had a rich brown complexion and she was beautiful. Not just in the sense that she had a nice, thick healthy body, but she was also fashionable. I could tell that she was from the city because she was obviously fashionable. In New York you had to have your "gear" and clothes correct or you would be a complete outcast. I "kept up" when I was in New York because I had to and, believe me, a lot of kids were doing crazy shit just to keep their clothes up-to-date.

As I watched Mona unpack, I told her some of the things she had missed in the first freshman orientation. I was mostly quiet though because I had learned that with girls you always had to "check the vibe." I had to observe and decide whether Mona was confident or insecure; whether she was high-strung or relaxed; and whether she wanted to be friends or strictly business. After about two hours I decided that she was very confident. So confident that she wouldn't be catty like a lot of women, nor would she launch some secret war-game competition between us. She was friendly, talkative, and I could tell that she realized that as a freshman she would need a friend and hanging buddy just like I would.

We were both hungry so we used our temporary meal cards and headed over to the cafeteria. In the cafeteria I was fascinated. I had come from a big family and one helping was all you could get. If you were late getting home from school, you'd be lucky to find your portion of the dinner left over. But here, in the college cafeteria, I could eat anything and everything I wanted. I went buckwild. I ate two dinners, which included two bowls of french fries covered with melted cheese, and cake and ice cream for dessert. Mona warned me, "Girl, you gonna get fat."

Sitting across from us were two juniors. One of them sarcastically asked me, "Have you ever heard of the Freshman 10?" I said, "No, what is that?" She said, "The Freshman 10 is the ten pounds most freshmen gain within the first two months of college. At the rate you're going, girl, it'll be twenty, not ten!" They all laughed. Just then a few brothers passed by our table with their trays. One of them looked good to me. I must have been staring because the other junior girl quickly said, "Don't even waste your time, girl! He hits on all the freshmen women, makes 'em all feel special. One semester later they crying and wanting to drop out and carry on. The boy been here five years and got it so good he don't even wanna graduate!" They laughed again.

I felt embarrassed that I had been so obvious. The big-mouth girl then added, "Freshmen women ain't considered nothing around here but pieces of meat. These dudes is like sharks smelling blood. But y'all are dumb and young, so I'll warn you. But you'll give 'em some anyway 'cause you still think the goddamn world revolves around you." Maybe she's telling the truth, I thought. Maybe she's lying. Maybe the guy I was staring at had screwed her and dumped her and that's the real reason why she's so bitter. Maybe the men ain't all that bad and it's just that she's ugly and full of gossip so they can't tolerate her. Maybe she's in love with the guy I was staring at and she just doesn't want him to like me or me to like him.

Later, I asked Mona what she thought of the girls at dinner. She said that Big Mouth was probably right. She said guys seemed to like playing mind games and hurting sisters. It made them feel large. She added that we should be careful because we were new. We would have to find out who every-body was before we started making any silly moves. It was good advice. Besides I didn't want to marry or even jump in bed with that guy. I was just enjoying the way he looked.

Wednesday was "pub night" and after a week of stand-ing on lines registering, buying books, getting special permis-sion from the deans to enter into courses that were already overbooked, I was down to go to the pub. I never drank alcohol. I heard that was the main attraction to the pub, but for me it was the music. Music always had a strong effect on me. I could listen to a gospel record and be overwhelmed by a spiritual feel-ing that made me want to cry. I could listen to jazz music and be submerged in deep thought about why the world was arranged the way that it was. I could listen to one of my grand-mother's blues albums and experience the emotions of the singer as if they were my own. Or I could listen to rap music whose beats drove me in so many different directions. It could make me feel overtly sexual and controlled by the drum beat. Or it could bring to mind the urgency of the poor condition of black people in this country. Rap spoke of many things—from Almond Joy to Public Enemy to Ice Cube was a trip from a hot sexual sweat to critical thinking to a directed rage. So I was going to the pub to feel the music and have it take me away in what I considered the most natural and safe way to "get high."

The pub played club music. Most college kids were not into hip-hop yet. It didn't matter since the beats were there. The place was jam-packed with people. Brothers and sisters all looking and smelling good. Some standing around talking. Some smoking, drinking, and dancing. I moved straight to the middle of the dance floor, moving my body with the rhythms and sensuality the music made me feel—not caring that I was dancing alone. I knew my bold ways would get me the attention I wanted. But when that attention came, I was determined to act like I didn't notice it. After all, half the battle in college, it was starting to seem to me even after only one week, was to be able to distinguish yourself from all the other women. It seemed to me that there were at least four times as many black women as there were black men at the college. Once I got into the groove I forgot about getting attention as I listened to lyrics about the "pain of love." And although I had fantasized about the pleasures and companionship of love, it was precisely the pain that I intentionally avoided. As I moved I wondered whether it was the men or the women who were at the root of the problem of our relationships with one another. I decided it was both. When I looked up I realized I had an uninvited guest. There was a brother dancing with me. It was cool though. I enjoyed his company and the challenge as we tried to outmove each other.

It was hard to wake up the next morning. I had a class called "Black Education." For the first time I had a professor, a black man, admit that racism was and still is a monumental problem that plagues America and destroys the lives of black people. He asked us to read a book called *Institutional Racism in America.* I must say I lost twenty pounds of high blood pressure from the class discussion because instead of having the usual discussion of whether racism existed or whether it was a figment of the imagination of over 30 million black people in America, we had a full exploration of its forms and manifestations.

After class I rushed to the college bookstore, excited because I did not know that books like the ones my professor

assigned existed. While searching the shelves of African Studies, I got sidetracked by the many other interesting books that
were available. I was overwhelmed and angry at the same
time. Overwhelmed, because here was a wealth of knowledge I
hadn't known about. Angry, because my high school teachers
were either completely ignorant, or had hidden this information from me. Overwhelmed, because I intended to read all of
these books. Overwhelmed, because I realized that when information is relevant to an individual's life and culture, learning
is fun, and an unrelenting burning passion that cannot be
subdued. Angry, because all of the students who did not "make
it" to college would never know that this "stuff" existed and
even their pitiful local public library might not offer such a
selection.

As I was flipping through the pages of Carter G.
Woodson's *Mis-Education of the Negro,* a tall, very dark-skinned
brother with a closely-cropped beard stood in front of me and
said, "Read it! Every college student should." I smiled and said,
"Yeah, I'm gonna check it out, but I have to read *Institutional
Racism in America* first." He said, "Yeah, I read that one, too.
It'll definitely open your eyes to what's going on in the world."
He held out his hand to me and introduced himself: "Nathan."
I told him my name and he invited me for a drink. When I told
him I didn't drink alcohol, he looked surprised. "I saw you at
the pub last night." "I don't drink but I do dance." "How old
are you?" "Eighteen." Suddenly, he seemed to lose interest. He
said, "Excuse me, I didn't realize you were still a baby." I calmly
said, "So, how old are you, old man?" "Twenty-four, senior,
political science/history double major." I reached up, grabbed
my copy of *Institutional Racism,* and said, "Peace, take it easy."

As I walked to the counter to pay, I thought about how ugly he was. He was black—black as the ashes from the incinerator of my old building in the projects. Or as kids around my way would say, he was "so black he was blue!" I decided he should be happy I even gave him five minutes of my time. I then dismissed him from my thoughts, paid for the book, and headed to my room to do some reading.

I read the book like a starving man would eat a fish sandwich. Each sentence prompted a new thought and I began connecting each thought introduced in the book to the things that had happened in my life or to the people I loved. I began to understand a little more about my community in the Bronx, how it was organized, how it was not organized, and how it got to be so miserable in the first place. I stayed up the whole night reading. Early in the afternoon the next day I was done. I checked the reading list and saw that the next assignment for this class was a book entitled *Black Bourgeoisie,* by E. Franklin Frazier. I happily went off to my 2:30 English class; immediately afterward I went directly to the bookstore to pick up *Black Bourgeoisie.*

That night Mona came in looking down and out. She was enrolled in the School of Engineering, which required a great deal of study and concentration. "What's up, girl?" She replied, "Work, work, and more work." I said it's good to be on top of things but you have to have something that makes you feel relieved so you can relax for a while. She looked through me as if she wasn't listening. I said, "All right! Let's work until ten and after that we can go to the 'hut' and get some tea and doughnuts." She told me she was down to take a break at ten and we both went to our rooms to do our work.

The hut was a cool place where you could get a snack without the hustle and bustle and bright lights of the cafeteria. Plus you could hear relaxing music, play games, watch television, movies, or videos. The best thing was the speakeasy on Friday nights, where students got to stand up and present their thoughts, works of poetry, rap, essays, and comments. When the speakeasy began, a brother got up and started going off on the black woman. He said that sisters on campus want to be down with the white women's movement, but the white women's movement had nothing to do with African women. He said that we, as African women, came from the opposite side of town and had a different set of concerns more relevant to our survival as a people. Too many black women were copying white women walking around campus half naked and then had the nerve to get mad when a brother took a long look. If black women want to be respected, he said, they had to respect themselves. He said that we must divorce ourselves from the white society's definition and description of womanhood and present ourselves in a light where a man can get to know our minds instead of just "running through" our bodies.

The student host opened the floor for discussion. I found myself standing up. Although I thought I agreed with most of his comments, I was always ready to test and see if somebody was sincere or if they were just talking. "I agree that we sisters could dress more modestly, brother, but I find that brothers like yourself say you have these high standards for women and then we find you chasing after the precise woman you say we should not dress like! Now, if I get lonely enough, and I think a miniskirt is the only way to get your attention,

I'll put it on." Everybody started laughing. Sisters said, "Right on, girl, word up! You tell 'em."

Looking like he was shocked to be challenged (I figured he probably gave this same speech every couple of weeks), he gripped his microphone and said, "With all due respect, my sister, I am not one of these brothers who says one thing and does the opposite, I don't chase after naked women. I judge a woman by her mind!" Of course, this sounded too good to be true to me, so I said, "Oh yeah? So where's your woman at tonight? If you are a fair-minded brother like you say you are, wouldn't your woman be here with you sharing in the discussion? Or, are you one of these brothers that talks about a sister building up her mind and then wraps her up in a sheet and locks her in the house so she can't use it?"

Suddenly, everybody was heated and involved in the discussion. Some were laughing so hard they seemed to be picking themselves up from the floor. Stuck for words the brother groped and said, "Yes! I have a woman but she's not here because she's in Loeb Library studying." I smiled and said, "It's real hard to believe there's a sister here at our university, where there are four black women to every one brother, who knows her man is onstage at the hut in front of all these women and she chose to let him come out all alone."

All hell broke loose. The sisters started clapping and the brother said, "All right, my sister, here, you take the mike." That's when I decided to sit down. Meanwhile, a sister got up on the mike, short hair cut like a man's, nappy, with long earrings and real dark-skinned. She said, "Now, I love myself. But I gotta wonder why nobody loves me when I am you?" The audience looked confused by her statement so she repeated it and silence fell on the room. She said, "Let me break it down for you. As you can see, I am dark-skinned, dark like midnight. This means that I am African. We, as Africans, and really before we even got that name, were the first people on this earth. We were created over two million years ago in the image of God. If Africans were the first people created in the image of God, then God must have been black. And, if God is black, and most of us say that we love God, why do we hate ourselves?" One sister responded angrily, "How do you figure we hate ourselves?" The dark girl replied, "Well, there isn't one brother in this university, my sisters, who wouldn't rather date you as a light-skinned, hazel-eyed sister than me as the dark-skinned sister I am. Brothers won't even look at me; they will automatically go to a light-skinned sister." Then she placed her hands on her hips and rolled her neck and said: "But we don't want to talk about that now, do we?" Once again, silence. "Well," she commanded, "all I am asking is that when you look at me you realize that I am you. And, if you hate me you hate yourself and who we are as a people." She placed the mike in the microphone stand and calmly walked off the stage.

Even though I had had fun shouting down the brother, the words of this sister, the truth of her words, stabbed me directly in my heart. Although she directed her comments toward the brothers, I, too, was guilty of the same kind of self-hatred that she spoke about. To be sure, I never wanted to be light-skinned. I felt good about being brown. But black was far too extreme for me. I hated black, dark black, and when I would see it, just like she said, I would not look any further. Not at the eyes, the lips, the teeth, nothing. So she taught me a lesson when I had no intention of learning anything in the hut that night. I thought about how I had routinely dismissed the brother at the bookstore the other day. I even went so far as to believe I had done him a favor simply by talking to him. So I was guilty of self-hatred and never knew it. Funny thing was, brown-skinned sisters hated to be put down by light-skinned sisters but I had never thought about how we all put down black-skinned brothers and sisters.

Mona interrupted my thoughts: "Why do you get so involved in this shit? People are just talking. It's a speakeasy." I looked at Mona and said, "Didn't she give you something to think about?" Mona spit back, "I already had too much to think about. I came here to relax, not to think. Besides, I can't solve the problems of the world." We paid the bill and left.

As the semester came to a close, everything became routine. It was one week before final exams and I knew I had grown both intellectually and spiritually. I had learned the valuable lesson that the more you think you know, the less you know. The more willing you are to learn, the more likely you are to seek and find only to discover that there is still so much more. The parties at the pub became pretty regular and after the first couple of weeks I started to memorize the faces. Some people became couples and some people just humped because it felt good for the moment. Although I longed for companionship, I discovered so much comfort and peace of mind in my new-found books, I continued my self-examination. I used Carter Woodson's book to begin to address my eighteen years of mis-education.

One day while sitting in the hut, I was cramming for my upcoming English exam. It was something I had to do since I hated the *Canterbury Tales* and the ramblings of old English "literary giants" who damn near nobody could understand. As I stumbled through my notes, up walked Nathan who, without hesitation, invited himself to sit down. "Every time I see you, you have your head in a book. Do you take time out?" "Time out for what?" I replied. Kicking back, he said, "Listen, I stay up late, live in your building on the third floor. You're on the seventh, right? So, come check me out, we'll talk and listen to some music." "What do you take me for, freshman meat?" "No, no, no, don't bug out. It's just that we all finish our work late at night. Anyway you won't be the only one there. Come on down and kick it with us tonight?" Just as I got ready to tell him I had to finish studying, he said, "I know you gotta study so I'll see you later."

Later that night I debated whether I should go down to see Nathan. I was bored. I put on my baggy pants and an oversized sweatshirt so I would look as unsexy as possible. I didn't want him to get the wrong impression, and, frankly, I didn't feel attracted to him. I was going for the conversation, which I had discovered was hard to come by, and was to be treasured if you could find a good one.

As I approached Nathan's door I heard voices and could smell incense. I was relieved that other people were there. I knocked and a girl I had seen around campus opened the door. She looked at me and almost instantly I could tell that she liked Nathan because she gave me the black woman "eye-roll." He couldn't see her reaction and when he saw me a bright smile stretched across his face. There was a brother there also. Nathan introduced them both. The sister's name was Tonya and the brother's name was Jamal. Another knock came at the door and a brother named Russell joined us.

I learned that they had been talking about Middle Eastern politics. Nathan had just finished reading *The Question of Palestine* by Edward Said. They were debating who was wrong and who was right in the Middle Eastern conflict. Nathan was the most talkative, as he knew all the names of the heads of state in the Middle Eastern area. Later that night I learned Nathan was a Muslim. Russell was a Christian. Nathan tried to argue the "Middle East" was actually geographically part of Africa. He told Russell that as a black man, an African, he should be on the side of the Palestinians. That it was not a question of Muslim versus Christian, but rather a question of white European domination of people of color all around the world.

Russell disagreed, and as the debate heated up he declared that the argument was not "going anywhere" and that he had an exam tomorrow and so he would be leaving. Jamal exited a few minutes later on Russell's heels.

The hour was late but my eyes were wide as plums. I was fascinated: I had just heard a conversation about a subject I knew absolutely nothing about! I was thrilled because I hardly ever had met people who were serious about learning and serious about understanding issues, people who could support their arguments with intricate details backed up by a number of books read on the topic. I felt embarrassed because I had assumed Nathan was sweating me and just wanted some pussy. Instead, it felt like an honor to be in his presence, to listen to his voice, and to be able to share in his wealth of knowledge.

Tonya was older than I was. A senior, she acted as though she had heard these types of conversations before. When she realized that even though it was getting late I wasn't budging, she got up, rolled her eyes, said she was going to bed and that we should all do the same. I enjoyed the little competition she stirred up, but I still had a ton of questions to ask Nathan, and besides, I wanted his reading list on the Middle East. Nathan got up and lit another incense stick. It created a sweet and fresh smell in the room unlike the usual funk of college dormitories. As Tonya walked out, Nathan walked her down the hall and I imagined him having to listen to her complain about why I wasn't leaving, too.

I looked around the room. It looked unusually clean and organized for a man. The books were neatly arranged in the bookshelf, *The Holy Quran* was prominently featured on its own wooden carved stand, and everything seemed perfect. As Nathan came back through the door I realized he was quite tall, about six feet. He sat down on the chair at his desk, smiled at me, and said, "Finally. What do I owe you for coming to see a lowlife like me?" His teeth were white and bright against his jet-black skin. "I guess I should pay you for the lessons," I replied. "Free of charge. We're here every night debating, discussing, and sharpening our skills." His lips were thick— thicker than the lips of any man I had ever taken the time to notice. His nose was wide and it struck me that this night was the first night I took the time to notice the details, the structure, the ins and outs of anyone's face whose complexion was so dark. His cheekbones were pronounced and formed like a masculine African carving. His eyes were big. But not big and dreamy like a Walt Disney character. They were big and powerful like the eyes I had recently seen on the African masks that were depicted in my history books.

"It's good to see you," he said. "I heard what you did a couple of months ago in the hut at the speakeasy. Man, Tarif came by after that and couldn't stop talking about you. You blew his head off!"

"I was just messing with him. Are you in the Nation of Islam?" I asked.

"No, I'm Orthodox."

"So how is it that you started drinking alcohol?"

"Sharp mind, good question. At the time that you saw me in the bookstore I was 'backsliding.' "

"Do you do that for convenience?"

He smiled, "Real sharp. No, it's a weakness." (This was the first time I had ever heard a brother voluntarily admit to a weakness.) "Ideally, I know what I'd like to be. But, I've always said, 'If you can wake up in the morning and like what you see in the mirror, you're doing better than most people.' What religion are you?"

"I was born and raised a Christian in a nondenominational church. We believe in God and we don't discriminate. My great-grandmother is the pastor and her fourteen children are the deacons and deaconesses."

He smiled again, "You know, you are beautiful. Not just your body or your face, although that all looks good, but there's a light that you have, a spiritual light. I feel the need to be around you and that light. It's very powerful and good but not many could stand it."

I wasn't sure what Nathan was talking about, but I was completely flattered.

"So," he said, like a lawyer or detective, "you don't smoke either?"

"Nope," I responded.

He laughed lightly and said with a sigh of relief, "A no-drinking, no-smoking, no-sleeping-around Christian girl. Well now . . . that's rare."

"How do you know I don't sleep around?" I teased.

"Because I would've heard about it. I've done some checking. Listen," he said, "give me your phone number at home. Maybe we can get together over your Christmas holiday. When are you leaving the dorm?" "In two days," I said. He said, "Yeah, me too. Come back tomorrow night and we'll talk before I go back to Brooklyn." By the time I got back to my room it was 4:30 in the morning.

I spent the next day packing up my few valuables and safely packing away my notes. Even though the semester was over, I did not want to throw away my notes. I figured I could keep them and somehow use them later. I had learned so much. I told Mona about my night at Nathan's. She told me to watch out because although Nathan seemed "pretty smooth, the bottom line is probably still the same."

That night I went downstairs to Nathan's. Once again, he and Russell and Jamal were arguing. Tonight's debate was over Malcolm X: What had he thought and who had he become the year before his death, and what was the significance of his philosophy anyway? Now this was a hot topic. Hotter than the night before. Everyone was just jumping right in and verbally slugging it out. Once again, I sat there and listened, not because I didn't have an opinion. I definitely had an opinion on this one. I sat quietly, because once again I was shocked to find conversation that went beyond the level of jokes like "Your mother's ass is so wide, and the last time you saw your father . . ."

Russell was frustrated. Nathan, he charged, was being dishonest because he knew good and well that Malcolm, at the end of his life, believed there were some good white folks in the world. Nathan disagreed, insisting that what Malcolm had said was that he realized that through Islam and the practice of internalizing Islam white people, who were usually power-hungry, unjust, warlike, and greed-driven, could become civilized. Nathan described Malcolm's "transformation" as an even greater challenge to white America to change the immorality of its ways. Russell searched the room for anybody to support not only what he was saying, but the style in which he was saying it. His eyes landed on me. Looking directly at me eyeball to eyeball, he said, "I hear you're a very nice Christian girl. Now I'm a Christian, too. Would you agree that after Malcolm's pilgrimage to Mecca he believed in the brotherhood of all men?"

For the first time, I was being dragged into one of these emotionally charged debates. These brothers and sisters were so much older than me. I was slightly intimidated, and so I chose my words carefully. I said that I believed Malcolm always believed in the brotherhood of man, before Mecca and even after his so-called transformation. This was a brotherhood that he believed could only be achieved by destroying racism and achieving equal power, resources, land, money and access to opportunity. Above all, Malcolm believed that without power black people would never be treated with justice or be considered as a part of the brotherhood of man. The black man would in fact be used, dominated, and destroyed by the same brotherhood because there could be no justice in a relationship where one group of people were kept nonproductive, dependent, and ignorant.

Jamal smiled and Nathan put his head down as though he felt embarrassed for Russell. Russell said, "Are you saying that during Malcolm's involvement with the well-known, race-prejudiced group 'The Nation of Islam' he believed in brotherhood?"

"Yes, and I'm saying he believed in justice. The Nation of Islam, in Malcolm's opinion, was the greatest vehicle in organizing black people for justice, productivity, morality, and self-sufficiency."

"Then why did Malcolm call the white man 'the blue-eyed devil'?"

"Because," I explained, "of the evil and devilish things that white people have done collectively to other races of people while pretending to believe in democratic principles, liberty, and justice."

"Are you a Muslim?" Russell asked, raising his voice.

"No, I am a Christian," I said calmly.

"Do you believe the white man is the devil?"

"I believe that he's doing a good job of convincing our people that he is, even if we as Christians were inclined to argue that he is not."

Russell was pissed and he blurted out, "That's not a Christian way of thinking!"

Still calm but indignant, I asked, "By whose book? In my Bible, Christ is for justice. He is for brotherhood but not at the expense of justice."

Russell looked at Nathan and said, "All right, man, I'm breaking out. I think you got a budding black radical on your hands!" In full sarcasm he then turned to me and said, "You gotta relax, tone it down some, even Nathan enjoys a nice white girl every now and then!" He smiled and slipped out the door.

The topics changed again and again and different people moved in and out of Nathan's room. As the early morning hours approached only Nathan and myself were left sitting alone again. Russell's parting words kept echoing in my mind. So I asked quietly, "Is it true?"

"Is what true?"

"Is it true that you enjoy a white girl every now and then?"

Nathan's eyes tried to avoid mine.

"Well, is it?"

"I don't know what you're bugging out about. There was a time, not too long ago in fact, when I couldn't get a sister like yourself to even look in my direction. Sisters got the attitude that blackness is some kind of disease." I knew his words were true but it still sounded like a poor excuse to me.

"Don't make excuses for yourself. If you like white girls blame it on yourself. Not on the sisters. What about Tonya? Was she too black for you, or are you guilty of the same things that sisters are?"

"Tonya," he said, "was desperate and lonely. Have you ever heard her say anything? Have you ever heard her join in the conversation? Hell, no. She just sits there on the edge of the bed with a lot of space between her ears hoping that since she's willing to overlook the color thing, I'll be willing to overlook the fact that she hasn't paid any attention to her own development. I don't know if you've noticed, but sisters around campus don't have much going on. They may go to class. And they may be on the verge of graduating, but in the final analysis there's not much real thinking going on in those pretty little heads of theirs."

"Yeah," I said, "what you're saying may or may not be true. Sisters might fall short of your standard but that's no reason to go and unite with a white girl, who, no matter what she says, is part of the problem. It's not the answer. It's a contradiction, an out-and-out contradiction. With sisters being four to one on this campus, it's wrong for any black man to be loving a white woman! Of course, the white girls might be 'more advanced' in some ways. But they've had greater opportunities, different environments, and a whole lot of time to devise ways to divide the black man from the black woman when we are, in fact, naturally supposed to be together." Nathan simply smiled and said, "Point well taken."

The university gave us nearly five-and-a-half weeks' vacation. Being home meant that I had to listen to everyone tell me how fat I had gotten, my "Freshman 20." Having been away from my family, I felt I could see more clearly the changes they had been going through during my absence. I felt that the family had grown further apart. My youngest sister, just thirteen years old, was showing signs of being fast, especially for her age. My other sister, in the absence of the pressure that I usually placed on her to get herself together, had become far too accepting and lazy about her lack of progress and direction in life. My older brother seemed self-absorbed and unable or unwilling to do anything about the declining status of our family. My mother was still exhausting herself chasing plan after fruitless plan in search of the American dream, hoping to rid herself of her welfare reality.

I went out with Chuck only to discover that although he was a true friend, someone who truly loved me and I him, there simply was no "heat" between us. The fact was, he was boring and had little to talk about other than his second year at one of the best science universities in the country, where he spent all of his time in the computer room or laboratory. While I admired him because he seemed to have his life so well planned, I couldn't find a sense of excitement and depth. Maybe the gulf between us was too great: between his ultra-middle-class, two-professional-parent family, two cars, the-sun-always-shines neighborhood and my government-subsidized, single-female-headed-household underclass reality. I tried to understand what was missing. I kept thinking it was his lack of a sense of struggle. But was this his problem or mine? Was I glorifying the need to struggle? Did I somehow envy his family because they had properly planned ahead and taken advantage of the few gains that were achieved during the rebellion of African people in America? Did my uneasiness have to do with the fact that his somewhat prosperous family seemed so content while the vast majority of our community was dying? Did they accept me because I was educated and would not, therefore, pose an embarrassment to their class pretensions, or did any of that matter to them at all?

Well, no matter whose problem it was, mine or Chuck's, I kept hoping Nathan would call. I dashed up the stairs every time the phone rang. But six days later, still no call from Nathan. I stopped running up the stairs and let my little sister answer the phone. I began to look up a few of my old high school acquaintances just to kill time. One day, while sorting the laundry with my mother and sister, the phone rang. My sister answered and handed it to me saying it was "somebody named Nathan." I smiled so wide I knew my family would ask questions when I hung up. Nevertheless, I was careful not to betray my eagerness to Nathan. I tried to act as though I hadn't been hoping that he would call.

"What's up, how ya doin'? I'm coolin'." Then, Nathan asked, "You wanna hang out in New York with me? We can check a movie or a club, and go get some dinner." I said softly, "Sure, why not?" I hung up the phone as my little sister danced around the room teasing, "Ooh, you cheatin' on Chuck, cheatin' on Chuck, cheatin' on Chuck!" I told her to shut up. I didn't feel I was cheating because I had never touched Nathan. Besides, we were just talking. And anyway, Chuck wasn't filling me up enough mentally and spiritually, not to mention physically.

My day with Nathan began in the early afternoon when he came to pick me up. We went to Manhattan's Lower East Side and he showed me the little news shops where political and economic journals from around the world could be bought. He stressed the importance of getting alternative opinions and assessments rather than relying on the ones given by the American government, and some "objective professors." He cautioned me about trusting the media. He told me how the news and television stations tried to control the flow of information concerning African people and all people of color. He said they attempted to shape public opinion and went so far as to create "facts" to lie to the people in the interest of maintaining their own power. He had a backpack full of information and showed me documents on different places around the world. He added that he thought I had done a good job of learning about domestic racism and the "black experience in America," but that I had to begin to see and understand how these racist institutions of power existed everywhere in the world, wherever African and Latino people lived and tried to organize to control their own lives, land, food, and resources.

Out of his inside coat pocket came what he called a gift. It was a copy of a book he had been impressed by called *The Pawns in the Game.* Later, we went up to the Metropolitan Museum of Art, which had a limited holiday engagement of the "Treasures of Ancient Egypt." Nathan explained everything that he said the tour guide had "left out." He pointed out the facial features of the African art—the wide nose, thick lips, and strong cheek and jawbones. He said that in the past these features had been considered beautiful, but that "white civilization" had taught African people to hate themselves. He said they did this for two reasons. One was to be able to control our minds and thus our dollars, gold, oil, land, and all the riches of African people. The second was to get us to abandon our own belief system, our own culture, our own way of organizing life, so that we would forget how to live and prosper and have to depend completely on whites for everything. At the root of all of it, he added, was greed and jealousy. He laughed a painful laugh and told me the story about how Napoleon in Egypt, consumed by envy, blew off the nose of the great Sphinx because the wide nose clearly confirmed that it was a great African creation that symbolized our originality and superiority in geometry, architecture, mathematics, and art. He told me that the result of all of these years and centuries of oppression and thievery over the Africans had resulted in our complete psychological, economic, spiritual, and practical dependency on white people. That our minds were actually so destroyed that we found it hard to do such basic things as love each other and see the goodness and value in ourselves. He ended my lesson by telling me that the reason the exhibit was called Egyptian and not African was because white scholars wanted the world to believe that the Egyptians were non-African, light-complected Phoenicians. This they did so African people would feel we had contributed nothing to civilization and that the great and original treasures of the world, that we Africans had conceived and created, were not actually ours.

Leaving the museum, we went to a health food restaurant and sat down to have dinner. Nathan smiled, and with a look of guilt said, "I brought you here because you were starting to look like 'two tons of fun' and I just thought I wouldn't add to your weight problem." He began to crack up, clearly amused by his own fat jokes, flashing his beautiful white teeth. My heart stood still as I realized that I had actually gained twenty pounds since starting college. But I played Nathan's remark off. Nathan started talking about his family. He had four sisters and no brothers. He had a hardworking mother and a father whose presence was "more like an absence." He asked me if I'd like to meet them? I said definitely.

After dinner, we went to his home in Brooklyn. Everybody in his family was very dark in skin color and his mother was overbearing and suspicious of any newcomers. She struck me as the type who would compete with any girl who wanted the affections of her son. Nathan's sisters were also possessive, and they inspected me as though it was their job to issue a certificate either authorizing me or keeping me from dating their brother. Because they didn't seem to take me seriously at all, I assumed that Nathan probably brought a lot of girls home.

After the whole phony exchange with his family, Nathan took me to the bus stop to put me on a bus that would take me back to New Jersey. He didn't try to kiss me, which was cool, because I didn't feel comfortable yet. Just before I got on the bus, he said, "You know, you're a beautiful girl, but we have to work on you. I like girls with natural hair. I've always wondered why you have that fake extra piece of hair weaved in the back of your head. Does it give you that much more of a sense of security and value?"

I was astounded. Nobody had ever mentioned my weave. I had always acted as if it were my own hair. How could he be so insensitive? "All I am saying is, I think *your* hair is beautiful. Maybe you can think of something else to do with it? Oh, and follow that healthy menu we had tonight, it's better for your system to eat light." I smiled meekly and got on the bus.

The next day I went to the store and headed straight to the exercise section and bought a Richard Simmons exercise album. I took it home, put on some workout clothes, and asked my youngest sister to be my instructor. She enjoyed being able to give me orders for a change. I gave one of my other sister's girlfriends, Gina, from the Bronx, a call and went to get my own hair braided into a natural style; cornrows going up into a small ponytail. (This was a style I used to wear to camp in the summer when I was younger.) For four and a half weeks, I exercised rigorously—two sides of the album every day. I ate only tuna on wheat bread and a glass of juice for lunch, and fish or chicken and salad for dinner. As my body was young it wasn't hard to reform and I was looking damn good for my return to the university. The odd thing was that Nathan had never called me back since the day we spent together. I blamed myself and my appearance for his disappearance and decided I would simply use my time constructively to correct my own problems. Plus, I wasn't gonna call him. I felt he owed me that courtesy.

When Mona saw me she said, "What! Get the fuck out of here! Girl, you lost all that weight. You look good! I'm jealous. You got your hair done, too." I told her about my date with Nathan and about all the things he'd said. Mona straightened out her face sternly and said, "Girl, why do you let him talk to you that way?" I said, "It's nothing but constructive criticism. He was right and look, it got me to fix the problem because I really did have a weight problem." She frowned, "It just seems to me that he's got too much to say. And what about him? Just what does he have to fix?" "Nothing!" I said. Mona shook her head in disbelief and said that I was "too absorbed in him."

I got annoyed and said, "So, what's up, Mona? You got something against men?"

"Don't get me started," she said defiantly. "I grew up in New York City all my life and I got tons of stories."

"So just 'cause you got stories, Mona, does that mean you give up on love?"

"Love!" she shouted. "Now don't tell me you love that nigga!"

"No, I didn't say that. I'm just saying, don't you think that if you take the time and try to find the right man things can work out for the better?"

"The right one! The right one," she threw her hands up in the air, "where the fuck is the right one?"

"Look, you're in engineering school, right? The whole point of being an engineer is to be a problem-solver: to fix things that are broken and make a more advanced, less painful society for everybody . . ."

"Either that," she interrupted, "or to get crazy paid in a short amount of time so you can tell everybody to get the fuck outta your face!" She laughed sarcastically. "My point is," I went on, "in social relationships things have to be fixed because our family structures have been so destroyed. Most of us, including you and I, find it hard to define what being a real man or woman is and what that means."

"Yeah, whatever. Just be careful," Mona cautioned me, "'cause I'm not as dumb as I may look."

"Mona, you wanna go jogging with me in the morning so I can maintain my weight?" I asked.

"I'll go if you're doing it for yourself and not for him," she quipped.

"Of course, it's just for me," I lied.

All during the first two weeks of our new semester I didn't hear from Nathan. I decided I wasn't going down to his room since he hadn't contacted me in what was now more than six weeks since our day in New York. I dealt with my disappointment by becoming even more busy than usual. I drowned my desire for good conversation by working extra hard in my new classes. I began checking out some of the organizations on campus that I always told myself I would look into, but never did.

Saturday morning when I woke up, I knocked on Mona's door. She was already awake trying to solve some of her difficult equations. I decided to go jogging by myself. Before I left I took a good look at Mona. Did she want to go to the hut tonight? It depended, she said, on whether she finished her equations or not. There was something in Mona's face that suggested that she was never happy or satisfied and was always frustrated over something. When I first met her, I would have never thought that somebody so pretty could have so many complaints. She claimed her frustration had everything to do with having chosen engineering as a major. Then why didn't she just change her major? She would simply shrug her shoulders and say, "I gotta do what I gotta do." For Mona, engineering was her ticket out of poverty. Failure was unthinkable, although I think she thought about it all the time. Failure was out of the question so she worked overtime to prevent it from happening. Whatever Mona's problem was, it had caused a deep evident sadness in her and I decided, as a friend and dormmate, I should try to help her out.

Later that evening I pressured Mona into going to the hut with me even though she still had work to do. I forced her to put it aside and pushed open her closet and said, "Let's get fly." I figured if we looked good, put her hair in a new style, and did our nails we'd feel better. Plus it would break the monotony of jeans and T-shirts. So we joked as her gloom began to lift.

The hut was packed. A scheduled performance hadn't started yet. Mona ordered coffee and I ordered herb tea. We sat there laughing about the first half of our year in school and how naive we were. It was a relief to see Mona smile, and I knew I had done the right thing by keeping her out of the library that night.

Just then, Tarsha and her sidekick Jackie came in and sat down at our table. Tarsha was a well-known figure around campus. She was in charge of "university gossip" and "the juicy information hotline." She used her gossip to keep everyone's attention on her. While she spread all of the "news" around, she disregarded the rumor about herself—about how she had gotten dogged by almost the entire Omega Psi Phi fraternity and had enjoyed every minute of it. She was respected by no one, but tolerated by everyone—at least for the fifteen minutes it took her to give you the scoop.

"What's up!" Tarsha said, always louder than everybody else in the room. "Hey girl," me and Mona responded almost at the same time.

"Girrl, I heard you lost all that weight over the Christmas break but I didn't believe it. But now that I look at you it seems like you a whole 'nother person."

"Thanks," I said sarcastically.

"Girl," she continued, "if I didn't know any better I'd swear you was smoking that crack over the holiday!" She laughed and so did Jackie. "Oh, wait a minute now, you got rid of that weave! Poof! just like that it's gone. Better you than me 'cause between you and I, I ain't ever gettin' rid of mine, it gits me too many looks." She laughed at her own joke. Then she turned to Mona and said, "You know my girl Sharnay works in the Center. She told me she saw you over there."

"What center?" I interrupted. But Tarsha ignored my question in her rush to give us the unsolicited list of everybody who had flunked out of school and the reason behind their dismissal. Soon the sound of her voice became so annoying that I just drowned her out and got into my own head. I could still see her lips moving, but I could no longer hear the words coming out. I began to look around the room scanning all of the faces. My eyes settled on a dark spot in the corner. There he was: Nathan sitting in the corner, purposely avoiding the lights and sharing a conversation that he, judging from the look of delight on his face, was obviously enjoying with a green-eyed, brown-haired white girl.

My face dropped to the floor and before I could pick it up, Mona flagged her and said, "Girl, don't you even worry about that." Tarsha chirped, "Worry about what? Worry about what?" "Nothing!" Mona reprimanded instantly. But nosy-ass Tarsha saw the unbroken stare I could not turn away from Nathan's corner table. She said, "You might as well forget that girl 'cause you won't even be able to . . ."

"Shut the fuck up!" Mona interrupted. "Don't you ever stop talking?"

Tarsha grabbed Jackie's arm and said, "You goddamn freshmen think you know every fuckin' thing. I was just tryna put you up on the scoop, but since y'all think the world revolves around you and can't appreciate a good friend well, fuck you then." And they left.

Mona looked at me and said, "Listen girl, don't even play yourself. I told you these men got games for days!"

I got up from my chair forgetting about Mona and walked toward Nathan's table. I caught his eyes even though I was halfway across the room. Our eyes locked and I was sure that he could feel my silent rage. The more steps I took toward him, the more powerful I could feel myself become. As the energy swirled around inside of me, I released it by coordinating my thoughts with the sway of my hips. Shoulders back, head up high, I arrived at the table and stood, blocking out the white girl and staring directly into Nathan's eyes.

"Nathan," I said with quiet force. He smiled a smile of pure innocence, his white teeth lighting up, and said, "This is Astrid." With an enthusiasm that ignored my anger, she said, "Hi! Here, have a seat. Gosh, your hair looks great! Where did you get it done?"

"If I told you, you still wouldn't know."

I looked at her intensely. Her skin was pale and completely devoid of color. Her nose was long and thin. Her teeth were somewhere between off-white and egg-yolk yellow. Her eyes were green, big, and empty. While her hair was straight, there seemed to be some desperate attempt at cornrows, as I saw ten braids cascading down her back. I looked at her and I felt superior, dominant, and far more beautiful. What offended me was the thought that Nathan, or any other black man for that matter, might be so foolish as to think of her as more beautiful. On the table lay *How Europe Underdeveloped Africa* by Walter Rodney. She apparently had put the book on the table in a conspicuous manner as if she thought that any passing black person would instantly think, "Now, there's a cool white girl."

"Your hair does look beautiful," Nathan said. He looked into my eyes and I could feel how much he liked me and how attracted he was. His eyes lowered from my eyes and he swept by my breasts, my newly achieved firm waistline, and landed on my mother-of-the-world hips. I felt his quiet desire and so did she. She knew she couldn't fight the African body and after I was sure Nathan had seen it all, I sat down.

It seemed to me that Astrid had decided to battle me on an intellectual level. She had assumed an air of mental superiority. "I was just telling Nathan," she said, "about my trip to Africa this summer past. Have you been there?"

"No, I haven't, but I wouldn't have actually had to go there to know it."

"Oh, sure you would," she said. "It's really different than America, and the Africans there are different than the blacks in America."

"Yes," I said, "that's a typical outsider's view. But if you had grown up black in America you would understand that white oppression manifests itself in the same way everywhere." I condescendingly offered an example. "An African girl in South Africa is forbidden to speak her own native language. An African girl in America does not even know her own language. An African girl in South Africa is forbidden a proper education. An African girl in America is forbidden a proper education. An African girl in South Africa is likely to lose her father to the gold or coal mine or racist murder. An African girl in America either doesn't know her father at all or may easily lose him to unemployment or murder. In both countries white people are the ruthless evil rulers and black people are the purposely confused and targeted victims. In both countries white girls enjoy the privilege of being white but want to sleep with the few surviving black men at the same time. So you tell me, Astrid, what's the difference?"

For a few moments her face filled with a plum-colored blankness, and I looked at Nathan's eyes shining with a pride he tried to hide. I could tell he received some devilish enjoyment and a tremendous ego boost from the vision of two women both going for the jugular vein over him.

"I understand your hostility," countered Astrid, "but there are some things you have willfully chosen to overlook. In both countries there are good whites who try to help, who sincerely sympathize with the blacks. There's a tremendous amount of working together and most blacks in both countries don't share your hostility, but are in fact very accepting and inviting to whites like myself." Then she looked toward Nathan, who did not return her stare. He looked between us into the space that divided me from her with a stern smileless glare.

"What is the definition of a 'good white'?" I said. "There is no such thing! Is that somebody who, while enjoying the money, privilege, and power that being white automatically offers them, does nothing but offer verbal sympathy to black people? Is that somebody who merely wishes that things will get better while having no intention of giving anything up, of returning stolen lands, stolen jewels, stolen culture? Is that somebody who sends a check to a pacification program for blacks that gives out a turkey on Thanksgiving Day and cookies and Kool-Aid over the summer? Or is that somebody like you, who joins black organizations to bless some beautiful black man with some dirty white pussy so the two of you can contribute some confused and befuddled mulatto children to 'the movement'?"

Astrid jumped to her feet and said, "Nathan! You know me. Don't let her speak to me that way. I don't deserve it."

I looked Nathan in the eye with the full power of black woman spirituality and said, "Nathan knows what's good for him and it's definitely not you. I'll see you tonight, Nathan," and walked away. Astrid left her book on the table, grabbed her knapsack, and ran out as though somebody might chase her. I headed back toward Mona.

Mona had a disgusted pissed-off look. "So, what did you do? Don't tell me. You went over there and beat up on that stupid little white girl when it should of been his black ass you was kicking."

"No Mona, them white girls always tryna take our men. Soon as they smell a little success headed a brother's way, they over there with their legs wide open and ready to cash in."

"Yeah," Mona replied, "they couldn't do none of that shit if brothers weren't willing. Besides, what's the difference between that white girl with her legs wide open and somebody like Tarsha with her legs wide open?"

I looked at Mona sternly. She was brilliant in all that mathematic and scientific shit, but she clearly had no interest in and no knowledge of the history of African people in this country and in understanding what were the factors and influences that produced the mentality of most of our people. I leaned toward Mona and said, "The difference is cause and effect. The white girl represents the people who, throughout history, have caused the destruction of the African culture, the

86

African family, and the African value system. Tarsha, on the other hand, represents what happens to African people, specifically women, after they have been destroyed year by year by the conditions that were created and caused by whites and their government and their educational system."

Mona rolled her eyes, gulped down her last bit of coffee, and said, "Ah, three cups—that should keep me up for the rest of the night. C'mon, I got work to do." We grabbed our stuff. As we left, looking out the corner of my eye, I could see that Russell had joined Nathan in the corner.

Back at the dorm, Mona complained that she couldn't study in her room because of her noisy and inconsiderate roommate. I told her to grab her books and things and come on over. She could study at my desk—all night if she wished. Mona went to the desk, clicked on her light and began studying. I undressed myself thinking deeply about what had happened tonight and asking myself, who was Nathan that he had so successfully intrigued me? Who was this man I was not initially attracted to, but was now mentally entrapped by? Why did he occupy so much of my thoughts? Of one thing I was sure: He was brilliant and I'd never met anybody like him. The endless knowledge that flowed from his deep mind had seduced me and I was addicted. Every conversation was like a new adventure. This was new for me, no boredom, no repetition, and a feeling far more powerful than simple sexual attraction. I fell asleep to the music of these thoughts.

I was awakened by the sound of whispers. My digital clock said it was 3:30 in the morning. I sat up and saw Mona standing, talking softly through a semi-cracked-open door with the chain lock still in place.

"Why don't you just leave her alone? I told you she's sleeping. Do you really expect her to take you seriously?"

"I just wanna talk to her for a few minutes, are you the police? Just tell her I'm here and let her decide for herself."

Oh my God, it was Nathan. I said, "Mona!" She turned around.

"Sorry he woke you up. I tried to tell him that you were already sleeping and to come back in the morning."

"It's all right." I pulled back my covers, put on my slippers, and headed toward the door. Mona looked at me as if to say, "I know you're not going anywhere with that see-through nightgown on and no goddamn bra." I put on my robe. I unchained the door, stepped outside into the dimly lit dormitory hall, and closed the door behind me. I folded my arms in front of me.

"Yes, Nathan?" I said with a firm sensuality. His big brown eyes filled with both a physical and spiritual glow. Then he said, "Man, I'm into you. No more frontin'. I can't deny it. Your brain got me going but it's scary. You're too powerful. I've never seen anything like it before. You got me going. You have my attention. Even when you don't see me you have my attention. Your spirit is so strong it's like an invasion." Nathan's words came gushing out like they had been held too long in a high compression tank. He had begun by looking into my eyes but now his eyes bounced around hoping to land somewhere where they did not have to connect with mine. I suddenly realized that as aggressive, talkative, and knowledgeable as Nathan was, there was also something shy about him. He was physically dominant and in every other way as well. But he seemed to lose "cool points" in my presence.

"Nathan, I know that you can feel that I want you. But I want you on my terms. I'm serious almost always and I don't want to play games." I was searching for the words that would allow Nathan to feel my sensuality and my desire, but also my strength. I wanted to possess him but I also wanted him to know that this female was also fragile and didn't want to be hurt. I told him he should know that "I'm in it for keeps. Not for a night or a couple of weeks."

He smiled and said, "Don't you think I know that? That's why I've been running for weeks. But I realize there's only one way to deal with a woman like you, but I didn't know there were any women like you, so you caught me off guard. That's something that almost never happens. Listen, I can't stay. I gotta go. I just wanted you to know that I'm here."

With my nipples hard-fighting to pop through my robe, I said good-night. Mona was at my desk still studying. I took off my robe and lay back down in bed, heated and surprised with desire.

The next morning I sprang up with new energy. I saw Mona fast asleep, overworked and exhausted, lying on the extra bed with her clothes still on. I took her shoes off and placed them under the bed. I put her legs back on top of the bed so they wouldn't cramp up. I jumped in the shower, got dressed, and went to a regularly held meeting of the African Student Organization in which I had become active. This was the group on campus that had undertaken to represent the interests of all African students. Since we were at a largely white university, we of course had many so-called interests. For instance, we had to fight with the university administrators to get the right to control the student fees of all black and Latino students on campus. The administrators claimed that separating student fees into racial categories was a form of reverse discrimination. They were dumbfounded, however, when we presented documentation and evidence showing that the structures and committees that were supposed to represent all students on campus had only invited white guest lecturers, presented white rock bands, held white beauty pageants, and sponsored events that centered around white European-American culture. We argued that we were entitled to control our own monies and activities both on the principle of self-rule and because of the way white student committees had almost entirely failed to address any of the aspirations or needs of the black and Latino students. Even in the few instances where these committees attempted to include African culture, they failed because aside from not actually being black themselves, they had been educated by a school system whose racist architects had refused to include a curriculum that sought to explore and understand people of color who, after all, represented seven-eighths of the world's population.

We also had to fight to keep the few black professors that we had. The few black courses and the comparatively low number of entering black and Latino students made our goals difficult to attain, and, once met, difficult to keep. Despite the myth in white America that said black students were underqualified and incompetent, the majority of black students in universities across America had to work four times as hard, struggle for goods, services, and education as their white counterparts, for whom these precious things were assumed to be automatically guaranteed and available. Moreover, black students had to preoccupy themselves with fighting off racial attacks, while still having to compete academically on the same level as everyone else in the classroom. Most white students never had to endure or overcome similar difficulties or obstacles. The pressures on black students were unrelenting.

Within the African Student Organization, among ourselves, we faced major challenges. We had to rule out self-pity, and learn to combat the contradictions our environment created in most black people that caused us to hate ourselves, to be envious of each other, and disunited. We had to learn to be responsible for ourselves, even though we were groomed in a society that fostered dependency in our community. We had to eliminate laziness and apathy. We had, most of all, to discover a way to turn our anger—and sometimes even our hatred—into something constructive, not destructive for our own people. None of this was easy.

Meanwhile, my classes were going fine and I could feel myself advancing with every lesson. I was learning the history of America from an African perspective in my black classes, and the history of America from a European perspective in my white classes. Of course, like every black student, I had many more white courses than black ones. Nevertheless, I was learning the international nature of our problems as a race and was feeling a stronger and stronger bond with my people whether they were born in the Caribbean, on the African continent itself, or in the Americas. And, like most students (black or white), I was stumbling through the courses that I hated, but needed to take anyway.

Later that night, after my classes and meetings were finished, I went to unwind in the graduate student lounge.

This was a place that was quiet and comfortable with couches, La-Z-Boys, and study tables. Freshmen were not supposed to use it, but the security was relaxed and the environment was inviting. I sat down in the comfortable La-Z-Boy and laid my head back trying to slow down the thoughts that began racing the second I opened my eyes each morning. Soon I felt a tap on my shoulder. It was Russell, Nathan's friend.

"Hey Russell, what's up?"

"Chilling," he responded. "I'm trying to finish this paper for my Quantitative Methods course."

"Good luck," I said, baffled by the course title.

"I can't believe I'm graduating but thank God it's finally over."

"Well, Russell, congratulations. I can't say that I can really relate since I just got here, but I'm finishing my freshman year here and believe me, I've been through a lot."

"Yeah, but I've watched you and you've grown a lot. Don't let anybody fool you, you came in strong, real strong. In fact, I know women in the senior class who are nowhere near your level. It's a shame when you really think about it."

"What is?"

"How can a brother marry any of these silly women we see around here? In five minutes they'll have a degree but they still won't have any common sense. Then the same women will turn around and call a brother irresponsible for not being able to make a commitment. But how can a brother make a commitment to an empty-headed, materialistic, self-centered college girl?"

"Funny thing," I said, "brothers and sisters have so many negative things to say about one another. It seems like we have to find some common ground somewhere, a place where we can start building."

"True," Russell said, "but in order to start building there has to be a foundation. How do you give a woman, who has already lived twenty-one years of her life in a state of total confusion and valueless chaos, a new foundation? How do you teach a woman that a brother's car, job, and wallet are less important than his integrity, direction, values, character, and family?"

I watched Russell as he talked. He was a serious guy, a practicing Christian. Brown-skinned with jet-black curly hair, he was considered handsome enough to have his choice of women, but he was finicky. Now he stood before me pouring his heart out about the poor selection of women in a university where there were four times as many black women as black men. Was he just talking or was there a specific reason he was telling me all of this? So I tested him.

"I think we all have weaknesses but I'm willing to overlook some of them and work on the ones that can be corrected. That's why I admire Nathan." Sure enough, his face soured at the mention of his friend's name. "Nathan," I went on, "has taught me a lot and I appreciate it so much. It's really the first time any brother has taken the time to show and explain things I never knew. I think, if we could ever really get together, we'd make a hell of a team."

Russell said flatly, "Yeah, Nathan's interesting. I'd say he's more of a contradiction than anything else. It's like I said about the foundation. It's hard to start building one at twenty-three years old."

I heard Russell but I wasn't really listening. I was completely taken with Nathan and as far as "foundations" went, from what I had recently learned, Islam seemed as strong a foundation as Christianity. Plus, Nathan had a certain charisma that Russell lacked.

Russell cut the conversation short and exited with the words: "Everybody has to learn for themselves." I interrupted by saying, "Yeah, but anybody can be helped." Russell didn't let my comment go. He said, "But they have to want to be helped. Anyhow, I'm in room two-oh-two. You probably didn't know that. Come by and talk with me sometime—that is, if you need to talk."

A week passed by and no sign of Nathan. I thought to myself, "Oh, he's still running." I stopped by his room and knocked on his door but he wasn't in. Then I did something intrusive. I read the mini-bulletin board on his door. His friend Rich was telling him about a party happening in apartment 2F at the campus of the agricultural school, which was about fifteen minutes away by bus. I jotted down the information on a sheet of paper and ran upstairs to plan what I was going to wear to the party I was about to crash.

I rang apartment 2F's doorbell confidently. I was crystal clear that I risked getting dissed. A brother opened the door and welcomed me in. The place was "back-to-back and belly-to-belly." The sweat was pouring off the walls. Inside there were several rooms. One was for those who were strictly there to dance to the music. One room was for the so-called intellectuals to sit around sipping drinks and talking. Another room was set aside for people who were doing anything that should not be publicly displayed. I slipped my way into the "coatroom," which was simply a bed piled high with coats, and relieved myself of my coat. I then began looking for Nathan.

I walked around slowly, laughing at myself as I realized that it would be damn near impossible to see him in the dark. But, to my surprise, in the corner was Nathan completely defying the organization of the party as he, two brothers, and one sister stood close together talking in the room where everybody else was dancing. I decided I would slide over by the corner, start dancing, and pretend it was a complete coincidence if Nathan happened to see me there.

I started dancing by myself. Within seconds a brother came out of nowhere and started dancing with me. If I had calculated things correctly Nathan would now be standing directly behind where I was dancing with his back toward me. So as the music played and the drum machines ripped, I maneuvered my dancing, playing off the full house and "accidentally" backing right into Nathan. He turned around to do a simple check and turned back around to his conversation. It must have taken him a minute to process what had just happened because that's how long it took him to turn back around, place his hand on my shoulder, and spin me around asking, "What are you doing here?"

Squinting my eyes as if I couldn't see him, I said, "Excuse me?" and jerked my shoulder back. Nathan, perhaps believing I could not recognize him in the dark and sweaty room, said, "It's me, Nate!" I then plastered a smile on my face and asked, "What, can't I party like everybody else?" Nathan said, "Yeah, it just bugged me out to see you here. Most freshmen aren't up on this spot." "Well," I said, "I know a lot of people—you'd be surprised. Besides, I told you before, I go where the music goes. Are you dancing or just talking tonight?" I knew I had to become more aggressive on a sexual level; otherwise my relationship with Nathan might never happen on more than a mental and spiritual plane.

Just as Nathan opened his mouth to answer my question, the sister he had been talking with in the corner when I first came in tapped him and said, "Nathan, here's your drink." Nathan held his hand up as if it were a stop sign and said, "Come on, now. You know I don't drink." The girl stared back hard at Nathan. She said nothing and simply walked away with the drink in her hand.

"Who's that?" I asked.

"Oh, nobody. She's just a friend of Rich's. I don't really know her at all."

"That's good." I took the opportunity to use the atmosphere to my advantage. I moved closer to Nathan and pressed my breast against his belly and placed my hand on his waist. "Damn, it's crowded in here." I knew he felt the warmth of my body and I felt the warmth and security of his. I looked into his eyes and motioned for him to bring his head down toward my lips. "I need to talk with you—no games, no running, alone." I slid my hand from his ear gently down over his sculptured face. Now both of my hands were on his waist.

"No problem," he said. "We'll meet tomorrow, you know where to find me."

I was disappointed, for no real reason except that I felt it was more of the same catch-me-if-you-can. He was definitely a ladies' man. Everywhere I saw him there seemed to be at least two women trying to attach themselves to him. But I sensed that he was looking for more than an attachment. Those girls were easy. I wasn't, and I could see that anything that came hard to Nathan was scary to him because he was used to commanding every stage and getting what he wanted through his charm without ever having to ask outright.

The next day reality kicked in, and I had to crash a paper I had neglected to write. This made it impossible for me to go mess around with Nathan. When I got back from the computer room where I was typing up my final draft, I found a note under my door from him. It said, "Even when you don't see me, I'm there." I smiled and decided Nathan was into the drama of the chase and was probably gonna turn me out if we ever did hit those sheets. With any luck it would be as hot and perfect as my own fantasies. Later that night I planned to pay him a visit. Maybe I would lock him in his own room and jump right on top of him. Or maybe I would just stop by and he would have special plans for me.

There was a knock at my door. When I opened it, there stood the white girl who lived in the room next door. I looked at her inquisitively and she responded to my look by saying, "Telephone." I went out into the hallway to pick up the pay phone, which was the only way to reach people in the freshman dorm. It was my mother's voice on the other end of the line. She was calling to tell me that my sister was pregnant. My mouth fell open as I tried to imagine any man lying on top of my thirteen-year-old baby sister. I thought of how naive and fragile and young she seemed to me and I thought of how sexually unaware I was at her age.

"I'm going to take her to get an abortion on Friday morning," my mother said.

"No! Mommy, I don't believe in that. It's wrong."

"If she doesn't get this abortion her whole life will be ruined. She's too young to have a baby."

"Yes, Mommy, I understand all that, but she has you, two older sisters, and an older brother. We can all help to take care of the baby."

"Look," my mother responded short of patience and annoyed, "I'm not taking care of nobody's baby. I have no time for this foolishness. I just called to let you know your sister will probably be upset after the procedure so maybe you can come home for the weekend or just give her a call or something."

"Mommy, does she want to get an abortion?"

"No, she doesn't, but she's too young to make an intelligent decision."

"Is she there? Can I speak to her?"

"No, she's not here and I don't even know where she's at. I'll tell her to call you when she gets home tonight. Listen, I have to go, I don't need to run up my phone bill. See ya, take care."

My heart was bursting. My sister and I had always been so close, and never did she mention anything about being sexually involved with boys. I felt mixed emotions. One of them was guilt. Had I left my sister at a young age unprepared and thus unable to make proper decisions? The other emotion was anger. I felt that my mother had not properly supervised her. She didn't even mention who the baby's father was, but knowing my mother, that was completely irrelevant anyway. Moreover, she didn't even know where my sister was most of the time. It's precisely that casual attitude between mothers and daughters that leads to young girls looking for real love and attention in all the wrong and premature places. So, since I had been away at school for the past eight months, my baby sister had found a new best friend. Only this time it was a man and their relationship was sexual, not sisterly. Spiritually, I felt decisions to abort were made too quickly with a disgusting ease of conscience. Abortion had become so normal in the black community that it was like pissing or shitting or something. No real thought went into the decision. There was no remorse or hesitation. Worse, there was no worry over what I had come to think of as the "spiritual tax." The cost your spirit and soul has to pay on Judgment Day for the reckless and arbitrary destruction of life.

I sat through my American history course in a daze, half-listening to the professor explain the institution of slavery and how historically it had been "overdramatized and oversold" by black people and so-called academicians. Too much, he said, had been made over the rape of slave women and the sale of slave babies when in fact, he insisted, most of the slaves, their masters, and their masters' families had been tightly knit units woven together by love and mutual need. He went on to say that most of the plantations in the South were not big with tens and hundreds of slaves and animals, but were in fact small farms owned by white families who had somewhere between one and five slaves. Within these relationships, he claimed, love had developed along with a mutual dependency. As evidence, he cited the fact that black women had actually breast-fed most of their owner's white children themselves, so naturally there was an intimate, even a maternal bond between the mammies and the little white children they lovingly cared for.

Now, usually I would have spoken out and protested such claptrap, but my thoughts of my little sister became inter-twined with the professor's obscene "lessons" and I felt vomit brewing in the pit of my stomach. With a reputation as a deep and critical thinker, this professor also taught a course on the Holocaust. How could he not understand that there can be no love in a master-slave relationship? Such a relationship, it seemed obvious to me, was based solely on power. The power of the white world with its control of food, land, resources, police dogs, prisons, and lynching ropes over the life of the powerless black slave victim. The slave had only two choices: either to submit and pretend to be a genteel figment of her master's imagination, serving him with the appearance of happy cooperation, or to fight back and have the flesh torn from her body until both her spirit and body were broken. Or perhaps she might plot the destruction of her master only to be betrayed by some other slave unwilling to risk the consequences of rebellion, and then hung from a rope to be picked and plucked by vultures. Was my professor so steeped in the insidious ideology of white supremacy that he had somehow convinced himself that black women had suckled the children of their white masters voluntarily? Had he actually believed that African women preferred suckling these foreign children over suckling their own children, who were left unattended and ofttimes hungry? Did he really believe that both love and lust were elements in a master-slave sexual relationship that, in reality, had amounted to a rape that had become so routine its victim had to either make it a "normal" function of life or lose her life or mind or both? And, most of all, I raged, if slavery had been "overdramatized and oversold," why then had millions of African people found it so hard to knit their lives, psyches, and families back together again—a hardship as exemplified by my own fatherless shell of a family, where my own African mother had become so petrified of the constraints of life that murder of the unborn was an easy call? I packed up my books and walked out.

That night I knocked on Nathan's door. I was depressed but sensed that Nathan would understand as he had a great understanding of many things. He opened the door with the usual warm smile. I closed the door behind me and put the chain lock on. Inside Nathan's room was cleanliness, healthiness, a careful arrangement of dim lights and candles, incense, and jazz. His smile widened and he said, "So, the lion has come to the end of her . . ." I interrupted, "I came to talk."

I told Nathan the story of my thirteen-year-old baby sister and my sentiments about abortion. He agreed with me and said that even though people tried to convince themselves that the seed was not a life, by spiritual law it was a life at the moment of conception. A life that, according to Nathan, Allah had already written a scroll for. He told me that he believed so strongly in the Creator that he feared the consequences of any evildoing. He admitted that most people were so ignorant and foolish that they didn't realize that there were consequences to our every action. He told me I should calm down and relax a little because a person with four sisters like himself could testify to the fact that there would be many more things that would be done by my family members that would be completely out of my control. He confided that his father, a former Jehovah's Witness, was an alcoholic. He said that when he went home from college during breaks he would often encounter, seated around the television in the living room, his drunk father and a couple of his sisters, who had either reefer, cocaine, or heroin in their systems. Tears welled up in his eyes but did not fall. But they fell from mine.

"Have you ever tried peppermint or coconut soap?" Nathan asked. I hadn't. He went into his closet and pulled out a robe and the soap and pointed me toward the shower, saying it would help me to relax. I went slowly. While in the shower, many thoughts raced through my head. Was this a set-up? But wasn't this what I wanted anyway? Did Nathan care about me or was this simply his procedure with women? As the water flowed down my face and the steam cleansed my pores, I decided to relax and explore and allow nature to take its course. I came out of the shower smelling like the Caribbean.

"Lay down," he instructed. "You can stay here tonight. I'll keep you company." I slipped under the covers and laid my head on the pillow. Nathan sat down by my side and said, "Have you ever read *Invisible Man* by Ralph Ellison and *Native Son* by Richard Wright?" I hadn't. Ellison and Wright, he said, were powerful authors. They dealt with the question of black manhood, African manhood, and what it meant. "You know, it's very difficult to be a man when you're black in America. Very few of us really know how. Most of us fake it and we do a good job because our women are so confused that they're not hard to fool." He turned toward me and said, "Sometimes I feel like the Invisible Man and sometimes I feel like Bigger Thomas, the big black killer in *Native Son*." Then, smiling, he said, "There's something special about you, girl, something spiritual and uncorrupted, something pure. That's why I ran from you. Because I know you are directly from God and I don't want to hurt you."

Nathan turned off the lights and only the flame from the candle he had lit flickered in the darkness. As he undid his clothes I noticed for the first time what I believed a real man looked like. His body was tight and defined, every muscle, every ligament. Not an ounce of fat. His legs were runner's legs, long, black, tight, and sleek. He got under the covers and I put my hand on his stomach and moved it softly to his chest, saying to myself, "So, this is what a real man feels like, hard and muscular, not soft and flabby like Chuck." My fingers moved in and out of his many grooves, inclinations and declines. I was young and fascinated. Nathan turned to his side and kissed me with his thick African lips. For the first time I felt secure, my body bursting with pleasure as his lips offered me a comfort, warmth and power I had never known. My body surrendered as Nathan took charge. He was the navigator of a willing ship in a tumultuous and inviting sea. I whispered in his ear, "Be gentle, this is a first for me" (a half-truth), and he entered into my body the stiffest, hardest, fullest, and most welcomed flesh I had ever known.

I woke up the next morning to shades wide open and the celebrating springtime sun beaming, a clean, fresh-smelling room and an empty bed. Nathan was gone. I panicked and wondered whether I was officially a "stunt" that had been "tricked" by an upperclassman. But to my relief, a brief frenzy led me to a note that Nathan had left on his desktop. It said, "Peace. You're deep and natural. Don't worry, you'll get yours in a box." I smiled, trying to decipher his cryptic message. I quickly concluded that he felt I was special and that that feeling would one day lead him to offer me an engagement ring, because rings came in a box. The note allowed me to feel that he still respected me because marriage was a topic hardly ever introduced by a black man voluntarily—at least, not in my world.

Nathan graduated. Mona and I completed our freshman year. My sister "survived." And Nathan and I had come together. He was my man and I was his woman. I wondered what would happen to us now that he was officially out of school and I had to return in September. But I was so happy and in love that I decided to cross that bridge when I got to it. My body was adjusting to making love on a regular basis, as it now became more of an overwhelming desire certain to receive regular fulfillment. Needless to say, being involved with Nathan had me three to five times more advanced than the average freshman going on to become a sophomore. With Nathan's encouragement, I read more books in my free time than books that had been assigned reading by my professors. I went to museums, concerts, bookstores, libraries, get-togethers, lectures. We went to parks and on walks and Nathan took me shopping, explaining to me the difference between low-quality and high-quality shoes and materials. We compared notes on our family trials and tribulations and he even had me, a Christian girl, participate in the Muslim holy fast called Ramadan. My whole diet changed to a completely healthy menu. My weight balanced out and for the first time in my life I maintained a fine figure. Under the challenge of a "dare," I had quit eating red meat for good.

Since the day after graduation, Nathan had been looking for a job. As May turned into June and June turned into July, Nathan became cranky and short on patience. He had expected simply to graduate and be rewarded for his degree, his intelligence, and his discipline. He had believed that the college degree would free him from poverty. Despite his deep understanding of racism, he believed that the degree would at least grant him tolerance from white people and some sort of economic integration and inclusion. He'd come home from his job search and interviews amazed that, despite a double major in history and political science, people were asking him, rather amazingly, if he could type, play football, coach a team, or drive a truck.

We began to discuss the prospect of starting his own business. I told him he was very talented and that together we could find a way to turn some of his skills into a profitable little start-up business. He confessed that, despite his college education, he had absolutely no idea how to go about starting his own business.

Meanwhile, I had found work as a part-time intern in a law firm. I would find out what the legal requirements were for starting a business. Two days later, after talking to my boss, a black male attorney who specialized in criminal law and had traveled throughout the world and served in many offices, I had a small understanding of what was necessary.

I arrived at Nathan's house with a Certificate of Incorporation form and a short pamphlet about tax rules and regulations for forming a corporation. Nathan said my enthusiasm always amazed him. Oddly, he didn't seem enthusiastic at all. He seemed distraught, discouraged, and depressed. Careful not to be too pushy, I briefly explained that we could get our friends together to be small investors, once we agreed on what type of business we wanted to have, and what type of services we could offer that people would be willing to purchase. I told him to take his time and when he finished thinking we could share our conclusions.

By late August Nathan still had not been hired anywhere and when we were together he seemed aloof. He resisted the conversation about moving forward with the business plan because he didn't seem to believe in it. He didn't believe it was feasible, or that it could be successful enough to pay his bills. School was set to start for me and the African Student Organization was off to an early start planning and organizing events for incoming black and Latino freshmen. The plan was to get them so involved that they would enjoy college enough to work hard and stay enrolled, something white universities had always failed to achieve on their own. I asked the organization if we could sponsor a speaker for the orientation. I suggested Nathan and said he was a positive example because he was a former student. He had graduated and that was what we were encouraging. He was politically aware and had a degree that qualified him to render both a political and an historical analysis. The argument was hard to sell since he was also my man, but my persistence won and they were willing to offer Nathan $500 as an honorarium for delivering a lecture and holding a workshop.

That night I told Nathan about the offer and said that I saw this as the beginning of his lecture career, something that could prove to be quite profitable. He gave me a half-smile and dismissed my help as charity. I argued that it could only be considered charity if he was actually not qualified to do what was being offered, but that I had simply used some contacts to get his qualified foot in the door. After all, this was how people made business deals all the time.

I was excited about returning to school and the first week of classes resumed. I was officially a sophomore. I looked at going back to college as presenting me with even greater opportunities to learn. Of course I would miss Nathan's everyday presence but, as he was my man, I knew we'd talk every day on the phone and get together on weekends. I spent my week organizing myself and getting my room ready. This year I again had what was called a "single," which simply meant a dormitory room for one person. I got it to ensure privacy for me and Nathan. I planned my academic schedule so I would have Fridays off, giving me three precious days a week with Nathan.

Friday afternoon I got to Nathan's house a little earlier than expected and he had a guest. He seemed so upbeat from his usual unemployed funk that I knew this must be somebody important. He introduced the brother to me as David and said that he was his "old running partner," his "man," his "partner in crime," the brother who had "taught me everything I know today." I was impressed with anybody who could claim credit for Nathan's brilliant mind so I smiled brightly and said, "What's up! Nice to meet you."

David was dark like Nathan, just a little bit shorter, and seemed about five or six years older. He grabbed my hand and kissed it. He smiled, revealing a beautiful set of white teeth just like Nathan's. He said, "You're even finer than Nathan said." He turned toward Nathan and said, "Yo, she's beautiful." David seemed even more polished and smoother than Nathan but that was to be expected since he was, after all, Nathan's "teacher."

Nathan signaled me to come into the kitchen. There Nate said to me quietly, "Baby, do you mind if we change our date until tomorrow night? I haven't seen Dave in over a year and he's telling me about a job he has lined up for me at an advertising firm." The name of the firm sounded important and prestigious. I was so happy I was through the roof. Not because I was particular about an advertising firm, but because Dave had so clearly lifted Nathan's spirit and I knew it would be easier for a man to help another man with a job than for his woman to help him. I personally didn't care who helped Nathan as long as he was relieved of the tremendous pressure he had been under. It was this pressure that was destroying his attitude and taxing our relationship. I gave Nathan a kiss and a warm hug and said, "I'll see you tomorrow then, baby. Good luck!"

Tomorrow came but Nathan never did. I ended up sleeping on the couch in his living room all night Saturday. I woke up about 4:30 Sunday morning and no Nate. My whole body was tense and my neck was stiff. I was worried that something terrible might have happened to him. By eleven o'clock I began receiving glances from Nathan's mother that clearly indicated I had "overstayed my welcome," at least in Nathan's absence. She, too, I thought, was anxious over her son's whereabouts. I packed up my little bag and left to get on the train to go back to school. I did not hear from Nathan for the rest of the day. I assumed that he had not come home yet and it took all of my discipline to keep from calling his house. At eleven that night I broke down and called. Nathan's mother answered with exasperation. Still no Nate. Monday I had classes back-to-back all day long. At the end of the day, I skipped dinner and went straight to my room to wait for the call I kept hoping to receive. I sat there stiff. I held in my pee, scared that if I went to the bathroom I wouldn't hear the phone ring. Still nothing but silence.

Tuesday night I packed up my overnight bag and got on the train to Nathan's. By this time, I felt someone was playing a game with me. I arrived at about 9:30. When I rang the bell Nathan's sister answered. Instead of inviting me in, she stood there as if she was uncertain about what I wanted. She knew what I wanted. I wanted Nathan. "Is Nathan home?" I asked, hanging on the end of my rope. "Yes, he just got back but he's upstairs saying his prayers right now and does not want to be disturbed." Resenting the fact that she was treating me like I had not been at their house every day for the past three and a half months, I was overcome with tears. I pushed her aside and ran through the door up the stairs to Nathan's room. I flung his bedroom door open and there he was: incense burning and bent over in prayer facing the East. Embarrassed, ashamed, and confused, I quickly closed the door so I wouldn't disturb him any further. By this time his sister was at the top of the steps looking like she wanted to kick my ass, and she sarcastically spit out, "I told you so. Now, can you wait downstairs in the living room?" It was more of an order than a question, so I went straight down.

Nathan finally came downstairs to the living room where I was nervously patting my foot on the floor. His head was down and his eyes were lowered. He looked like he had seen a ghost. Something told me not to touch him so I didn't. I decided that instead of blurting out "Where the fuck have you been?" I would be cool and wait for him to explain. There was silence. Finally, I said, "What's up, Nate? Are you okay?" He said flatly, "I'm fine." He didn't look up. "Listen, I want to do some reading tonight in my *Holy Quran* so could you do me a favor? Could you please leave?" The request was abrupt but not hateful. I knew something was wrong but he looked too far gone for me to reach him at that moment. I picked up my bag and said, "Nate, I'll leave. But please, let me help whatever the problem is. We're supposed to be partners—not you on the inside and me on the outside." Nathan said, "Yeah, I'll call you."

At around 10:00 P.M. on Wednesday, the next day, I was sitting at my desk doing my homework. The phone rang. It was Nathan. "Hi," I said softly. "I miss you. When can I see you?" Nate replied solemnly, "You can't. I decided it's best if we don't see each other. I'm asking you not to come, not to call, not to do anything."

I tried to speak but my voice had packed up and left.

"I know you'll want to be friends but we can't be friends either. We need to just eliminate all communication."

"Why?" I squeaked.

"It's not you. You're beautiful. I'd even say you're as perfect as any man could ask for. It's . . ."

I began to cry, repeating softly, "Why?"

"Because it's the way it has to be. I'm no good for you."

Then I became angry and hysterical and my voice jumped out all over the place. "Whose decision is that? Whose decision is it as to whether you are good enough for me or not?"

"You'll be all right in a few days, you're a strong woman," he said as if I was sitting there in a blue suit with a big red "S" on my chest.

"I didn't date you to be 'all right.' I was 'all right' when you met me. I dated you because you complemented me and I complemented you. So stop saying that dumb shit, 'you'll be all right,' that's not the goddamn point!"

Then he said "Take care," and I heard the click as he hung up on me.

I called back four times and got the busy signal. I dialed again and his mother answered and coldly announced, "He's not here." I jumped on the train and went to his house. His sister just opened up the upstairs window and shouted out, "He's not here." Two weeks passed. Nathan's family grew tired and angry over my repeated calls and impromptu visits. So I looked up the address for the advertising firm he was applying to and headed to Madison Avenue. When I got there the receptionist confirmed that he was employed there but in order to get upstairs I would need a pass. The receptionist called him on the phone and then told me that my pass was denied. I decided to wait outside until 5:00 P.M., figuring that we would see each other when he got off work. But he knew my ways and didn't come out. He wouldn't accept my calls or my visits. He wouldn't accept me.

I buried myself in three times my usual amount of schoolwork. When anybody asked about Nathan I responded with silence. Not because it angered me, but because the whole thing was too painful. It was hard enough to think about it, but to discuss it would have destroyed me.

Seventy days, seventy prayers, and twenty-five lost pounds later, at 7:00 P.M. I received a call. It was hard to hear the voice clearly because there was so much noise in the background. "I need you, please come. I need you." "Nate! Nate! Is that you?" The background music and chatter was so loud I wasn't sure if it was him or if I was bugging out completely.

"I'm at Mickey's on East Fiftieth Street, please come now, I'll wait." Click.

Two hours later, I walked through a crowded bar filled with men and women dressed in business-style suits, trench coats, laughing, drinking, and smoking. A ton of smoke filled the air. Allergic to cigarettes and disgusted by the smell of them, I was anxious to find Nate fast. I found him bellying up to the bar ordering "another rum and coke, please." I looked at him. He had obviously been drinking for at least several hours. I sat in the stool next to him as my respect for him began to plunge at an accelerating rate.

Nathan smiled and said, "I can't believe you came. You look so beautiful." He leaned over to kiss me, missed, and fell. I was shocked. I leaned over to help him up and he said, "That's okay. I can get up myself." He lifted himself up and moved toward me to give me a hug. I recoiled. "You smell disgusting. You know I hate the smell of alcohol." He said, "Please don't," stumbling into a nearby booth and asking me to sit with him.

Baffled by his fall from grace, I sat down wanting to know what had happened to my strong Muslim man. "Nate! What's going on?"

"I got the job!"

"Well, I can see that. What else is going on?"

"I'm down here with all these dressed-up perverts. They like to play with little boys and go home and say, 'Hey, honey, how's the kids?' " He started laughing.

"Why did you leave me Nate? I don't understand this. We were strong when we were together. Not like you are now. Where did you go that weekend?" His laugh was a harsh and bitter bark.

"I was with my lover, David! He helped me get this way, you know. I tried to fight it. I tried to fight the demons but no matter what I did and how hard I tried the demons kept coming back and coming back."

The blood seemed to empty from my body and spill all over the floor. I sat lifeless for what seemed an eternity. Old scenes of love, prayer, respect, education, and mutual history flashed and raced through my brain. I lost all sense of desire for Nate. There was no longer any relationship to fix—at least as far as I was concerned. It was just one human being helping a dirty, drunk, and confused human being out of a bar before some tragedy like robbery or murder came upon him. I helped Nate up, walked slowly through the streets of New York with him to the train station. I paid his and my train fare and took him back to my room. I laid him on my bed where he fell fast asleep. I took off his shoes, coat, and opened his necktie and the first few buttons of his shirt. I grabbed the chair from under my desk and sat in it, where I slept until morning. When I awoke I gave Nate a bowl of hot water, a wash cloth, and two aspirins. My face was blank and my actions merely functional. I sat back down in my chair and waited. The room was filled with silence and shame.

"So . . . Nate is gay."

"No!" He spit back in the strong voice I was accustomed to hearing. "I never use that term, it's a lie. Do I look happy to you? Was Mona happy?"

I gasped in more than a mouthful of air and began to cough. He silently with his eyes confirmed, yes, Mona, too.

"I love women. I love you. I think you're beautiful. But I'm sick. It comes in spurts. I'll be fine for months and then when the pressure mounts up, the feeling comes back again. The demons start calling me and I find myself thinking about some perverted activity."

"What about Islam?" I asked.

"Islam is pure. Islam is perfect. I use it to stay strong. But sometimes I fail. Islam does not fail. I fail."

"Explain to me how something like this can happen to you. Somebody whom I look up to?"

"It's racism."

Right then I got pissed off. I felt he was using something I felt strongly about to make excuses for himself to further manipulate me. "Please! Take responsibility for your own shortcomings."

He responded, "Black Nate, Nate the spade. You so black you blue. Who can see you. Yeah, I liked women like every other young brother does. But women didn't love me. It was always a joke, a crack, a snap. David was a friend of my older sister. They were in some real estate courses together. He came by my house for the first time one day with my sister. He looked at me and began to tell me how handsome I was. He had all kinds of information about blackness and the beauty of African people. My sister thought it was good that I have a role model. She said I needed a strong man to fill in for my father. So she brought him over to the house after class all the time.

"Only thing she didn't know was David liked little black boys. So instead of loving women who didn't seem to love me, or have anything decent to say, I loved David, the first person to tell me anything positive about myself at a young and impressionable age. By the time women started to admire me and my blackness, my mind was already twisted and I couldn't relate. I was confused and looking for help. But I don't have to tell you how hard it is to get good help in our community.

"My junior year in high school one of my teachers took an interest in me for what he said was my brilliance and intelligence. He took me under his wing and he introduced me to Islam. I loved Islam because it gave me clarity. I understood what I must do as a man. It gave me a set of guidelines and a purpose. But I had been so corrupted and misled by that time that I agreed with Islam intellectually and spiritually but had to fight with my perverted emotions and the fact that at a young age I was taught to look at men in a perverted way and women in a negative way.

"When I met you, you were a change and a challenge. See, I could pretend that 'my problem' was under control by clinging to Islam and not having to deal with women in any real way. The women made that easy. They were empty-headed, misguided, and had no self-respect. To put them off all I had to do was keep pointing out their faults so they would never see my faults. I knew they would never be able to catch up to me intellectually. They couldn't even decipher my games. I did have sex with them, but I didn't have to answer to them.

"Then you came along. Beautiful, intelligent, aggressive, political, and spiritual. I couldn't find any angles. I was genuinely turned on. I was aroused sexually, and in every way. But I was confused so I tried to stay away. But you kept coming and coming. So I turned more and more to Islam. I prayed for strength and direction. I entered the relationship with you out of a true love for you, a real attraction, but still knowing that I wasn't the man that you deserved. That's why I left. Because you deserve a real man. But in America it will be hard to find because we've all been so destroyed in one way or another."

"So, I was like an experiment for you."

"No, I wouldn't say that. Believe me, I am not gay. My feelings were and still are real. Nothing physical happened when I saw David. Nothing. Just painful memories of incomplete manhood. But the memories haunt me to this day and it's gonna take time for me to get my program stabilized and on track. Believe me, if I didn't love you, I wouldn't be here disgracing myself with the story that I have never told anyone. But I had to tell you because I believe you are of God, a mirror for me to look into. You're a challenge for me to be stronger. But, honestly speaking, it will take years for me to catch up with you. And when I picture myself inside my mind's eye, I see one person not two. That's because I have to repair myself before I can unite with someone as sure and true as you are. So I freed you because I love you. I don't want you to suffer through years of my problems."

I sat motionless trying to digest all Nathan was confessing to me. Yes, I could see how racism had scarred us all one way or another. I could see that we have all had the course and direction of our lives affected and for some rearranged by racism. But I was no longer attracted to Nathan. He now sat before me a shattered husk of a man. I was concerned about him as a human being. So just as he set me free, I would set him free, and the pain inside me would soon wither and perhaps my wisdom would expand. I would continue to fight the racism that rearranges the minds of our people. I would have to if we

African women were to save our sons. "But Nate," I said, "you lied to me. That's the thing that hurts me most."

Nate stood up and slowly collected his few things. He looked me in the eye and said, "If people lie to God each and every day, in their prayers, in their promises, and in their actions, what makes you think they won't lie to you?"

three

Nikki

"Yeah, right . . ." Brian sipped his beer sitting on Nikki's couch with his feet propped up on a chair. His voice was low and relaxed, the calm sound of a working man after a hard day's work and a cold drink. He was speaking with authority on the topic of women. If anybody was an expert on the subject it was Brian. A college junior majoring in business and mathematics, he was also a track star. In between his studies and athletics, he managed to hold down a part-time job at UPS. For me, as for many women I knew, Brian was a fantasy: an intelligent brother who had his shit together, was rumored to have a big dick, and was comfortable with being a strong black man. I listened carefully as he continued:

"See, where you brothers mess up at is trying to handle too much at one time. You need to find yourself a 'good woman' and cool out with her. That way you can concentrate on all the other things that gotta be done. You see, once you start all that lying, you gotta remember what you said. You be standing there sweating and fighting, got women screaming and crying all the time. Who needs that? I mean, a brother like me needs some peace of mind."

Art, the brother Brian was talking to, was unimpressed. He had his own ideas about women. Art was a basketball player whom everybody called "Slick" because of the way he would routinely fake out his opponent before taking him to the hoop. The nickname also came from his easy way with the women on campus. It was strange to me how these two managed to be best friends when their outlook on life was so different. Even though they were hugely competitive with each other, it was clear to everyone that they shared a real brotherly love. Slick wasn't giving Brian an inch:

"Man, you give these bitches too much credit. These ain't the times of your mom's or mine. These girls are 'hoes! They don't have no respect for themselves. Man, that's why you gotta 'stick and move.' Don't invest no time in them and damn sure don't give them none of your loot. They living fouler than the dudes. They be lying. They be gassing a nigga's head up, making him think he was the only one. Then you catch the nasty 'ho sucking your best friend's dick. Nowadays, when you catch 'em, they don't even have the decency to make up a good excuse. They start popping shit about 'It's my body. You don't own me. I can do whatever I want to do.' That's when you gotta bust they ass. That is if you give a damn."

Brian smiled his calm cool smile. It wasn't the first time he had heard Slick's philosophy. He looked as though he thought Slick was just talking. I remembered him once telling Nikki that he knew Slick wanted to have a girl and a relationship just like theirs but "he likes to front too much, that's all." Brian continued to lecture: "See, your whole attitude is wrong. That's why you keep meeting women who act like that. You don't have no respect, man. First off, every woman is a bitch to you. So you attract those kind of women because all you want to do is 'stick and move.' A nice girl ain't gonna be down for that."

Slick jumped to his feet. He always let Brian get him hyped up. "Man, what you looking at is experience. You can laugh if you want. You can preach all that shit. What the hell is a 'nice girl'? I'll tell you what another name for a nice girl is: 'a sly bitch,' 'cause the 'nice girls' be the worst ones. You know how many nice girls line up after a hot basketball game with their panties and a toothbrush in their overnight bag just waiting to get fucked? Ask me how many 'hoes I had on their back who had boyfriends, fiancés, husbands. Man, you ain't even gotta do nothing for pussy these days. You should know that."

These were the conversations I enjoyed listening to. I was living at Nikki's apartment for the summer. I had to take a summer course and didn't have the money for a dorm room or an off-campus apartment. The commute from college to home was too far. Nikki and I had met during the school year. I would see her from time to time at the campus student center. We belonged to different student groups but they both had offices in the same center. I was a member of the African Student Organization, which sought to protect and advance the services and rights of African students. Nikki, whose major was in management, was part of an organization that raised money and sponsored all the entertainers, conferences, and speakers. My organization was highly political and idealistic. We didn't have time for money. Nikki's organization was strictly money and business. They didn't have time for causes, movements, and politics. So we stayed separate. We even badmouthed each other from time to time.

But I used to watch Nikki because I found her interesting. She was always dressed up like a woman. While most of us wore jeans and sweatshirts, Nikki wore expensive dresses and suits like a professional. Her outfits were always complemented by the right accessories, designer bags, soft leather shoes, things that most of us didn't think about or at least delayed because we knew we couldn't afford them. She always had long fancy fingernails and perfumes that filled the whole student center with a pleasant and sweet smell. She drove the latest model BMW. Even though she was a member of an organization she never hung out at the center like the rest of us. She always moved in and out swiftly, as though she had a full schedule outside of her activity at the center. Nikki was light-skinned and from Texas, about five-foot-nine. She always had a fly haircut. Her big green eyes drew the attention of many men but you could tell that she was always in control. Her body was thick but not fat. She had big athletic legs, from her high school days as a track star, and a small waistline.

Nikki liked watching me, too. One evening I was in the downstairs office at the center waiting for the secretary to bring out more paper for the copier. Nikki came in to copy some bills. She came over to me in a friendly and confident way and said, "I see you around here all the time. You know, people have a lot of respect for you."

I smiled and thanked her, and introduced myself. She put her hand on her hip and said, "Come on. I know your name. What do you think, I'm stupid? I've seen your name in the school paper enough times." Her big eyes looked me over from head to toe. "You're a real pretty girl, too. I just thought I'd tell you. Most of the time us women don't compliment one another without becoming suspicious, but I like the way you hold your own ground and stand up for yours."

Yes, Nikki was unusual. She was bold and unintimidated. She quickly assumed control of the conversation. Leaning over to me so no one would overhear her, she said, "Listen, I want you to have some things that I think would make you look nice. If I pulled them together, would you accept them?"

My mind raced around for a response. I thought to myself if she was offering clothes, I could definitely use them. Like many college students I was broke and repeating the same old wears. But then I wondered why she wanted to give them to me and what she wanted in return. I rejected the notion of her being gay because everyone knew and was jealous of the fact that she was going out with Brian. Many women had tried to take him away from her, but couldn't. So I decided to accept her offer.

We drove in Nikki's expensive new car to her apartment to get the clothes. The BMW had a plush leather interior, fancy air fresheners, and a computerized display board with an Alpine car stereo that sounded as clear as speakers in a recording studio. She punched in a tape that had hip-hop, reggae, and rhythm-and-blues music. She bobbed her head and feet to the music. You could tell she loved it a lot. When the beat excited her, her foot would lay heavy on the accelerator. Within seconds we were going over sixty miles an hour on small residential streets. While terror gripped my heart, she handled her stick shift with ease as if she were only doing twenty or thirty miles per hour. Minutes later we arrived at her off-campus apartment.

I was surprised. It was not furnished with the usual cheap wooden student-just-getting-started furniture. She had a leather couch and a love seat. There was an area for dining with a dinner table and chairs. There were candle holders on the table with two used candles inside and hardened wax dripping down the sides. On the walls were pictures of children in playful poses. I assumed they were her relatives.

She motioned for me to come into the bedroom. She put her things down and immediately swung open her closet. I could see instantly that she had all kinds of clothes. Her closet was overstuffed with her belongings. She started to go through her things and I continued to look around trying to piece together the puzzle of this young woman whom I found to be a mystery. Her room was very feminine. Or at least the way a girl's room is portrayed in a Disney movie. Her windows boasted curtains with frills and plenty of lace. The walls were painted a pale shade of lavender. She even had a vanity table with a big mirror on the wall. On this table was what seemed like every color of nail polish available, polish remover, cute little dishes, cotton balls, knickknacks, hair sprays, body paints, and seemingly every brand of perfume ever made. Pasted on the mirror in a shape of squares were small photos of Nikki in different clothes, including bathing suits and fancy hats. It seemed from the pictures that she thought of herself as some kind of model.

Meanwhile, Nikki began making a small pile of the items she wanted me to have. It included a couple of leather skirts, silk shirts, dress pants, and a couple of dresses. She went to her vanity table where her jewelry box was and took out some costume jewelry to go with some of the outfits. Then she began to look for a belt that went with a pair of the pants. She ended up pulling out a box filled with what seemed like a hundred pairs of panties, the Victoria's Secret type, all kinds of tropical fruit colors with different types of cuts, styles, and strings. There was no shortage of matching camisoles and bras. I had now concluded that Nikki must come from a financially well-off family. There was no way the average college student could afford all of this. Not even if she just came from a regular old middle-class family.

Just then the belt popped up. Nikki pulled it out from the back of the closet from behind the box the panties were in. She got up from the floor exasperated from the search. Taking a deep breath and with a friendly smile, she said, "All right, that's everything. I'll get a nice bag to put it in." I looked at her curiously and said, "This is some expensive stuff. Do you want any of it back?" She put her hand on her hip and rolled her eyes at me as if I had said something ridiculous. Then she said with attitude, "Don't even try it. That's why I asked you if you minded in the first place, so you wouldn't start freaking out acting all suspicious like there was some trick involved. I already told you, I'm giving you these things 'cause I like you. You have guts. You're a fighter. Most of us don't give a damn about nobody but ourselves. So if I give you these things, it's like I helped out in some way. I don't have no time to join any movements or go to any more meetings. And no, I don't want the clothes back."

"Thanks. I'm sorry," I said, feeling a little embarrassed.

"Besides, girlfriend," she said with flavor, "I can see that you so into the black thang that you need somebody to help you out in other areas."

"Like what?" I said, but I really understood exactly what she meant. She meant that I could use some new clothes, a new hairstyle, and all that. To be honest, I had stopped caring so much about that stuff since Nathan and I had broken up. Because I didn't see any guys on the horizon that were serious-minded and worth the effort, I had let myself go.

"Come on, girl. You know what time it is. Why would somebody as pretty and intelligent as you are not get all you can get? You already have people listening. Now it's time to turn on the charisma that I can tell you have but refuse to use. Here, sit down. . . ." She pointed to the chair at her vanity table. She took the rubber band out of my hair. Then she pulled out her curling irons, her crimping irons, her combs, and barrettes. She said, "I hope you don't mind. And I hope you're not in a rush." To tell the truth, this whole experience was so different from my normal routine of debating and politicking and community service, I was entertained. I wanted to know more about Nikki because I felt her to be so completely different. I agreed to the "makeover."

Nikki and I rapidly became friends. She made me feel comfortable. I was flattered. I had seen her slight other people whom she didn't like. She had a way of isolating those she wanted to prevent from coming near her, leaving them with nothing but the air of mystery that surrounded her. I was glad she had befriended me. She was helping to revive my spirit. She had me dressing up, painting my nails, and "using my body" as she put it. She told me that if I was to find a man I had to put more music in my hips. Much of what she was teaching me, I already knew, but had deliberately pushed to the back of my mind and agenda. Some of the other stuff, however, was strictly news to me.

Friday was Nikki's "girls' night out." She told me to meet her at her apartment at eight o'clock sharp. First, we were to pick up Latasha, one of her other girlfriends, and then head to some happening club. When I knocked at the door, I was surprised to see Brian Davidson's tall, dark figure. I recognized him immediately; I had seen his picture in the sports pages in all types of painful yet victorious poses. He was even more powerful-looking in person. He was wearing a tank top and long shorts. As he opened the door, he rolled his eyes at me. It was obvious he wasn't expecting my company. I looked toward the dining room and noticed the table was set for two. Even though I wasn't an eater of red meat, my nose never lied to me, and I could smell the steak broiling. I immediately became annoyed. I felt that even though I was invited I was being made to feel like an intruder. I wondered why Nikki had me come over if she was supposed to be chilling with her man. I introduced myself.

Brian's face changed from aggravation to respect. He took my hand with his big, warm strong hand and said with seriousness, "Keep up the fight, sister." He offered me a seat. It was always curious to see how men reacted to the outspoken political women on campus. He sat on the opposite end of the couch assuring me that Nikki would be out in a minute. Soon Nikki emerged from the bathroom followed by a cloud of shower steam. She had on her bikini panties, no bra and was still slightly wet on top. She smiled and said, "Girl, don't even panic. You know how it gets. I have to feed Brian and drop him at work by ten. I have to stop by my mom's for a second and then we can go. Oh, we gotta pick up Brian at three-fifteen. You know he works the night shift at UPS."

If I had known all this I would have stayed home. Then Nikki said in her lively way, "Girl, you can have some dinner, too." I glanced toward Brian expecting him to give me a disgusted look. Instead, all I got was a welcoming smile. I was surprised. Nikki quickly steamed some vegetables for me and gave me her baked potato and salad. We all ate together. On Brian's plate was steak, homemade gravy, baked potatoes, bread rolls, spinach and salad. I had never pictured Nikki as the cooking type. She seemed more like the on-the-go TV dinner type. I was wrong.

She was a perfect hostess. She pranced around her kitchen now wearing her bra and panties, plus her heels. Brian, it was obvious, was completely in love. I imagined it was probably Nikki serving home-cooked meals in her sexy slinky panties that kept him enraptured. But there had to be more to their relationship than sex. I could see that he clung to her every word no matter how trivial. There was no trace of the blank, disinterested stare that some brothers displayed when a woman was talking. He took no notice of me at all. In fact, he had barely looked in my direction since opening the door and greeting me. That was fine with me. I saw it as a sign of his loyalty to Nikki. When dinner was over, Brian disappeared into the bedroom looking tired, like one does after a heavy meal. Nikki stayed with me. As she quickly washed the dishes and cleaned the kitchen she said, "Don't worry, girl. We'll get out of here soon. I know you're ready to loosen up after this hectic week. I know I am!" She laughed as she went into the bedroom to change her clothes.

Alone for the moment in the living room, I realized how much I envied Nikki. I, too, needed someone like Brian to smile at me and wrap his big arms around me. I, too, needed to feel safe and secure. But instead, tonight all I would have is the beat, the rhythm and the rhyme to seduce me and then help me to forget that I would be in a club filled with undesirable men who probably had no principles or real goals in life. Suddenly, I realized that I had been waiting for Nikki for nearly thirty minutes. Where was she? I was ready to leave.

I got up to use the bathroom, which was adjacent to the bedroom. The bedroom door was open a crack. With a single glance, I saw Brian's long legs naked and spreadeagled across the bed. Nikki was sitting between his legs on her knees with her head in Brian's lap. She was sucking his penis ferociously as though she were in a bobbing-for-apples contest. I froze. Brian's head lay on the pillow. His eyes looked glazed and the veins popped out of his strong neck. He moaned as if there wasn't a better feeling in the world. Nikki was now licking Brian all over, always coming back to the center. She ran the tips of her long nails over his skin lightly and he let out a gentle moan. Then she grabbed his balls and gave a last pull on his penis with her lips. That's when I heard him grunt. Then in a shocking move he began to whine like a baby while his body shuddered. Nikki pulled her head up and caught my eye at the door as my foot pushed forward in an attempt to make it look like I was heading toward the bathroom. I saw her smile at me, letting me know that she knew I was watching.

Once in the bathroom I flushed the toilet even though I hadn't used it. I turned on the faucet and splashed water over my hot and embarrassed face. As I dried it with a towel, I wondered how I could fix my face to appear that I had not seen anything. It wasn't that I was Miss Innocence. I knew Nikki and Brian were a couple and that's what couples did. I had been in positions of passion before. But never had I seen a woman so confidently in control of the sex. Nikki had made her man cry. That was a surprise.

In the car I sat in the back of course. Nikki glanced at me through the rearview mirror. When we arrived at UPS Brian gave her a big hug, and thanked her for the dinner. He slid his tongue into her mouth for a last taste and told her he loved her and would see her at three-fifteen when she came to pick him up after work.

I joined her in the front seat. As soon as I looked at Nikki she started laughing. I started laughing, too. Then Nikki said with no shame, "That's right, girl! Some women think they're too cute to suck dick. Take it from me. That's a female who wants to lose her man. If you really want to keep a man you have to suck it and do it right. You can't be sloppy and biting him now, girl. If you do it right, you can turn 'em out. They'll give you anything you want! Me and Brian been together for a year and a half now. He's my heart. I love him. Any woman who tries to steal him is looking for a fight."

"Do you think y'all been together because of the sex or because he loves you?" I asked.

"Both!" she said. "Listen, don't be stupid. Stupid women separate the issues. Never underestimate the power of sex. It's about eighty-five percent of any relationship."

I rolled my eyes in disbelief.

"Girl, men are freaky. All men. You'd be surprised the things they think about. Most women don't know so they lose out. Men like the little things—like good smells. A sweet-smelling woman can steal the attention away from a regular plain and simple clean-smelling girl. Girl, you know, I have flavors for days. I have fragrances specifically for my neck, the back of my knees, my feet, in between my breasts, and my you-know-where!"

I smiled, listening intently to the most dramatic woman I had ever met.

"For men," Nikki said, "it's all about pleasure. It's the way you stand, walk, bend over. It's the variety, the positions, and keeping it interesting. It's your underwear, colors, styles, cuts. It's environment. Things like how bright the lights are. How soft the linen is. What it smells like. Some stupid women lose their man 'cause their house is too damn dirty. While she sits around trying to figure out what's wrong and goes out and gets a fly haircut, the real problem is that she hasn't changed the sheets for three weeks and her underarms stink!"

Listening to Nikki was like going to the theater. I was no dummy. I was mentally taking notes even though I disagreed with some of her points. The fact was she had a good man for over a year. I had none. Plus her talking kept my mind off her driving, which made me nervous. The car began to slow down on a back street in Newark. It was pitch black except for a small, faulty streetlamp. She stopped the car. I thought she was lost. Still smiling, she casually said, "Hold on a minute, I'll be right back." I tried to damp down my rising panic and said, "You're getting out here?" Nikki didn't respond. She popped the trunk and went out to the back. She pulled a Macy's bag out and started walking toward the curb. I heard her call out "Sandy." Just then a tall, thin woman emerged out of the doorway. The flickering light lit one side of her face. I could see that her face was dirty and her lips and hands were swollen. A sick feeling shot through my body, a feeling of fear, sympathy, disgust, and anger. I remembered that look from the projects. Sandy, I could tell, was probably a heroin addict. From the looks of her skin-tight dress she probably was also hooking. Nikki took some clothes out of the Macy's bag. I heard her say, "Here. It's getting cold out. I figured you could use a couple of sweaters and a pair of long pants. Are you all right? Are you taking care of yourself?"

I wondered who this woman was and how Nikki met her. I had always thought of myself as someone who did community service, but I had never been brave enough to bring clothes to drug addicts who prostituted themselves for dope in back alleys, at 10:30 at night. Nikki got back in the car. We sped away as if nothing had happened. She didn't say anything about it. I was smart enough not to ask.

A few minutes later we slowed down again. This time we were on a busy street—the houses old-style, broken-down row houses badly in need of repair. Although it was late at night, there were plenty of kids outside. Hair uncombed, shoes dirty, language foul. Everybody looked unhealthy. The only clean-looking, well-dressed youths were the ones who were obviously hustling. Everybody had one thing in common. They all knew Nikki. "Hi, Nikki!" "What's up, girl?" "How's college?" "Yo, give me a ride up to Fat Boy's house!"

Nikki looked at me still smiling and said as she parked, "Come on, girl. You don't have to sit in the car." Assuming we were coming to pick up Nikki's other girlfriend, I followed Nikki into one of the ramshackle houses. The door opened into a living room that was furnished with cheap furniture—the kind covered with plastic slip covers. We walked through the living room into the kitchen. Nikki ran and hugged an older woman, whom, from her complexion, hair and eyes, I took to be Nikki's mother.

Nikki introduced me with pride as if she were proud to have me as a friend. As I said hello, her mother looked me over with a phony smile. I could tell at once that she was possessive about Nikki. As Nikki rattled on about my political work on campus her mother cut her off, making it clear that she wasn't interested in any of my accomplishments.

"How's school?" she asked. As they talked, I kept wondering where Nikki got the money for her fancy car, nice apartment, designer clothes, and expensive furniture. It was obvious that it wasn't from her mother, whose circumstances weren't much better than my own mother's.

"Yeah, me and my mom go everywhere together," Nikki said with a little girl's innocence. "She's my best friend." I figured she was telling me this more for her mother's benefit than for mine. It was as if she were letting her mother know that even though I was a new friend, I was no threat to their tight relationship. I was starting to feel uncomfortable. I took my *Essence* magazine out of my pocketbook and pretended to read it. Just then Nikki's mother asked, "Did you see your dad while you were out?"

"No, I didn't."

"He's supposed to be out jogging. I don't know what fool jogs this late at night. He left here about six o'clock. It's ten-thirty now. By now he should have reached Philadelphia." She laughed sarcastically.

I didn't look up from my magazine. But I could hear Nikki exhale as though she wasn't interested in hearing her mother's complaints. But the complaining continued, "Now, of course, he's been jogging every single night for the past month. I guess that makes him a professional."

"Now Ma, you did your dirt in your day. So ease up off Daddy."

"That was the past. The past don't matter. I'm talking about what's happening right now, today. See, your father's problem is that he wants to kick dirt in my face. I never did that to him. I always conducted myself with class. I didn't bring no men folk to our house. I didn't leave no telephone numbers laying around. I may have gone out to play, but I came back in time to have his dinner on the table. Now your dad came in here the other night with some Virginia Slims in a gold cigarette case in his back pocket. So I asked the fool why he started smoking at such an old age and isn't it hard to puff on a cigarette while jogging at the same time? But he, he's a magician you see. He has answers for everything. You know, Nikki, you should talk to him. He loves you. He'll listen."

"Is that why you asked me to stop by, Ma? I asked you not to put me in the middle of this stuff. I love both of you.

Besides, like I said, you did your dirt, so what's the big deal? I have nothing to do with it."

Her mother's eyes glistened with tears, but they did not fall. She poured herself a drink and said, "I told you, I stopped messing around."

"But you didn't stop for Daddy. You stopped for your own reasons. As you grew older, you got tired of running. You lost your desire, and changed. Daddy's a man. Do you really expect him to lose his desire because you did?"

I got up, embarrassed, and asked where the bathroom was. I wanted to let them finish what seemed to be a very personal conversation. When I returned there was a man in the kitchen. I assumed it was Nikki's father although he looked a good deal younger than his wife's faded beauty. He stood there in his jogging shorts and sweatshirt with strong runner's legs. He smiled at me as if he were twenty years younger and single. As Nikki introduced me he walked toward me with his eyes roaming over my body. He held his hand out. Instead of the generic innocent greeting, he gave me a warm inviting touch, pressing two of his fingers firmly into the palm of my hand.

"So you're the little girl I saw on the cable station debating with that, uh, politician? Girl, you did a good job!"

I smiled and turned slightly away from him so as not to anger the mother any further. But he went on:

"Yeah, when my baby girl told me you were one of her friends, I said, 'Baby, you're in good company.' But you know, you're in good company, too. My little girl is a genius. Did she tell you she's a mathematical wizard? I'm real proud of her."

He took me to see Nikki's trophies, certificates, and awards from high school. He even had a pair of her infant baby shoes! While flipping through the pages of her "modeling portfolio" he told me Nikki was his favorite, "the best one." He added that of his five children she would probably be the only one "smart enough to make something of herself." I watched him carefully as he slipped slyly in and out of two separate personalities. One was the proud father. The other was the young-looking older man who wouldn't mind meeting me in a hotel room later that night. Meanwhile, Nikki's mother attempted to act like she didn't know what he was doing and it took a lot of vodka for her to convince herself. Nikki's father finally took note of her reaction, said goodnight, and headed upstairs. Then the front door swung open and a man who turned out to be Nikki's brother came running in.

"Baby girl!" he shouted as he picked her up. "How's school? I know you busting those grades out!"

Nikki's mother exploded: "Good grades! What you know about good grades, boy? Did you walk outta here with my color TV this morning? 'Cause if you did you better find a way to buy it back or pay me back!"

He frowned, eyebrows connecting in the middle, and said, "Ma. Why you always gotta show out when company come?" He turned to Nikki. "Baby girl, who's your friend? Damn, she's pretty. Big titties and all . . ."

The mother threw her hands in the air and said, "She's not interested in you. She don't want no fool who don't have no money and every time he gets hold of a dollar smokes it up."

The brother shot the mother a hateful look. Nikki stepped in between, placed her hand on her brother's shoulder, and guided him into the hallway right outside the kitchen, but we could still hear their conversation.

"You seen Todd?" she asked.

"He's around the corner at the spot."

"How do you know? You told me you stopped smoking."

"I did, baby girl. I wasn't buying nothing. I took the shortcut through that block on my way to Geeter's. Baby girl, you got fifteen dollars?"

"You know I do. But I can't give it to you 'cause you don't know what to do with yourself when you have money."

"Listen, don't be a big mouth. I'm in a program. I ain't living like that no more. I need the money to get around. I'm looking for a job."

I heard her pocketbook snap open. Later she told me she gave him fifty dollars.

After saying good-bye to everyone, we headed to the door. As soon as Nikki opened it, I could see a brand-new 190 Mercedes Benz blocking Nikki's car from leaving. Before I could take another step, a dark figure startled me as it emerged from the darkness on the porch. Nikki smiled a sweet little girl smile and said, "Todd, what's up, baby? What you doing here?"

"You know my lookout told me he seen your ride. I decided to check on 'my stuff.' "

"Your stuff is straight," Nikki said, running her hand down the side of her body. "And nobody been messing with your 'stuff.' " They both started laughing, and Todd hugged and then tongued Nikki down.

"You still coming tomorrow night?" she asked in a seductive, begging voice.

"Yeah, but it'll be late. Fucking around with you the other night I lost out on some loot and had to bust some ass."

"Don't be so tight on the dollar," Nikki teased.

"I have to be tight on the dollar with you spending my money."

"Look, handsome, I work."

"Yeah, but you spend more than you work. But it don't matter. My girl don't have to work 'cause I got that covered." Todd's face was that of a man totally in love. It was as if I wasn't even standing there. His big rough hands were moving all over Nikki's body. He grabbed her butt and let his hand settle there like he knew that ass well. Nikki was facing me so I gestured that she should give me the keys so I could sit in the car and wait. She let go of Todd and said, "Oh, I'm sorry, girl. I'm all rude and everything." She started to introduce me, but Todd wasn't interested in meeting me at all.

I got the point. I took the keys and sat in the car. Eventually, Todd walked Nikki over to the car. As he was pulling away in his Benz he leaned out the window and said, "Don't forget, I want curry chicken, and you wear the blue one." He smiled and winked, then left.

Nikki smiled at me. "Girl, next time you gotta say 'Come on, Nikki, I gotta go' or something. You know how men are. They'll take up all your time if you let them."

She laughed, turned the music on, and sped away without bothering to explain anything.

As we headed toward Latasha's home, I tried to understand Nikki. Why would she gamble her relationship with Brian when she had told me that she loved him? When he treated her so well? What did she need Todd for? How did she work out the two relationships when Brian practically lived in her apartment? And wasn't it peculiar how different Brian and Todd were? Who was the girl in the alley? I also thought: I can't get one man, Nikki has two. Todd seemed as into her and under her spell as Brian obviously was. I had watched with a mixture of dismay and admiration the way she used her body, speech, stance, clothes, everything to manipulate men. I had always thought of myself as attractive and even calculating. But Nikki had me beat.

When we reached Latasha's house she was standing on the curb in her pumps, in the dark, unafraid, waiting for us. She was not a college student. Or at least I had never seen her on campus. She was short, brown-skinned, hair with finger waves, sporting big earrings, boasting a tight dress. Her face was rugged and experienced, but not unattractive. As soon as I opened the car door to let her in she started talking.

"Nikki, you know that guy Mark I met at the club that time? Girl, he can go! You know how backed up I was anyway. When I got him in my bed I tried to break his back. He surprised me though, girl. He got right with me. We did it three times. He was much better than boring-ass Lakim with his no-hitting-on-nothing self."

"Mark, which one is that?"

"Tall, light skin, wavy hair, mustache . . ."

"Oh, yeah! The one fine-ass Troy brought to the club a long time ago!"

"Hey, whatever happened to Troy?"

"Girl, he got married!"

"They say the good ones always do."

Nikki laughed and said, "He ain't that good. He still comes around sniffing and begging for my stuff! He had the nerve to come messing with me one afternoon. When we were done he opens his briefcase and asks me to pick which of his wedding pictures look the best so he could blow it up, buy a frame, and give it to his wife as a wedding present. His wife had never even seen the pictures yet."

The car filled with laughter.

"Nikki, you know you're the shit! Let her have him. Let her have all the headaches. We'll take his pockets!"

"Speaking of pockets, did you tell Lakim about the pregnancy?"

"Yeah, he's so stupid. He went for it. So now I can get my coat off of layaway next week. I told him the abortion costs five hundred dollars. He told me he knows a place where I can get it much cheaper. Girl, that's when I screamed on him. I told him: 'What do you think I am, some cheap 'ho or something? I go to a good doctor, a private doctor. He's the only one I feel safe with and it costs five hundred dollars!' Girl, I had him apologizing and damn near in tears. He promised me his whole check and I get his check next week. The only thing I could do to keep from busting out laughing was think about my new coat and those fly matching boots. That's how I stuck to my story so good."

Then Latasha asked Nikki, "What about you? Did you get your money?"

Nikki looked at Latasha through the rearview mirror sternly: "Did I get my money? Girl, please! I got fifteen hundred dollars. I told three different fools. You know how I get once I get in that mall. I had to go on an all-out campaign."

I couldn't contain myself: "Nikki, you told Brian you were pregnant when you weren't?"

Nikki cut her eyes at me and said, "No, girl. I told you Brian's my honey. I wouldn't mess with him like that."

I decided to keep my mouth shut. Nikki and her friend were obviously out of my league.

The club was live. It was different than partying on campus where everybody knew each other and things often got boring. This club was a place most students would never go to. Most college kids didn't party with people from the community. And people from the community were never invited on campus. Not unless they wanted to pay three to five dollars more than students paid for the same event. Prices were deliberately hiked up to discourage their participation. Community folk usually thought of college kids as uppity. College kids usually thought of community folk as low class, uneducated, and prone to start fights. The club I was being taken to was in a neighborhood where people seemed down to earth. A place where you could be yourself. Guys didn't act like they were cuter than the women. Women weren't acting like they didn't want to dance. There seemed to be an unspoken agreement that we were all there to party, get loose, and forget our problems.

Nikki seemed to know almost everyone—especially the men. More important, she knew all the workers and bouncers. We didn't have to pay to get in. When the guy at the door saw Nikki's face, he lit up like a flashlight. Nikki, who I was quickly learning had a knack for planning things perfectly, had left her coat in the trunk of the car and was now using her body to get everything we needed. She boldly went up to the doorman.

"What's up, Big R?" she said, swinging her body back and forth.

"Jam-packed tonight," he said, watching her breasts bubble out of her tight, V-neck, cinnamon-colored sweater.

"I brought my girls. You know Latasha and . . ." She introduced me. Before I could say hello, his attention had bounced to Nikki's small waistline and then moved to her light-skinned legs that were provocatively exposed by her tight brown miniskirt. Next thing I knew we were inside the club, easing our way through the packed house. Latasha tapped my shoulder, leaned over, and said, "Follow Nikki straight to the bar. She'll hook up everything."

As we got to the bar I noticed immediately the bartender, who had a beautiful mud-brown complexion, a round face, and round brown eyes. His beautiful teeth glistened in the small light at the bar. But I realized swiftly that it was Nikki who brought the pleasurable look to his face.

"Ahhh, shit," he said. "My girl. What are you having?"

Nikki quickly said, "Two rum and Cokes, and one cranberry juice with a twist of lemon for my other girlfriend." As he turned away to prepare the drinks, she tapped his arm and asked, pointing at me, "Vernon, do you know who this is? Have you ever seen her face before?"

"No, but I wouldn't mind knowing her."

Nikki then told him that I was the girl on campus that was "giving those damned racists hell" and looking out for black interests. He responded with a simple "well, all right." Then he turned to Nikki and said, "Donovan said to call him in his car as soon as you got here."

Nikki went to the other side of the bar and picked up the business phone. Fighting to eavesdrop through the loud music blaring in the club, I could only hear a few words: "Yeah, baby, I know, I had to make a few stops. Okay, baby, in ten minutes." Nikki drank her drink down and waved good-bye to Vernon. To me she said, "I'll be right back." I turned to Latasha but she was already on the dance floor working up a sweat with some brother.

I moved through the club looking for a corner in which to unwind and groove to the music. When I found it, I started to move first my hips, then my feet, and then up my waist. I started up slow, but I knew as I let the rhythm hit me I would be transformed. But I had to let go of my thoughts. The tragedy with Nathan still haunted me. I quickly snuffed out that thought and let it go. I thought about organizing on campus and let it go. I thought about the countless men who killed my interest in them as soon as they opened their mouths. I let that go. As I painted the walls of my mind black, I felt free. Dancing was my narcotic.

The only way I knew hours had gone by was when the deejay put on a record I hated and I lost my musical high. At that point, I spun around on my feet and found myself face to face with an uninvited greasy partner. Now, I didn't mind a brother coming up and dancing with me; many had. But this one had jheri curls. As a rule, I couldn't stand to see a black man with a perm or jheri curls. This particular man had sweat, Vaseline, and curl activator sliding down his face. I moved away to find myself a new spot. I glanced at my watch. It was nearly 2:30 in the morning. I began to panic. True, I was having fun, but I realized I hadn't bumped into Nikki all night. She was my ride home. I wasn't interested in stumbling around this particular part of town in the middle of the night. Plus, public transportation didn't start running again until 5:30 A.M. I began looking for Latasha. I spotted her at the bar talking to Vernon. She obviously had had too much to drink. Her words were slurring and she was trying to throw herself at Vernon, who didn't look even mildly interested. Why should he? I thought. He must see women like her every night. I tapped Latasha's arm and asked if she had seen Nikki. She laughed and said, "Don't worry. Nikki will be here at two forty-five like clockwork. We'll meet her outside on the other side of the club."

"How do you know she'll be there?" I asked. Latasha rolled her eyes and said, "'Cause it always works like that, okay? She's with Donovan. He owns this place. He's paid. Why should she stay here and shake her ass in a club when she has the guy that owns the club, who'll give her anything she wants?"

At a quarter 'til, Latasha and I were standing outside across the street from the club. A Jaguar pulled up to the curb. Nikki was in the passenger seat. Donovan was driving. He looked about 47 or 48 years old. The color of chocolate cake, he had a black, silky clipped beard and a mustache. He was sporting a nice fat diamond pinky ring. He also had a conspicuous, princess-cut diamond wedding ring. As Nikki eased herself out of the car, he grabbed her hand as if he wasn't ready for her to leave.

"Next time don't stay away so long."

"Two weeks, Donovan, that's not a long time," Nikki said with homegirl attitude. "Now go home and play with your wife and kids."

He leaned his head out of the window and said softly, "I told you I'd give them all up for you. But you just keep running, and you know you're too fast for me. . . ."

Nikki bent over. She leaned in his car, letting her breasts rest and spread against the top of the window. She licked her lips and said, "Just think of me as something you like to eat a lot but can only afford to have occasionally." Then she stood up, put her hand on her hip and shifted the weight of her body to one leg while seductively resting on her toes with the other one. "Good-night, Donovan."

He smiled as he started the car and said, "Just remember, I never eat anything I can't afford." He motioned to Nikki to come closer and when she did he handed her a stack of fifty-dollar bills and simply said, "See you soon, I hope."

As Latasha and I got in Nikki's car, I noticed that Nikki was now wearing a completely different outfit than the one she had on in the club before leaving to see Donovan. Latasha couldn't stop kissing Nikki's ass for having gotten the money out of Donovan. I suspected she admired Nikki for being able to do things with men that she had tried, but failed to achieve.

After dropping Latasha off, we swung by UPS to pick up Brian. As he got into the car, Nikki casually mentioned that the "sorority party" that she and I had gone to was "boring." She told him she had decided not to pledge AKA but instead would pledge Delta. Then, in a sweet, innocent voice, she told him how she had to go back to her apartment earlier to change her clothes, having spilled ink, she said, on the brown mini-skirt while she was writing her mother a check. She added that she told her mother to "stop chewing the tops off of her pens" because it made them leak.

I began to pity Brian. He was too beautiful a brother to be played like that. Too desired by many others and too rare an opportunity for any woman to blow off while she weaved a web of lies and deceit. But I didn't dare say anything. Brian was too enthralled with this long-legged Texas girl whose every step had turned him into obedient Play-Doh. The thought of her cheating on him had apparently never crossed his mind. He was simply happy to have this light-skinned beauty add, as he put it, a "touch of class" to his life. Besides, Nikki smiled at him with the face of an angel.

As the weeks and months passed, I realized more and more that my friendship with Nikki was peculiar. I knew that she represented some of the traits that I hated most. At the same time, there were many good things about her that kept us close. I had read somewhere that a man could be judged by the men he surrounded himself with. I assumed that this adage also applied to women. Why, then, did I continue to hang out with Nikki? We were such opposites. Perhaps I was living vicariously through her wild sexual adventures. Maybe Nikki was doing things with men that I secretly wanted to do but didn't have the guts to act out. In the end, I decided that I didn't respect Nikki's way of life. Nor did I want to live her life. After all, I had been scarred as a child by the carousel of male faces I saw going 'round and 'round my household.

But I wasn't completely off the hook. I figured it was the power Nikki had over men that kept me fascinated. It was a power I wanted to have. To be in control. To call the shots and not be left with a heart full of tears and a mind full of questions. I felt I could learn this power. I could get for once what I wanted: one successful relationship rooted in mutual love and respect. The kind of relationship I originally thought Nikki had with Brian. So I decided to study her. To see what I could learn. I was convinced it was more her style and attitude than her looks. After all, I knew a lot of cute light-skinned girls who weren't controlling their relationships. Their emotions had been dragged around and casually tossed in the gutter, too. Watching and learning from Nikki wouldn't be difficult. It may sound strange, but even though I didn't respect her, I still loved her. She'd been a loyal friend to me and was very considerate. She'd often sacrifice her own schedule to take me home from late-night organizational meetings and rallies. She unselfishly shared anything she had. Moreover, she loved children and had been supportive of community service projects that involved children. She empathized with my feelings. And she had a good sense of humor and was able to lift me up when I was down. She never tried to influence me to do harmful things like drink and smoke. She was constantly reminding me not to neglect myself or my studies. She was someone special.

The most skillful episode I watched her pull involved Barry, a married, middle-class businessman. He became so obsessed with Nikki that he arranged to have a private answering service with the phone company receive her calls and instructions concerning their meeting times. She used him like a washing machine. She acted strict with him, like a mother. He, in turn, acted like an obedient child, serving her every whim. She told him that if he wanted to take her out to dinner, he would also have to take me, her "starving" roommate. Nikki would leave the time on his answering service. He would arrive in his car. We would meet him downstairs. We would end up at one of many fancy restaurants. He would charge our shrimp-and-lobster dinners on his credit card. By the seventh or eighth time, I watched as his face grew worried when the bill came.

His lust, however, was great. So he swallowed the bills, which by now I imagined had him going broke and his wife in an uproar. Barry would sit at the table and try to romance Nikki as though I wasn't sitting there with them. When he would get up to go to the bathroom, Nikki would tap my foot under the table, laugh, and remind me to order everything I wanted.

My heart dropped the night that Barry showed up at Nikki's door while she and Brian were enjoying a quiet time at home. I figured the game was finally up, Nikki would definitely be busted this time. I tensed up at the thought of the kind of fight that I was sure was about to happen. I was sitting reading on the couch when Nikki had answered the door. Barry stood there in the doorway like a whipped puppy waiting to be asked in. Brian demanded, "Who is it?" Nikki, to my astonishment, casually said, "Oh, it's for her." I looked up from my book and saw her pointing at me. Then she shot Barry a mean look, which let him know to follow her lead. I put my book down and said, "What's up, Barry? Come on in."

Nikki went back over to Brian, bent over and kissed him with her tongue, and said, "Come on, baby. Let's go in the back and give them the privacy they need."

As they went to the bedroom, I motioned to Barry to sit down. He sat. I rolled my eyes at him in disgust. In about seven or eight minutes, about the amount of time it must have taken Nikki to tell Brian her next lie, Nikki emerged from the bedroom leaving Brian inside. She was finishing tying her robe shut. Then she put one hand on her hip and moved close to Barry, pointing her finger until it landed square in his face. "Look, sweetheart," she said in a bitter voice, "if you come here and I'm with my man, you tell him you came here to see her."

"Okay." He whispered as if he had violated some rule.

"And do not come here unless I invite you. I'll call you. No surprises. You got it?"

"Got it." He fell right in line.

"Now get out." She opened the door. He left meekly.

Over the next several weeks and months, there were many times when Barry would call the house and end up talking to me. One day I finally summoned the courage to ask Barry why an attractive, successful, married businessman would allow himself to be abused by a woman the way he was abused by Nikki. He told me that he was "addicted" to the sex. I told him he struck me as a man who could get sex from anyone he wanted. He didn't disagree, but said that what he wanted was good sex. Nikki was the only black woman he knew who would have anal sex with him. He had always had, he confessed, a wild fascination with big butts. With Nikki he not only got the best sucks ever, he got to have sex with her from every position and in every area imaginable. He described her ass as the "best feeling in the world." I could tell he was becoming excited just telling me about their sessions together. He told me about the day he came by with groceries for our apartment. Nikki had her own little picnic eating strawberries out of the crack of his ass. When I asked him if his wife knew about his ass fetish, he said, "No, she's too conservative." Yet he claimed that seeing Nikki helped make his marriage work. He was willing to do whatever Nikki wanted and most of all he vowed never to stop sexing her. His explanation left me speechless.

After a while I started to think of the men Nikki dated as suckers. Perhaps that was the only way I could continue to live with Nikki, by blaming the men she exploited instead of blaming her. Besides, as far as I knew, it was only Brian and Todd who were under the illusion that they were Nikki's only man. Nikki swore she loved Brian while I knew she definitely feared Todd. He was a stone-cold street guy. The rest of her men, I reasoned, were willing participants in her game. Perhaps they really didn't mind being used by Nikki; after all, they each had a girlfriend or wife at home who apparently loved them blindly.

Whenever I tried to talk to Nikki about how she was living, she would remind me that I couldn't possibly have all the answers because I didn't even have one man to speak of. She told me that I would be wise to take some tips from her and loosen up a little. No man is attracted to an upright young girl who takes the world so damn seriously, she said. After spending most of my summers alone, I finally decided to take Nikki's advice. It seemed that no men valued a woman like me. My attempts to be strong and straight were not only not appreciated, they went unnoticed. Meanwhile, Nikki's seemingly carefree and spontaneous attitude won thumbs up from all kinds of men. I convinced myself that I, too, could be simple like Nikki. I would dress up, act less intelligent, and take less notice of my surroundings. I would make many fewer comments and would try behaving in a manner altogether more spontaneous and less worried.

I knew who I liked—Kyle. I had met him at a week-long annual retreat the African Student Organization had hosted. These retreats were troubleshooting sessions for politically active students from all around the country. By meeting at the end of the summer, we were able to get a jump on planning collectively and effectively for the entire upcoming school year. Thus, we were united nationwide on our political goal and theme for the year. These retreats were held exclusively for seasoned student organizers. That way we could concentrate on strategy and specific projects without having to orient any newcomers. The retreats were held in the student cabins on the agricultural campus.

I had spotted Kyle the first day of the retreat. But, as Nikki had always said of me, instead of moving in on him I overthought the situation and hadn't yet even introduced myself. Tomorrow was the last day of the retreat. I didn't have much time. Besides, I noticed another sister definitely checking him out, too. Danielle was a sister I respected. But men were scarce, and I decided if I wanted Kyle for myself I had to get rid of her. She must have felt the same way, because all week we found ourselves battling over him. We both tried to outspeak one another in an attempt to grab attention. But I remembered what Nikki had said. She said attraction was 85 percent sex. I was ready to junk the intellectual path and go straight up Nikki's style.

So I let Nikki do my hair and pick out one of her "won't fail" dresses for me. The dress was black, tight, short, and sleeveless. In fact, when Nikki finished with me, I looked beautiful. It had become unimportant to me that I looked completely inappropriate for the retreat I was attending. Nikki smiled and laughed in her wild style. She threw her hands in the air and then on her hips. Pleased with her finished product, she said, "Totally irresistible, girl! Let Danielle try to mess with you now."

I stood in the mirror admiring myself. My self-confidence escalated. I took a deep breath. Nothing could stop me now. I was about to make it clear to Kyle that I was his only choice. My object, Nikki said, was to fill him with so much desire that he would come to me.

As I got out of Nikki's car she handed me her Ralph Lauren overnight bag. I had seen her use it all the time. I turned up my nose and said, "I won't be needing that yet. I'm just trying to get his attention, exchange numbers, addresses, you know, stuff like that." She continued to push the bag toward me, saying, "You never know what might happen. My motto is it's better to be prepared." She smiled. I took the bag.

When I got to the retreat everyone was already assembled. They were engaged in a heated debate over whether the campus should be opened up for the neighboring community to use. I stood on the side, scanning the area for a chair. The place was packed. Just then Kyle caught my eye. His eyes opened wide, as though he had never seen me. He motioned me to come over. The dress was already working its magic. Kyle was usually so deep into his work that you had to hit him with a wet cloth to get his attention. Now he was trying to accommodate me like I was an out-of-town guest. I thanked him and sat down by his side. I balanced my legs on the tips of my toes and sat up to emphasize my curves. When I made points in the discussion, I leaned over and let my cleavage speak for itself, all the while acting as though I was unaware of the effect of my actions. In fact, I pretended that I was sitting there in my usual sweatshirt and jeans.

By lunchtime I was like an open jar of honey. Danielle was rendered invisible in her faded jeans and semi-clean sneakers. Her intellectual performance melted away into obscurity as my dress radiated heat around the room. When anyone asked, I casually lied. "I'm all dressed up because I'm going to my cousin's wedding as soon as I leave here," I would say. When I looked up, I saw Kyle coming my way. This was the moment I planned for. He smiled and said, "So where's the party at?"

"There's no party around here on a Sunday unless you make your own."

He raised his eyebrows and said, "Is that right? So where are you headed? I know you're not looking this good for a retreat."

"Oh, so you like my dress?" I put one hand on my hip and raised my leg a little so I could assume a cute little stance. "I'm going to my cousin's wedding reception when I leave here."

"Damn, I thought you were coming with me."

As I got ready to respond, Danielle interrupted, "Can you believe that students who are involved in our struggle could actually argue over the point of community inclusion in campus life?"

I smiled at her and said nothing. I was headed for the kill. She turned to Kyle and said, "Can I fix you a plate of food? We have a little bit of everything."

Without even looking at her, he said, "Sure, I'll take some fried chicken, thanks."

Danielle went off to prepare his food. He seemed glad. Then he asked, "So, is this your first, second, or distant cousin getting married?"

I rolled my eyes and lied, "All I know is I'm glad it's not me."

He looked surprised. "Oh yeah, you got something against marriage?"

I looked at my nails and said, "Oh, right now I'm just cooling, taking it easy. I don't want to be tied down."

"So what's the answer to my question? Is it your first cousin, second, or a distant?"

"It's a second cousin. Why do you ask?"

"'Cause I figured if it was a distant cousin you wouldn't mind skipping it and coming with me," he said with confidence.

"It depends."

Just then Danielle returned with a plate packed with food. She was pleased with herself. Kyle just took the plate without thanking her.

"It depends on what?" he asked, turning back to me.

"On what you wanna do," I said as though I was open to suggestions. Then I added, "I gotta make good use of my dress." I laughed.

"Check this out," he said, "You want to come home with me? There's a nice club that gets some live people and music. They be rocking even on Sunday nights."

"Where's home?" I asked as though it really wasn't important to me.

"Baltimore," he responded, looking into my eyes to see if I was bluffing.

Now I wanted to say, *Baltimore,* are you crazy? I have to go to class in the morning. But it didn't go with the carefree and open image I was trying to project, so instead I said in a voice as unexcited as I could make it, "And how will I get home?"

"I'll bring you back tomorrow, of course." He held up the keys to his car. "I drove up here with Brad." He pointed to a brother across the room who had also participated in the retreat. "Brad can pick up his girl. We can all hang out together."

Inside I was urging myself on, to be adventurous. Otherwise, I knew I'd end up spending the rest of the night watching Nikki and Brian as usual. So I said, "All right, we can do this."

On the way to Baltimore, Kyle and I talked about records, singers, fashions, and basketball. It turned out he wasn't involved in community service, politics, or much of anything. He was just giving his friend Brad a ride. He said he had a little business transporting students in his car for a minimal fee. That's how he maintained himself while in school at the University of Maryland. He charged, he said, less than a train, plane, or bus. Besides, he enjoyed traveling because he liked meeting people. We went to Kyle's apartment first. He lived off campus in a small, clean apartment across the street from a beautiful wooded area. He dropped his bags, showered, and changed. Then we went to Brad's. Lastly we went to pick up his girl, Yolanda. When she came downstairs she was wearing a miniskirt and a tight, low-cut top. She had on three gold chains, one of which held a crucifix.

Instead of being excited to see her, Brad looked vexed. He got out of the car to intercept her path to the car door. Then he asked, "What did I tell you about wearing your skirt so short? Go upstairs and change."

She immediately became steamed. "That's it. That's all you have to say after being away for a whole week?" She threw her hands up in the air in disgust.

"Don't act like you didn't know that I hate that skirt."

"You're not my father. I wear what I wanna wear. Now, are we going or not? 'Cause I could be taking care of other things."

"You're supposed to be my girl," Brad tried to reason with her. "If I don't like the skirt, then who are you wearing it for?"

Yolanda completely ignored Brad's demand. Brad let it drop. They got in the car. The club was decent. Baltimore seemed to have a surplus of lonely women, so I found I was one of many women there with a tight, short, black dress on. I kept my confidence high anyway. Kyle and I were getting along real well—dancing to the music, riding each other's bodies, feeling free. It was when the partying and friendly conversation was over that my body tightened with concern and uneasiness. I thought about my plan of not thinking too much. I tried to refocus on the "fun stuff."

When Kyle and I got back to his apartment we talked and laughed some more. I cracked on the "funny dancing" the country folk did. He laughed about the rugged, combat boot-wearing black-power sisters back home at the retreat. But then the time for joking was over. Kyle was standing close to me, hands extending toward my body. Before I knew it he was tonguing me down. As he moved his hand over my breasts and down to my thighs, I felt him place his hand under my dress. He was pulling on the top of my panties. My body jerked. It was my natural reaction to a man who was moving too fast. But was he? After all, I had set him up. I had measured out, organized, and calculated the whole thing. I had bended, twisted, and shook more than a chocolate malt. Yet something inside of me was freezing up. He stepped back.

"So, what's up, girl? I know you're not a little tease."

I put a carefree look on my face and said, "Sometimes a little teasing can be fun."

"Yeah, and too much can be a pain in the ass!"

"And who's to say how much is too much?" I said playfully, trying to avoid the inevitable.

"I'll say when," he responded with confidence, grabbing my waist and pulling me close again. He began kissing my neck and then licking up to my ears.

My body was saying, "Yes! Go! Yes! Go!" My mind was saying "No, don't do it, don't do it." My heart stood by, watching and warning that it was not even remotely involved in this misadventure. So I pushed him away gently and started jokingly running away, easing myself around the table as though he should try to catch me. My mind raced. Why am I here? What am I doing? He caught my shoulder, went for my back and pulled the zipper on my dress down. My dress was now opened. I laughed like I liked it. Finally he grabbed me and playfully wrestled me down to the floor. I began to understand the thin line between the games that women play, our indecision, and so-called date rape. He began kissing me all over my face. I thought to myself: Why not? It feels good. But a split second later I was completely unexcited. There was no love here. My mind searched for an excuse. Within seconds

I was whispering in his ear to let me get up and go to the bathroom.

"Come on, woman, I'm ready now."

So I teased and stalled, "Wait 'til you see what I have for you. Then you'll really be ready."

"Damn! All right. But don't try to front, girl. You been sticking those titties in my face and licking those juicy lips all night. I'm ready to taste it all."

I picked up the bag Nikki had prepared for me and dashed into the bathroom. I put the bag in the sink and opened it up. Knowing Nikki she had something good in there for me. I wasn't disappointed. I pulled out a beautiful, red silk teddy. It was high quality, obviously expensive. As I stood admiring it, I caught a glimpse of my face in the mirror. It must have been my own eyes that startled me and woke me up. The spiritual voice inside of me said, "You're pretty ugly at this moment." I knew it was true. I did not love Kyle. Was I acting like my mother, whose loveless relationships had driven us apart? No, I told myself. I wasn't looking for money or support. I was just trying to have a little fun.

"Come get in this bed, girl." Kyle was getting impatient. "Don't keep a brother waiting."

Yes, I thought, Kyle was handsome. But the truth was I wasn't ready to sleep with him. I wanted love first, not sex. If I had sex, would he even call me back again? Men called Nikki back. I began to panic standing there in my bra and panties. What could I do? I couldn't just come out and say forget it. Kyle would think I was crazy. Maybe I was crazy. Maybe I should just go and explain my confused feelings to him. No, that wouldn't work. He doesn't even know me. He doesn't even know me! All right, I thought, I'll go out there. I'll apologize for everything. I'll risk making a complete fool of myself. But I would pay him back cash for the club and even the gas and tolls. I decided I would just be bold, straight to the point. I opened the door slowly. As I turned left, wearing my panties, I walked slowly down the corridor to the bedroom. Kyle was quiet. He was so playful and eager I half expected him to jump out from behind the bedroom door. Maybe he would tackle me. Then I wouldn't have a chance to explain fast enough.

As I entered the bedroom I saw him stretched out on the bed in his silk, black, bikini underwear. He lay quietly on his dark blue satin sheets with the matching pillowcases. I exhaled nervously. Then I laughed. The sucker had fallen asleep. Good! I thought to myself. He'll be much calmer when I break the news to him. He's a good guy, I thought to myself. He'll understand. I tapped his shoulder. "Kyle," I called. He didn't respond. I tried to wake him but he was a hard sleeper. His head tilted to the side. I put both of my hands on either side of his face to wake him. Just then I noticed his teeth were clenched tightly over his tongue.

Oh, my God! Terror shot through my body. He's dead! Oh shit, he's dead. I began to shake and tremble. I didn't know what to do. I didn't know who to call. I started to cry. I tried to think. My eyes darted around the room. I searched for the phone. I found it, pressed o for operator.

"Oh my God he's dead. Oh my God please help me."

"Who's dead? Calm down, ma'am. First, who is this?"

I ignored her question. I didn't want to give my name.

"We need help."

"Where are you located, ma'am?"

My mind went blank. Where was I? No, it wasn't that I had forgotten. I really did not know where I was. I didn't know the address, phone number, nothing. So I said, "Baltimore."

"Baltimore's a big place. What's your address, ma'am?"

I cried, "I don't know where I am!"

"This is an adult I'm speaking to, right? You're not a child, are you? What do you mean, you don't know where you are?"

I quickly lifted the shades on the window. I searched the block for a street sign. I was overwhelmed. All I could see was darkness and a patch of forest. I dropped the phone and started searching through Kyle's papers on his dresser. I found an opened phone bill. I located the address and ran back to the phone. Now 911 was on the line. I gave them an address and they promised to dispatch an ambulance.

I hung up. I was afraid to turn and look at Kyle's stiff face. So I ran into the living room and picked my dress up off the floor. I couldn't pull up the long zipper in the back of my dress. I started to cry and pace the floor wildly. I wondered how I would get home. I ran into the bathroom and looked in the mirror. My hair was a mess. Just then a knock came at the door. Three large white men entered the apartment.

"Where's the body?" one of them asked.

I led them to the bedroom. They looked at Kyle and mumbled some medical terms back and forth. One of them looked at me and asked, "Are you a relative?"

"No."

"What is your relationship to the subject?"

"I'm his girlfriend," I lied to try to dignify my predicament.

"What's his name?"

"Kyle," I said, not knowing his last name. I glanced for the phone bill; I knew his name would appear there. I picked it up and acted like I knew the last name all along.

"Johnson," I said. They saw what I did. One of them smiled. They began to glance at each other.

"Do you know of any prior illness?" they asked.

"No . . ."

"Has this happened before?"

"I don't know what you mean. I don't even know what happened."

"Do you know how we can contact his parents or a close relative?"

"No, I don't." The medical worker rolled his eyes like he had experienced this scene a hundred times before. Then he chuckled.

The other two medical workers looked as if they were restraining Kyle. One pulled out a solution and placed it under his nose.

"Kyle!" The medical worker commanded with authority in his voice. "You've had a seizure. We're in your apartment. We're not going to hurt you."

Kyle awakened in a panic. He looked at everyone in the room suspiciously. His face turned violently angry. The anger then turned to disbelief and uncertainty. They lifted him up and began to walk him back and forth.

"Do you know who you are?"

"I'm Kyle." He sounded groggy.

"Do you know who she is?" they asked, pointing at me.

"No," he said, looking at me as if at a complete stranger.

"Is this your girlfriend?" they asked, pushing the issue.

"No," he said with conviction. My soul filled with shame. I felt like a whore.

They bundled Kyle into a waiting ambulance. I accompanied him. They said they had to run some tests on him. It appeared that he had had an epileptic seizure. One of the medical workers explained that when such a person regained consciousness it was not uncommon for the victim to experience a partial or complete memory loss for the first half hour or so. That's why Kyle hadn't recognized me. But I thought, no, he really didn't know who I was. And for a moment I had apparently forgotten who I was as well. At the hospital a nurse gave me directions to the train station. I took the first train smoking home at five that morning.

Later, when I told Nikki what had happened she laughed so hard she nearly died. I couldn't laugh about it, though. I realized that I deserved what I had gotten. I wasn't Nikki and never would be. I couldn't handle the fast lane. As far as Nikki was concerned, I blew the sex that night, an opportunity to let go. For my part, I accepted that she would never understand how I felt. We were just two different people.

So here I was listening to Brian and Slick argue about women. I had come to admire Brian. He was always honest, with the best of intentions. I secretly wished he was my man. By watching him, I learned how many brothers are good men but naive to the ways of some women. As much as I hated to admit it, I agreed with some of the things Slick was saying. In many ways Slick was dealing with the real world; Brian was dealing with the way both he and I would have liked the world to be.

That night Brian and Slick's playful argument ended in disaster. Slick kept pushing the issue of women who couldn't be trusted. Brian kept offering his girl Nikki and their relationship as one of many examples that Slick was wrong. Slick grew tired of beating around the bush. He confessed that he had a friend "back home" who knew a drug dealer who was "banging your girl Nikki." Brian leaped from his chair like the proverbial knight defending his queen. He swung at Slick and called him a liar. Slick told Brian that he loved him like a brother and would never lie to him or try to hurt him. But he was tired, he said, of watching Brian get played out. Then he said, "I know plenty of bitches who want you, man, but you're caught up with this 'ho." Brian swung at him again. Slick ducked. Brian accused Slick of being jealous. He pulled out his knife and accused Slick of wanting to fuck Nikki. Slick said, "I already did."

Brian cut Slick that night. The police came. I helped Slick clean up the cut, which fortunately was superficial, and played down the incident to the cops. Nevertheless, they took them both into custody. Neither wanted to press charges, and so they were released a few hours later. When Nikki got home I told her what had happened. She got excited that Brian and Slick had fought. She said that Slick had a "big mouth" and was "too damned nosy," and that he deserved whatever he got. I asked her about Brian. I told her he had been emotionally devastated by what Slick said. She got up and laughed.

"Girl, don't you know the flavor by now? Brian belongs to me. I'll just tell him something he wants to hear, give him a little something to make him feel good. What did you think? Did you think he would listen to Slick? No, honey, he'll listen to me. Slick can't do for him what I do for him."

She must have been right. Brian listened to her and didn't even try to confirm the truth of what Slick had told him. In fact, Brian and Slick stopped speaking to each other. Then one afternoon Brian came home early from practice and found Nikki's lips wrapped around Todd's dick. Well, Todd threw Brian out of Nikki's apartment and beat Nikki's ass.

Months later, Brian showed up at my dormitory room. He said he finally figured out that he should have been with me and not Nikki. He told me he had always respected me and the way I carried myself even before meeting me personally at Nikki's place. He said he could smack himself for overlooking me.

"How come I couldn't see it? You were right there in my face—respectable, intelligent, and beautiful, too. I'm a fool."

He asked me if I thought we could hook up. I told him I thought he was special, adding, "Always thought you were fine with your dark, beautiful self." I confessed that I always knew he was there and wanted him for myself. Then I apologized. "But, I'm sorry, as much as I want you, I can't, 'cause Nikki's my girlfriend."

Later on I discovered Nikki's terrible secret. She had been molested by one of her father's friends. She had been raped in the basement of her own house when she was twelve years old. It had a strange effect on her, she said. And I learned that the woman we had brought clothes to in the alley in Newark was her sister. Probably there were other secrets about Nikki's early family life that she had not shared with me. Perhaps it was these secrets that caused her to want sex all the time. Instead of becoming terrified of men she became fascinated with them. Her parents didn't know about the rape. Besides, Nikki said, my mother, father, sisters, and brothers are all just as sexual as me. Sex is good. It can be used for power, for escape, or for nothing at all. She asked me never to tell anybody about it. I agreed, but asked why she had decided to tell me.

"Because I've always respected you, might even have wanted to be you. Besides, you're my girlfriend."

four

Joseph

At twenty-one, if a sister is educated and single without children, she is as deadly as a nine millimeter. I was beautiful; after all, my skin was as rich and as dark as wet, brown mud, a complexion that any and every pale white girl would pray for—that is, if she believed in God. My butt sat high in the air and my hips obviously gave birth to Creation. Titties like mangoes, firm, sweet, and ready. My thighs and legs were big and powerful, kicking Vanna White and Cindy Crawford to the curb.

The bugged-out thing was that I was not unusual. Sisters in the projects, inner cities, urban, and rural areas are deeply attractive and even in the pain of poverty have the appearance of royal queens. Nobody could give greater comfort to a man than a sister who loves herself and uses her thick warm lips and big sensual eyes with an ancient soul and innocent exterior to make him do what he would not normally do: react spontaneously, abandoning all beliefs and philosophies. (Which is why on any given day you can see white men driving in and out of our communities like slave masters, seeking the "dark experience" from sisters who, when trapped in poverty, might well sell what their ancestors blessed them with.)

Well anyway, skip the poetic shit. I was fly and I knew it. But just because you're fly doesn't mean that you're smart. Not smart in the sense of reading nine hundred books, but smart in the sense of street smarts: to know when you are getting played; when a brother is lying to you through a sexy smile and hot lines. Or to know whether just because somebody's in love with you means they can do anything for you as a woman. So there I was: big, beautiful, dark, young, and dumb.

I met Joseph at a rally. He was on stage surrounded by other African men all enraged at the murder of another young brother gunned down by the police. On his face was the black man's dilemma: How to survive in America as an African man without going to jail for killing some *unjust,* white motherfucker dressed in the police robes of legality for killing your kids. How to balance being a man and naturally wanting to protect and provide for your community, but having been educated in the finest white institutions that teach you that violence can only be used by white people and their armies to maintain white property and white superiority. And that, when you are African, even in the face of murderous injustice, you should just pray, cry, beg, but damn it, don't act uncivilized and strike back.

My first attraction to Joseph was the fact that he was fed up with white racism. That he had definite thoughts and that he had the desire for revenge. This was a strength to me, especially after having gone to college with a bunch of ass-kissing black boy-men who overintellectualized our condition as Africans in this country. Who would think of every reason not to defend themselves. Who stood like their mothers, and batted their eyes like their mothers, and laughed like their mothers, and cried like their mothers—and not like their fathers, whom they had never met! Joseph was a welcome plea-sure. Not only was Joseph angry, he was intelligent, respected, and admired by other men, which in some sense meant that he had some semblance of power.

After tripping on the deepness of his mind, I fell into his big compassionate eyes; and his thunderously moving thick lips and the passion that he spoke with, I wanted to feel per-sonally, sexually. I wanted to feel him in the same way thou-sands and even millions of African women fantasize about loving their minister, who, for the most part, is the only "sober-minded, paid black man" that they see all week. Of course, if you mentioned this, each and every one of them would deny it and say the thought alone was adulterous and blasphemous and even inconceivable, or that only a whore would say such a thing. But let me assure you: they lie! Believe me, most African women in the country don't want to deal with thinking about the disappearance of our men. What happened to them? Why are we so desperate and lonely that we sit mesmerized in our community churches fantasizing about the one surviving black man? And while we escape truth, we are left with the unpleas-ant reality of sharing our men and acting like we don't know it.

I leaned over and asked my girlfriend, Sonya, who was also at the rally, if she knew the speaker. She smiled and said yes. I pushed, "Is he married?" She said, "Yeah, married with two children. He's beautiful, isn't he?" I said, "Word up." I acted cool on the outside to my girlfriend, but on the inside I was boiling. I felt I had known the speaker for a long time. I was seduced by his mind and strength, and moist in my panties because of his charismatic and sexual power. But, damn, he was married! Fuck it, I wanted him anyway. After all, in our community there weren't many men like him and I had been lonely for a long time because I was never any good at having sex for the sake of sex. It always had to be connected to something much deeper, like a purpose, a spirit, a love.

So I plotted, as all women do. No matter how much we may deny it, we must admit that we have the ability to calculate things down to the smallest detail. We calculate how we stand, how we sit, how we talk. Whether to wear a skirt that grips your butt and rides your hips and shows your underwear. Whether to wear a bra that squeezes your mangoes together to make them more voluptuous. Whether to wear sandals and to use your toes as items of pleasure, or whether to look completely disinterested in a man you'd kill for.

I decided to ask around and see when the next "event" would occur in which he would be featured, and what organization I could join to be next to him. I didn't feel phony in doing this because I was already legitimately involved in the movement for justice and power for African people. At the time, I was deeply involved in the divestment movement directed at getting American corporations to stop investing money in and doing business with South African companies. I didn't think it would strike anyone as strange that I was joining one more effort.

My investigation into Joseph's whereabouts and whatabouts was easy: I'd just get on the phone with one of my friends and talk about a dozen other things and then casually mention his name to see if they knew him, or simply to get a response—any kind of a response. I found out one thing for certain: all the women had clocked him, but added he was a one-woman man, a dedicated father, a respected individual, and impossible to "git wit."

My confidence level, however, was extremely high. Mainly because I had been sick that spring and had lost a bunch of weight and was looking more delicious than a chocolate cake. I had been fasting so my skin was more flawless than ever, and because I was always reading, traveling, exploring, and thinking, I was sure that the power of my mind could change any situation I concentrated on. I, too, thought I was desirable and hard to get. I too had high standards. I wasn't interested in the usual garbage like what kind of car a man drove, or what kind of house he had, or how much money was in his wallet: rather, what kind of mind did he possess? What kind of vision? Did he believe our world could be changed? Did he care whether we as African people could build, own, and control our own institutions? Was he as articulate about solutions we could use as a people as he was about the problems that we faced? Of course, these kinds of standards meant that I was going to be lonely most of the time.

I learned from Sonya that Joseph would next be speaking at a community event on Wednesday night. She agreed to accompany me. When we arrived, the place was jam-packed with folks hungry for information and leadership. Brothers and sisters who had the common sense to know that something was wrong with this country. To know that they were tired of cooperating with the painful control and domination of white America, but more than anything that they were scared. Scared of the repercussions of thinking about taking action against white racism. Scared they would be hung like Nat Turner, set up like Marcus Garvey, killed like Medgar Evers, Malcolm X, and Martin Luther King, Jr. So instead of fighting directly they would defer to a young, educated African man with several college degrees who, they figured, must know a way out of this hell called America. So they came with heads and hearts full of hope and fear.

Sonya and I waited anxiously for the other speakers to conclude their remarks so we could hear Joseph. At last, he came out onto the stage and gave warm greetings and then fired up the crowd. He talked about the long list of deaths we faced at the hands of police, and the generations we lost with the murder of any young African man. He spoke about the need to unify as a people, to stop believing that we were powerless victims. He added that while we had civic organizations such as fraternities, sororities, churches, and community centers, we neglected our greatest strength, which was our collective power as consumers. He urged us to consider that if we would stop giving our money to products, institutions, and people that perpetuate racist oppression, we would then be in a much better position as a people. He praised the family unit as a foundation of our society.

After hearing a drumroll of applause, I said to myself: Hold up, the brothers and sisters here have faith in this man, they see him as a way out. Or, at least, if not as a way out, then as a man capable of giving direction and insight. Suddenly, my sexual desire turned into respect for him. I determined that even though he was gorgeous—dark eyes, nice butt—he'd be better off serving the community instead of serving me. Of one thing I was sure: I wasn't the type of woman that a man sexes and leaves. I knew that if we started, one adventure would lead to another, and then another. When the sexual energy that he exuded met up with my sexual power, why, we would be twisted and soldered together like those African carvings in which a naked man and a naked woman are inseparably inter-twined in an athletic sexual embrace. I was drifting. I settled on the idea that I should respect Joseph. I shouldn't start any trouble by taking his mind (or his body) off his community mission.

The next few weeks were full of work. If there was anything to be said about me, it would never be that I was lazy. In fact, I was a workaholic. While I had come to believe that we as African people had a thousand legitimate gripes against this system of white racism and the people who controlled and ben-efited from it, we only had ourselves to depend on to overcome our predicament. So I was up early in the morning. It had been more than a year since I had been with a man. I was doing aer-obics every morning at six and this particular month I was fast-ing all day in solidarity with some of my friends who were Muslims. Their holy month was called Ramadan. I was no ex-pert on Islamic affairs, but I thought the idea that you occa-sionally sacrificed the usual pleasures in order to concentrate on the Creator was a good one. I didn't mind them calling God "Allah." Nor the fact that they prayed five times a day and remained humble throughout the day, only breaking their fast at sundown. Even then, they were not allowed to eat just anything. Pork, for example, was forbidden because it was considered a filthy animal that Allah forbade the believer to partake of. Anyway, Muslims all over the world observed this holy month, and since I agreed that it was good to acknowledge that there was a greater force than man, and that sacrifices had to be made to receive blessings, I fasted to show support.

That afternoon I was on the busiest avenue in town, walking and reading papers at the same time, something I often did. The hot sun was beaming down, making my already chocolate complexion double chocolate. I had my tight jeans on. Real tight, like skintight. On top I wore a silk camisole that was very thin, but not quite see-through. My nipples were sticking out and my hair was cornrolled into a ponytail. On my feet were pumps. I suddenly felt somebody's eyes on me. I looked up, and sitting in a parked car was Joseph. He was doing some work in his car, but evidently my blockbuster screaming hips caught his attention. He was now looking out the car, his eyes stuck somewhere between the "V" of my crotch and the top of my thighs. His eyes were big and sensual and his gaze was steady and strong. He looked as though he could well imagine tasting my Georgia Brown skin. My nipples got harder, but I remembered that I was, after all, from the projects, so I had to throw on my attitude and act like I wasn't turned on. But the lustful thoughts that I had banished earlier now returned with a vengeance.

Later that week I found myself attending a student committee meeting. I showed up, books in hand, ready to go. I walked through the door and quickly saw about eight people sitting around a table, one of whom was Joseph. My heart melted like an orange Creamsicle on a torrid summer day. Cool now, sister, cool now. I sat down, introduced myself, and set to work on how best to organize black students across the country into an African student network. With moist panties and a body that wanted to be touched (but a mind that told me to slow down), I argued that most African students were confronted by the same problems but usually found themselves "fronting." Fronting basically meant that you acted as if you didn't really have any problems, that you had everything under control. It was a survival tactic many of us had been taught in order to conceal any inner weakness or vulnerability. Meanwhile, you found yourself spending your guaranteed student loan, which was supposed to purchase your books and pay for your courses, on fancy shit from Gucci, Fila, and Chanel, trying to hide the fact that your family was on welfare and you came from the slums. That you were mentally harassed almost daily by your family at home, who didn't have the luxury of living on a college campus, which, to those who came from the projects, seemed the plushest of places. They called you every other day on the hall phone in your dormitory to unload their new problems, then they told you to do well and they would talk to you tomorrow. Instead of developing solutions to our mutual problems, black students came on campus and fronted like each of us was better than the next brother or sister. We tried to blend into a predominantly white educational system, and by doing so we retarded ourselves to the point where we were too embarrassed to acknowledge each other in the presence of white people. So we avoided the usual greetings so common among us of "peace," "power," "forward," or any of that black shit.

Perhaps it was just my imagination, but I felt Joseph looking at me with what I took to be admiration. He started with my braids, got lost in my eyes, and danced with my tongue as I spoke. He slid down my neck, sucked on my breast, or at least his eyes did. He settled in my chair where my Alabama butt had spread all over, healthy but not sloppy.

For the next five months I would see Joseph at meetings once a week. I was convinced he wanted me as bad as I wanted him, but then he'd do things that made me think that maybe I was wrong. He was an older man, and sometimes he made me think he was playing with my head and enjoyed the fact that, although he never had put his hands on me, I was on him like his own skin. I realized that if I wanted him, I'd have to push up on him because it didn't look as though he was about to make the first move. I had him between my sheets many nights, through my dreams and fantasies and visions, but I wanted him there in physical form, making me sweat and moan. I'd have to make my move.

Four weeks later, I finally had gathered enough courage: I called Joseph at his office and said, "I'd like to have a talk with you."

"What about?" he asked.

"Oh, a few things."

"Oh, really." (As though he suspected something.)

"But, in this talk, I need just me and you, not a committee, a council, or an organization."

"Okay, when?"

"Whenever you can do it."

"Next Monday," he said, "I'll come by and pick you up at about two o'clock."

"Okay." I hung up the phone and felt an ancient African drumroll in my stomach. I was scared but I wanted him more than I feared speaking up.

Monday came a month later, or at least it seemed that way. Joseph drove up, got out, rang my bell, and went back to sit in his car while I came downstairs. I got in his car feeling stiff on the outside and like jelly on the inside. My mouth was dry. We rode in the car. He poked fun at me in a friendly sort of way, something he had done often since we had become friends working together on the student committee. About fifteen minutes later, we arrived at a small, quaint Jamaican restaurant. We walked in and were soon seated together at a table.

Our initial conversation was a little strained, perhaps because we knew we were about to do something we weren't supposed to do. We avoided each other's eyes; at least, I avoided his. After about twenty minutes of this excruciating back and forth, I guess it became apparent to him that I couldn't get up the nerve to say what I wanted. My emotions were battling inside of me: right versus wrong, propriety versus desire, young versus old. Why was it that I couldn't find the words to say what I wanted to say? Finally, he simply asked, "So, what was the reason we got together today?"

I shifted my big brown eyes with long black lashes downward, and said shyly, "I really don't know how to say what I want to say."

He said, "Okay, let me say it. It has something to do with you and me."

I said, "Yes."

"You're attracted to me," he said, as if it were obvious.

"Well, actually, I felt that we were attracted to each other."

"Oh, did you? What gave you that impression?"

At this point I could see he wanted me to juice up his ego. I wasn't going to let him front like he hadn't been sweating me all these months. I saw him countless times outlining the contours of my body with his eyes. I could see he was impressed with my intellect, my ability to express myself, my dedication to our people. I replied, "The way you look at me. The fact that you go out of your way to pick me up in your car and drop me home."

"Well," he said, "you know I'm married. Do you care about that?"

"Yes, I care. I'm not trying to get you to leave your wife. I respect her. (Can you imagine?) I'm just into you and it has nothing to do with her. (I must have been crazy.) I'm highly attracted to you, I respect your mind and your way of thinking. Besides, I think you're beautiful: your lips, your eyes, your spirit. I want to be around you, be with you, I want to talk with you, I want . . ." By this time, I could see that he was with me, but he hadn't said a word. He hadn't agreed to anything, but somehow his eyes looked helpless, as though he had fought off the offers of many women before; as though he had seen many women, prostitutes, lonely mothers, disobedient wives, professional polished women twice a week in the hair salon, beauty queens, the whole nine yards.

But I was sure he had never seen such a combination as he was confronted with now: a young, sultry, big, brown-eyed, voluptuous, wholesome, intelligent, spiritual, ghetto girl who, because of his mind, wanted to dedicate her usually picky self to him and only him. No matter how much he might deny it, over the past six months she had seeped into his soul. His values must have battled incessantly. He loved his wife: after all, she had given him two beautiful children, plus years of support and love. They had been together through thick and thin. She was down with him when he was down and out, and she celebrated alongside him during the good times. He was hugely possessive and, I knew, would never have allowed his wife to do what he was about to do with the ghetto girl. But the attraction was too deep, the temptation too overwhelming.

"I want to touch you," I said.

"You're too young and you deserve more than to be waiting on some old married man," he replied.

"Sounds good, Joseph, but I don't want anybody else but you. You know how it is out here for black women. We don't have many choices. Our men have been ruined by America. If I could find the same qualities in another man—and, believe me, I've looked—I'd take him. But you're the only one for me. I can feel it all over my body. I think about you all the time."

Joseph motioned to the waiter for the check. We left in silence, still two separate entities.

We got into his car, Joseph not saying a word. He hadn't said much in the restaurant, yet he was eager to start the conversation. His silence turned me on. It meant that I had already won. I knew that this was not just a case of my having a pretty face, but of him understanding that if the already deep feeling between us was now to be expressed sexually, he would be stuck—stuck with two women, his wife, whom he loved very much, and me, his young addiction.

In the car, while we rode in silence, I saw him looking at my legs. Before he had picked me up, I had been careful to spray myself with the softest, most seductive perfume I could afford, and was wearing my black lace pantyhose with the curlicue design up the calves. These were stockings that have been worn by many women who were trying to entice married men whose wives had long since retired from the fashionable niceties that make life interesting. He placed his hand on the top of my knee and slid it slowly up my thigh, pushing my skirt up toward my butt. Then he slid his hand into my "V" and ran his fingers over my crotch. He said, "You may be young, but you're a big girl. Big, brown-eyed, big-legged girl." Niagara Falls couldn't have been wetter. I relaxed my head against the headrest and thought, if this is the foreplay, the sex is gonna make me a slave to the rhythm. But that was as far as Joseph was willing to go before he let me off.

Another month passed and Joseph and I were still just talking, working together, flirting, and teasing. Once again, I determined to up the ante. I decided to stop by his office at the insurance company where he worked. I would make it appear as if I just happened to be in the neighborhood. My appearance would be deliberately enticing, but I'd act casual, as if looking that good was an everyday thing.

In the elevator up to his office on the third floor, I tried to catch a glimpse of my reflection in the piece of mirrored steel on the wall. I had already looked at myself a thousand times. Earrings, handbag, pumps—all matching. Silk dress hugging my curves so tight that they were about to start their own lib-

eration movement. I walked into the foyer and let the receptionist know that I was there to see Mr. Brown. She asked me to
wait with a kind of snarl in her voice. But she was as insignifi-
cant to me as any old white woman.

I sat down on the couch and picked up a copy of *U.S.
News & World Report*. The lead story on "Black-on-Black
Crime" claimed to be an examination of why young African
men in America seemed to be killing each other at an alarming
rate. The more I read, the angrier I grew. There was nothing in
the article that so much as hinted at the system of oppression
that was principally responsible for creating and maintaining
the conditions of violence in which our people found themselves so hopelessly trapped. I hated reading such articles
because they made me feel that no white person deserved to live
comfortably and unmolested in so unjust a world. The emotion
building inside me, I suddenly realized, would not fit with my
seductive appearance. I needed to refocus my thoughts.

Looking up, I saw standing before me a short, dark-
skinned woman with about forty extra pounds around her
waist. Matronly in appearance, with the standard white strand
of pearls around her neck, and a Plain Jane haircut, she was
whispering to the receptionist that she should not forget to
remind Mr. Brown to pick up his laundry from the cleaners,
that it would be ready after five o'clock.

I froze, feeling numb, instantly realizing that this was
Joseph's wife. I felt funny inside, scared mostly, because even
though I hadn't actually made love with Joseph, I still felt like
a thief in the night creeping around someone else's house. I felt
like somebody had turned on the light and there I was, exposed
and guilty, stolen goods clutched in my hand. What should I

do? Run and give the stuff back? How would she react? Would she be like the overly protective ghetto girls I knew and just commence beating my ass with murderous intent? Or would she be like the uppity and polished college girls I knew who stupidly assumed that no woman had anything over them, and so foolishly thought that no man of theirs would ever violate their trust?

She looked in my direction as if to say, Who are you? Her eyes gave me a black woman's lookover. My beauty was not to be denied. But the look in her eyes seemed to say, Well, there are many men and women employed here, I know she's not here to see *my* husband. She threw her head in the air as if she hadn't a care in the world and hadn't noticed me, and virtually bounced back into the elevator.

I thought, Oh, she's taken the college-girl approach, she must be stupid. Stupid, because after all the years of marriage she had forgotten how sensual, sexy, and commanding her husband was. Stupid, because she should have known what her husband liked and that I was it. Stupid, because she had neglected to study her man's likes and dislikes, or to watch his behavior, or to calculate his next move. Stupid, because she had let herself go, become sloppy in appearance. Not in terms of her clothes—they were all top of the line, but sloppy in terms of her body. She was not old enough to look as old as she did. Her extra weight added a good nine or ten years to her. She no longer looked powerful. I was glad that my titties were juicy, that my body was firm, that my butt was warm, and that my spirit was adventurous. Glad that Joseph and I could talk for hours and keep the conversation interesting and exciting.

"Mr. Brown will see you now."

I collected myself, walked through the inner doors, down a corridor, found his office, and entered. Joseph's eyes widened. Bubbling like champagne, I said, "Hey!" He simply stared. "I was in your area and had to pick up a few things for school, so I stopped by," I lied. No reply. "I knew I'd see you tonight at the committee meeting, but I thought it would be nice to swing by maybe for a little lunch."

Joseph's stare intensified and I imagined that by now his dick had to be harder than two bricks. I went over to his desk and leaned over toward him a little, letting him see the top curves of my cleavage. I acted like I had no idea of the effect my actions were having on him. "I was hoping that if you couldn't make lunch, you would at least talk with me for fifteen minutes about some ideas I had."

Joseph opened his datebook, and said, "When can I arrange to spend a little time with you?"

"What, you can't go to lunch?"

He stared into my eyes as though he wanted to rip my clothes off, and said, "Not lunch, real time. I want to . . . see you."

If I could have kicked my heels together and blasted through the roof, I would have. I was so excited I could have fucked him right there on the desk top! "The midwestern delegation of the student network is having its annual meeting in Chicago in two weeks," I pointed out. "Are you going?"

"Yes," he said slowly, "I'm scheduled to do a workshop there."

"So, we can meet there. It's a date."

He got up from behind his desk and, still staring, he came toward me and backed me against the wall. He leaned against my mangoes and my body temperature seemed instantly to double. He ran his hand down the side of my body, moving with every curve, stopping at the bottom of my butt cheek. He squeezed my butt hard and pressed his thick wet lips against mine, sliding his warm juicy tongue into mine. I sucked his tongue forcefully, as he did mine, and we exchanged juices like there was nothing sweeter in the world. I moved my hand down and without warning I grabbed his balls quickly and then let go. I felt that if we didn't stop, we would be butt-naked in his office, which was located on a corridor with what had looked to me like at least five other offices. He looked at me and said evenly, "I'll see you tonight at the meeting, but I'll really see you in two weeks in Chicago." Acting as coolly as I could, I picked up my purse from the desk, where I had put it, and waved good-bye with a dreamy look, from a spell left unbroken.

Sonya and I flew to Chicago together. We looked forward to sharing a hotel room at the conference. Despite the unspoken competition I felt between us, Sonya was a good friend, cool and intelligent. And, while I didn't feel that it was I who needed to compete with her, she seemed as though she always had to have one up on me. I, in my arrogance, felt this to be impossible, but somehow Sonya had worked it out in a way that made her feel comfortable with me, and that was fine with me as long as I didn't have to deal with a cranky attitude or aggravating whining. I hadn't told Sonya anything about me and Joseph, which was hard because she really was my good friend. I couldn't tell her, though, because Sonya, like many women I knew, secretly lusted after and admired Joseph. I was sure she had even fantasized about him, but she, like many women who knew they simply couldn't "get it," hadn't even bothered to try. Moreover, had I told her (and I would have given her graphic descriptions—I was good for that), I feared she would have turned into a green-eyed monster and exploded with jealousy. So I kept my mouth shut.

We checked into the Hyatt Regency, a beautiful hotel. We had a double room, Sonya on one bed, me on the other. We had to unpack, quickly shower, and change because our first meeting was at four o'clock at the nearby university. Dinner would be at six, after which we could either go to a party or be free until the next morning, when a full day's work would get under way.

At the meeting I got pissed off. If there was one thing college students were guilty of, it was being unrealistic, or, perhaps more accurately, unreasonably idealistic. We fought each other over dumb shit like whether African people ought to be Pan-Africanists or communists. Simply put, Pan-Africanism was the belief that black African people, no matter where they were in the world, ought to unite. If you happened to have been born in Haiti, Jamaica, Cuba, South Africa, Kenya, England, Los Angeles, or Brooklyn, and you were black, then according to Pan-Africanism you belonged to one people. The continent of Africa was home base, to be built up and supported by African people all over the world. It was to have a communalistic or socialistic economy rooted in pre-European African values. Its borders were to be defended by one massive continental army, equipped with the latest technological weapons. The idea was that a free, independent, and protected Africa, in full possession of its authentic culture and priceless resources, would be able to exercise enormous influence and respect in the international arena. Instead of being seen as beggar nations, unable to feed their own people, forced to take out yet another loan from the International Monetary Fund, which everyone knew could never be repaid, and which only plummeted the continent into a perpetual cycle of economic enslavement, Africa could stand tall, rock-steady on its own two feet.

The black students who supported communism, on the other hand, wanted a radical change in the power equation in America. They also wanted to unify poor people throughout the world. They battled ethnic nationalism because they didn't believe in racial separatism. They believed that class was more important than race as a basis of unity. That it was a question of rich versus poor. Sometimes these students seemed to prefer communism because, deep inside, they didn't believe black people would ever lay aside their petty internal gripes to unite in a common cause.

Neither the Pan-Africanists nor the communists did much for me. I was more practical-minded. I believed that we should organize where we lived. That we needed to dedicate our skills and devote our resources and attention to the African youth in the communities we lived in. It seemed obvious to me that you helped your own first and foremost. What fool would argue with African nationalism when Irish nationalism, French nationalism, and Jewish nationalism, to name just a few, had been powerful and successful forces for many years? I suspected that these students didn't really want to do any work. They were lazy and perhaps took their status as privileged students for granted. They loved endless conversations and, for the most part, were content to play intellectual gymnastics for four years, then graduate and join AT&T. They didn't really care about the "brothers and sisters back home," having always felt inwardly superior to "them." These students sometimes seemed filled with loathing for their own kind. Political "activism," for many of them, was an indulgence; the real payoffs were the "good jobs" they looked forward to obtaining upon graduation. Of course, they'd get those jobs at a price: keeping silent about the conditions from which they had themselves emerged. They were eager to put as much distance between themselves and the underclass kids from their communities, who were not likely to be college-bound, as they possibly could.

I couldn't wait for the meeting to end. Finally, it was over. Everyone headed out to dinner. Clad in our standard college attire of jeans and sweatshirts, Sonya and I stepped into the dining hall. People were continuing to talk at the tables, some told jokes, others laughed, hollered, and screamed. Some people, I noticed, had already paired off. Joseph entered, talking with two students, one male, one female. They sat down. I tried to avoid looking excited, but Sonya was on me like a homing pigeon. She had a habit of "diggin'." Maybe she suspected something. Maybe not. What I did know was that I had to begin plotting my disappearance and rendezvous soon, or Sonya would definitely be on my case.

"This food is horrible," I complained. "It's making me nauseous."

Sonya snapped, "Well, why don't you stop eating it?"

"Yeah, I'm gonna throw it away." My plan was to act sick later that night, so I would have an excuse not to go with Sonya to the party later on (there was always a party at these revolutionary conferences). That way, with Sonya gone, I could shoot upstairs to Joseph's room, which I knew he had reserved five floors away from all the students. Carrying out my plan wasn't going to be easy. Nosy-ass Sonya would probably have a heart attack when she learned I wasn't intending to go to the party. Because if I wasn't there standing by her side, it would become obvious that nobody was asking her to dance.

"Sonya, let's go back to the hotel, I don't feel well."

"Yeah, I wanna get out of here myself and lay down after that ridiculous argument at the meeting."

Back in our room, we relaxed by watching *Cry Freedom*. That is, if you can relax watching a movie that's supposed to be about Steven Biko and the oppression of black African people in South Africa. Oddly, the movie was less about Biko than it was about some white reporter.

At about nine o'clock Sonya got off her bed, ready to shower to go to the party. It was now or never.

"Sonya, I'm not going to the party tonight."

"Word," she said.

"Yeah, I don't feel too good."

"That never stopped you from shakin' that big butt." She started cracking up.

"No, seriously, I ain't going."

"All right, all right, I'm not gonna sweat you for a party. Maybe I should just stay home, too."

"No, Sonya, I think you should go. There's crazy cuties here and maybe you'll meet you a man, a politically conscious, politically correct brother."

Sonya paused. "Maybe so. I'll go for a little while, at least take a look around." Forty-five minutes later, she was showered, dressed, and out the door.

I was relieved. It wasn't that hard to convince her to at least get out of the room for a little while—long enough for me to change into something I knew Joseph would like. He hated jeans and all that boyish stuff we sisters were wearing in college. Out of my suitcase came my lace undies, and a smoking red dress slit up the side with shingles on the end. The dress hugged the waistline, accentuated the butt, and gripped the mangoes just enough for Joseph to keep tabs on my nipples. I carefully put on my stockings and garters, slipped on my pumps, and wore my hair out. I was ready.

I took the elevator to Joseph's floor with butterflies in my belly and knocked on his door. Joseph opened the door slowly. He had a suite, not at all like the room Sonya and I shared, but one with a living room, kitchenette, and a big bedroom, with carved lamps and a plush carpet. He stared at me intensely and gestured for me to come in. I walked in working every curve I had on my body, knowing I was wrecking his nerves with each step. I sat down on the couch.

He asked me if I wanted something to drink and opened the door to the cute refrigerator full of juices and liquors. Joseph knew I didn't drink alcohol so he must have meant did I want some juice. He poured some cranberry juice into a tumbler and handed it to me. He came and sat down beside me; my body temperature rose several degrees. He took his finger and ran it down my hot, red, tight dress starting at my shoulders and straight down over my nipple. It sent the red alert throughout my body. He took the glass out of my hand and placed it on a nearby table and, without getting up, he began to suck the cranberry juice off my tongue and lips. Kissing Joseph was an art in and of itself. It was like sex. We both licked and sucked everywhere. It was unafraid, unashamed, uninhibited, sensual sucking kisses. Joseph had his hands all over me. Without even taking off my clothes, he wet my nipples through my dress and teased my toes with his tongue through my stockings. He ran his hands up the inside of my leg and found his way to my panties. Since I didn't have any panty hose on, he pushed my panties to one side and pushed his thick thumb into my pussy sending me off into the pleasure of blackness. I cried out in the sounds that have no meaning other than "more."

Joseph eased up, grabbed my hands and started licking my fingers and directing me toward the bed. He hadn't spoken a word and, still silent, he unbuttoned my dress down the front and the middle; it fell to the floor and there stood my titties at attention, stockings, garter belt, and Joseph wanting my young firm body. (A figure I supposed he had not seen in a long while.) He pulled the sheets back with one hand and with the other he unfastened my bra, and it too fell to the floor. He sat me down at first and then laid me down.

When my body hit the cold sheets, I broke out all over with goose bumps. Joseph sucked my mangoes lightly, just enough to further entice me, then stood up to undress himself. He turned down the lights and stood before me in the semi-darkness at the side of the bed. If my titties were at attention, then he was in full salute. I sat up and put both of my hands around his waist and began to suck and tease his dick, prompting his cool to give way as he let out a sigh of total pleasure. I licked and teased bringing him almost to a point of no return, but then withdrew wanting to make sure I had saved the best until he was inside of me.

I laid Joseph down and placed my big hungry body on top of him, wrapping my thighs around him, riding him like Black Beauty until we both broke out into a sweat. Joseph was on my neck sucking as though there was maple syrup there. He was on my neck, behind my ears, and on my throat, and then it happened; almost at the same time our bodies shook and we flooded one another with our "more than approval."

Even though I was on top, Joseph collapsed and went to sleep. I laid there feeling better than I ever had, but scared. I had known Joseph for a year now, we had bonded as friends and we were of like minds politically. We had merged in soul and spirit and now we had deepened our relationship in the most personal and explosive way. This was no fling. This was critical—critical because it was forbidden, and because it could probably never "be," it was bound to cripple me emotionally if I ever lost it.

By five in the morning, I knew I had to get back downstairs to my world, where Sonya was probably going berserk looking for me. In order not to awaken Joseph, I tiptoed around his room, found my tote bag, pulled out my jeans and sweatshirt, quickly slipped them on while stuffing everything else into the bag. I got in the elevator, went down; the doors opened to a big, empty, soundless hallway. I reached my room, slid the card-key into the door lock, undressed, and got into my bed quietly. Sonya was sleeping heavily. I laid my head against the pillow and dropped off to sleep feeling like I had released a year's worth of tension. I was in love—deep, deep love—with a married man.

The next morning as I stepped out of the shower, I wiped the moisture off the bathroom mirror with my towel, only to discover that my neck, shoulders, and top of my breasts were covered with purple passion marks. I gasped! What could I do? Nosy Sonya would have a thousand questions. She wouldn't suspect Joseph because he had told the students that he was heading back home last night after dinner, having already fulfilled his obligation to chair the first day's workshop. Besides, I doubted Sonya's ego would have allowed her to believe that I had successfully won the choicest and most desired prize. I pulled out a clean pair of jeans and a sweatshirt and put them on, hoping they would conceal the tracks of Joseph's love.

Over the next two months, my relationship with Joseph grew stronger. Because he was married, we didn't have as much sex as I would have liked. The bugged-out thing was how that circumstance brought us closer together and more than guaranteed that when we could find the time and place the loving would be even more intense and special. The real problem was elsewhere. Because of the tremendous energy flowing between Joseph and me all the time, our deepening bond was hardly a secret anymore. Even in the presence of other people—committeepersons, conference participants, peers, businesspersons—our spiritual bond, at the very least, was palpable. African people are very spiritual. When two people are loving and sexing and bonding the way Joseph and I were, they radiate a "vibe" that other spiritual people can feel. Joseph and I were exposing ourselves in just this way to every seeing eye. I think Joseph knew that people were catching on, but he was so far gone that either he didn't care or couldn't be bothered to pay much attention. The only reality was our reality, and it would take a ton of bricks coming down on his head for him to wake up.

Joseph's wife caught on. How did I know? Because she started doing strange things like dropping the two children off at his office and asking Joseph to drive them to their activities instead of taking them herself. She started going along with Joseph on his business and activist trips even though she never had before and he had always been seen as a loner. She began to pop up at his office on odd days, breaking her usual routine that I had pretty well memorized.

And since she changed, Joseph changed, too, under the pressure. He could not say no to his children. He could not say no to his wife. He certainly couldn't tell her that she was not welcome on his out-of-town trips.

Joseph began to miss dates that we planned on, agreed upon, and longed for. Once, in fact, I was left sitting in our little Jamaican restaurant with my sweet-smelling perfume and moist body in my seductive silks, all by myself, wondering, waiting, and hoping that eventually he would show up. Joseph, too, became frustrated for several reasons. One was because he knew he had an obligation, a commitment to his wife and children. After all, he had always been Mr. Commitment, Mr. Building-a-Strong-Black-Family. He was also frustrated because he wanted to see his "sweet little addiction" with whom he had merged on so many levels, with whom he now had so much more in common than his wife.

When Joseph and I would finally hook up, we'd argue. Argue because I was lonely, I had been stood up, I had been horny, starved for good conversation. But mostly, we'd argue because we missed each other and felt ourselves to be under the sway of circumstances somehow beyond our control.

I knew I had to get myself together. I had to deal with his new reality. I had promised myself that I would never try to break up his family because I didn't believe in families breaking up. I sucked my teeth and said to myself, If we were back in Africa and Joseph were a great man, a community leader, he could have more than one wife. We could all agree to that, know it openly, be thrilled just to be involved with and connected to such a great leader and spirit. But we were not in Africa, we were in America, where people said they were Christians and any other way of life was the way of the "infidel." So men married one woman and hid their other "wives." When they got caught, they called the other woman with whom they had shared their intellect, spirit, body, and soul "whores" who were to be dismissed and denied even though they had been around and loyal for years.

What could I do to draw Joseph closer to me? What could I do to grab his attention and make him understand that I loved him, needed him, and that the plain fact was that over the last year he had become a part of me—a part of me that I never wanted to sacrifice or give up.

After careful thought, I came up with a plan: I'd tell Joseph that I was pregnant. Surely the idea that I was carrying his baby would bring us closer. It would make me "family" and he would never leave me. It wouldn't matter, I thought, that I wasn't really pregnant because once I had said I was he'd have every reason to keep loving and sexing me, because the dangerous deed had already been done. And that's when I'd actually try to get pregnant. I'd throw away all the birth control and we'd hump like there was no tomorrow.

I called Joseph on the phone. "Hey, baby, I know you're busy, I know you're under a lot of pressure, but I've got to talk to you, it's important."

Joseph said, "Sounds serious."

"Well, you know, I miss you and . . ."

"I miss you, too! You don't have to explain. I would tell you to come to my office, but Margaret . . ."

My heart dropped. That was his wife's name. He had the nerve to call out her name. He had never done that before. Maybe I was crazy but I only wanted him to say my name, to speak to me, to think of me.

He continued: "Margaret comes by sporadically and I don't want the two of you to run into each other." Joseph got quiet. "All right, baby, come Thursday afternoon at about three o'clock. I know for a fact that she's gonna get her hair done at that time. You can meet me at my office and we can go out for a late lunch, or early dinner, and then we can talk."

"Thanks, Joseph, I do need the time. I'll see you Thursday; until then, stay sweet."

"You know I love you . . . right?"

"Yeah, baby," I said, "I love you, too, take it easy."

Thursday came sooner than later. I found myself sitting in the foyer of the insurance company Joseph worked for, with the same crabbed receptionist. I imagined her reporting my comings and goings to Margaret. I rolled my eyes at her ugly face and then buried my head in a copy of *Newsweek*. The topic of the week was "Unwed Black Mothers" and their unmanageable and "illegitimate" children. My reading was interrupted by two brown-colored legs coming through the door out of the corridor where Joseph's office was located.

Staring down, I thought the shoes were somewhat familiar, although I couldn't remember where I'd seen them before. My eyes began moving up slowly, all the while I was praying it wasn't Margaret. When I got mid-waist, I swallowed hard, and went eyeball to eyeball. It was Sonya. She had a stern look on her face. I spoke first, slow and curious.

"What's up, girl? What you doin' here?"

"Just taking care of something I should have taken care of a while ago," she said snottily.

"Oh yeah, well I hope it works out for you," I replied.

She snarled, "Hopefully it will work out best for all of us!" She turned on her heel and abruptly made her exit.

Now I was really nervous. What had happened? Why was Sonya here? I knew she wasn't fucking my man! Naw, she wasn't even his type. Fuck it, who cared? That's when Dog Face barked, "Mr. Brown will see you now."

I got up feeling my uterus had dropped out. I had arrived confident that my plan was going to bring Joseph and me even closer, but here I was in front of his desk. He looked down and out like he had come to the end of his rope. He didn't even look up to check my legs, my lace stockings, or my big brown eyes puddling up with tears.

"Joseph," I called.

He looked up.

I looked in his eyes, I could feel he still loved me, but he didn't look determined anymore. He looked defeated. "What's up, baby?" I said.

"I guess you saw Sonya on the way out?"

"Yeah, what did Inspector Clouseau want?" I joked.

"She knows about us. She came to tell me that she's not the only one who knows and that she's more disappointed in me than in you because I'm older and far more respected. She claims that she expected much more from me, that I had, after all, been the one who told everybody about the family unit. She asked me how I could take marriage so lightly and why would I sacrifice all that was at stake, not only for me, but for this community that looks up to me. She asked if I realized that you were young and naive, even though you're extremely intelligent and confident. She asked if I realized that you never had a father and nobody in your neighborhood ever had a father, so she said you had no respect for or any real understanding of what a 'family unit' was—other than a useful piece of political jargon."

I got pissed off, and said, "Why doesn't she mind her business! She always thought she was a cut above just because she came from a two-parent family, two-car garage, middle-class okey-dokey community."

Joseph interrupted, "I think she was being helpful."

I sat there boiling, thinking, Yeah, Sonya was being helpful all right, but if she could have she would have gotten her black ass between Joseph's sheets. If she could have sat side by side with such a strong-minded man and exchanged thoughts on an equal level, she would have, but instead she comes tripping in here on her moral high horse, tip dippin' into my life and most precious reason for living. I remembered a line Aretha Franklin had sung from my mother's old record collection about life being unkind: "Now you're the key to my peace of mind."

Joseph brought me back to earth. "Baby," he said, "as much as it hurts me, I think it's over. We gotta cool out. I'm about to lose everything, and I've realized one thing: it's either I keep you and lose absolutely everything else, or I give you up and honor my commitments for life."

Feeling as if I had been stabbed in the stomach, I gasped for air and it slipped out. "I'm pregnant."

Joseph looked like his heart fell in his lap. He remained silent for what seemed an eternity. Then he lifted his head and said softly, "Get an abortion."

five

Mona

It was the middle of the week and I was up early shopping in the grocery market for food. I wouldn't need much because on Monday I was scheduled to fly to Zimbabwe, a country located in southern Africa that used to be called Rhodesia. I was excited; it would be my first journey home to Africa. Plus, I would be visiting a country that had recently experienced a revolution, and won. The prospect of meeting African men, women, and children who had actually been so oppressed and disgusted that they had picked up guns, driven tanks, and launched missiles to kill their racist enemies was exhilarating. I had never met any Africans like that.

I was to stay in Zimbabwe for the entire summer—about two months. First, I would visit the "big city" called

Harare. Then, two weeks later, I would travel out into the country past Bindura to the small village of Mtepatepa. There I would live with someone from the local area while working in a medical center. After all the lies I had been taught about Africa in public school and in college, I was looking forward to experiencing Africa with my own two eyes. Until now, I had only my inner spirit, my reading and research, and my own appreciation of African people born in America on which to base my understanding and opinions. Now I would become an expert with primary sources. I would be able to say I had been there.

Raising money for the trip was hard. I almost didn't make it. At one point, I began to despair. So, I got down on my knees and asked God if it was His will for me to take this trip to Zimbabwe. If it was His will, I prayed that He help provide a way to make it happen. Then, at the last minute, Adrienne, an older girlfriend of mine who was a lawyer specializing in international affairs, gave me the last eight hundred dollars I needed. Adrienne had attended the same Africa program when she was doing her undergraduate work at Princeton University. She told me that she thought my participation would be the greatest experience for me ever. It made me feel good to see a sister, a black professional woman at a prestigious Park Avenue law firm, still have enough love in her heart to help a younger, economically disadvantaged student like myself at the moment that I was about to be counted out. Adrienne was a godsend.

I was also grateful to be leaving because I'd been a little depressed. You know, the man stuff and the loneliness. I lived under what sometimes felt like a blessing and a curse: so much love in my heart, so much love to give, and no man balanced enough to give it to. It seemed that every time I embarked on a relationship it would end up with pain. So, I slowly pushed my cart through the market trying to avoid the depression foods like chocolate and cakes and cookies and hot-buttered microwave popcorn. I knew that these foods would only depress me more, by adding excess weight to my waistline. But the advertisers were tricky because there I stood in the aisle with a bag of hot-buttered microwave popcorn that claimed to have "less butter and less salt." I thought to myself, "Less than what?" Just then, another cart bumped into mine in the crowded narrow aisle. I reached my hand back to move my cart out of the way and a voice shot out, "Hey, lady, move that damned cart now before . . ."

I screwed up my face and got ready to fight. When I looked up, to my surprise, it was Mona, my old friend from freshman year. She started laughing and said, "Hey, girl!" I got happy and said, "Hey, what's up?" We embraced. It had been so long since we'd seen each other. I hadn't even seen her around campus anymore. She looked me in my eyes with a high level of concentration, something most people never did and said, "Yeah, well, I've been in the area but I took the year off and I'm working. I don't know how much more of that engineering curriculum I could've taken without having a complete breakdown." Then she smiled and added, "I have an apartment about eight minutes from here. You should stop by and see me soon."

An alarm went off in my head: I remembered what Nathan had told me about Mona. She was a lesbian. I wondered if I should accept her invitation to stop by and see her. For a moment, I considered accepting and just ducking her and never showing up. My consternation must have been obvious because Mona chuckled as though she knew exactly what was running through my mind. Or perhaps she was used to people reacting with fearful anxiety to the fact of her homosexuality. Mona said, "Oh, come on, girl. We go way back. Getting together is not going to hurt anything." Then she added, "You'll be safe, don't worry." I figured this was her way of letting me know that she could tell I knew she was gay. My mind started racing for an excuse and I quickly said, "Oh, you know what? I am finally going to Africa. I'm scheduled to leave for Zimbabwe on Monday and I have a whole lot of packing to do."

I looked in her eyes and she was obviously disappointed. Not necessarily disappointed that I wasn't coming over, but disappointed in me as a person for being apprehensive. She stepped closer, bent over, and whispered in my ear, "What's a matter, girl? Are you homophobic or something? What are you afraid of?" Then she pulled away from my face and looked me dead in the eye again. I thought to myself, Homophobia, a fear of homosexuality. Am I guilty of that and should I be?

It was a deep question to ponder right there in the aisle, so I put it aside and said to myself, This is Mona. I lived with her in the same dorm for a year and it was cool. We had been through thick and thin. Why not stop by and check her out. The only thing that was different between now and two years ago was that I was now fully aware of her lifestyle, which made me uncomfortable. Before, when I hadn't known that she was gay, I was real relaxed and we chilled, had fun, and I was myself. So I said, "I tell you what. I can stop by on Sunday evening. By that time I'll be packed and ready to fly out on Monday."

She smiled happily and said, "All right, girl, since I know you like to eat, I'll cook dinner. So don't eat before you come. I'm gonna stuff you with healthy, good-tasting foods. And we got so much to talk about."

I took her address and phone number. She took mine and we agreed to meet at six o'clock.

By Sunday morning I was finished packing and had everything stacked by the door for my departure. I was ready to throw everything in a cab and go straight to the airport. Even though the plane wasn't leaving until four in the afternoon on the following day, I was advised that on an international flight you should arrive at the airport about two hours early. I would definitely be on time. The phone rang. It was my sister, the middle one, and I could tell from her voice that she was fighting to hold back tears.

"What's the matter?" I asked.

"Me and Leon had a fight. It was terrible. The baby was crying through the whole thing. You should've heard the things he said to me. Well, he packed his things and left. This time he said it's for good. He said he got a new girl and another place to stay."

I remained quiet for a minute. I thought it was good that Leon had left for good. He was a fool who created more responsibilities for himself than his dull mind could handle. I knew my sister didn't want to hear that, though. She always resisted the truth. What she wanted was to be comforted.

"Can you come over? I'm so depressed. I know you're leaving tomorrow. I'm sorry. But I need you to do me a favor."

"What's the favor?" I asked. I didn't trust my sister and her ill-thought-out schemes.

"Just something. I'll explain when you get here," she said.

"I'll come, but you'll have to pick me up. The trains are too slow on Sunday and I'm supposed to do something tonight around six."

By mid-afternoon, my sister arrived, sporting a blue and purple bruise on the side of her eye. I grew angry, too angry to say anything. I could feel the heat rising from my ankles all the way up until it had consumed my entire body. I got in her car and said nothing. Finally, on the turnpike headed toward her apartment, I asked, "What happened to your face?"

"Me and Leon were play-wrestling the other day and he accidentally kicked me in my face."

"What do you think? I'm stupid? How is it that you were just 'playing' with the man who just packed up and left you today? That bruise can't be more than two days old."

Her face clouded with a painful expression I had never seen before. Holding back the tears, she said, "I'll tell you everything. Just give me a chance. Let me do it my way."

When we arrived at her apartment she went next door and picked up her baby, whom she apparently had left with the neighbor. When she returned, I held my niece, who was only three months old. I looked at her beautiful innocent face and thought to myself, Little girl, if you're gonna survive in this cruel world, you're gonna have to be a lot smarter and stronger than your mother.

My sister sat down and began to explain. She said that when she first met Leon he was a different person. He was loving and attentive. She said they used to do everything together. But ever since the pregnancy he had turned against her. He had undergone a dramatic change. She didn't think it was because of the baby. After all, it was Leon who was always flushing her birth control pills down the toilet because he said they weren't good for her. Since he flushed her pills and wouldn't wear a rubber, she figured he must want a child. He was ecstatic when she first told him she was pregnant. But after about six months, he started disappearing, coming home drunk, acting stupid. One night her girlfriend called her from a club called Cheetah's and told her Leon was there humping some other girl all around the dance floor. She told her that he had been there last week, too, but she hadn't wanted to say anything. When Leon got home, my sister had asked him about the club and the girl. By way of an answer, he gave her a black eye.

At this point my mind drifted from my sister's exact words and entered its own realm. Her words were painful to me and moved me to want to do something violent to Leon. My intellectual mind attempted to calm my emotions down, rationalizing that Leon was just like some other black men who had been raised without a father and without a clue of what a man was and what was required of him. But my emotional mind spoke up louder and louder, blocking out my intellect, as I envisioned several different violent ways that I could deal with this fool. The idea of physical violence against women was something that I rarely had to think about and had never had to personally deal with. I felt that when the sickness of a physically abusive man combined with the kind of vulnerable woman who exuded the feeling of not being in control, there would always be violence. Other women radiate danger—that if you ever even look like you're thinking about hitting them, they'll blow your head off. Well, I was the latter kind of woman, and I had never been hit or been in the presence of any man who even remotely looked like he was going to strike me. My sister was finishing her story and telling me her scatter-brained scheme.

"So the reason why I didn't tell you about the hitting thing was because I know how bad your temper is when you get mad. And I thought you might kill Leon or something. And I understand that you probably think he deserves it, but he is the baby's father. How would I explain to her that she never met her father because my sister, her aunt, killed him?"

"That's a stupid question because you'll have to explain to her why she never met her father anyway because the fool isn't strong enough to hang around and handle his responsibility as a father. Either way, dead or alive, he is gonna be absent."

My sister paid me no mind, and said, "I called you here 'cause I want you to talk to Leon. I was never good at talking; you always was. Besides, he respects you a lot more than he respects me. He talks good about you all the time. He reads anything you write in the paper and everything anybody ever prints about you. He looks up to you. When we used to fight he used to ask me, beg me, not to tell you anything about it."

I looked at my sister and felt sorry for her. It wasn't her fault she was so weak-minded. My mother was not the same person when she raised her that she was when she raised me.

"I knew he was gonna leave," she continued. "So I took his Rolex. I knew if I took it and hid it, when he left he'd have no choice but to come back for it. His grandfather gave it to him before he died. It's the only expensive thing he had. So when he comes back for it, I want you to talk to him and convince him not to leave me. . . . I love him. Besides, I can't afford this apartment without his income, not to mention the other bills."

"You what? You love him! Don't be ridiculous, you don't love him. You're just used to him. He's like a bad habit you think is good for you just because you been doing it for so long. Listen: You see this child?" I asked, holding up the baby. "Do you love her?"

"You know I do," she said.

"Well, she's the one who's important. She doesn't need to suffer because you keep making bad decisions. If you love her, you'll become strong for her. How could you love him when he doesn't love you? Does a man who loves his woman bash her face in when she's six months pregnant? Does a man who loves his child leave her when she's three months old? Both of you don't know the meaning of love, but I'll tell you what I'm gonna do. Give me that Rolex."

"What for?"

"I'm gonna sell it first thing tomorrow morning. I know I can get at least two thousand dollars. I should get a lot more, but the pawnshops always cheat you anyway."

"But he's gonna come looking for it," she said, concerned more for Leon than for herself and her own child.

"Yeah, and you're gonna tell the bastard that you haven't seen it. You don't know where it is. Then you're gonna play a mind game with him the way he plays a mind game with you and you're gonna say, 'Maybe you gambled it away one of them nights you was out drinking.' "

Later that afternoon I called a locksmith service and had the locks changed. Because she lived on her building's fourth floor I didn't have to worry about the windows. I called my mother and told her that my sister and the baby needed to stay there for about two weeks. I promised to get the money from the watch in the morning. She was to take it and budget it for the rest of the summer. Leon sure wouldn't have made two thousand dollars that summer at the job he had anyway. I told her that just as soon as I got back from Africa, I would get a part-time job and give her money for the baby. We had a talk about life. I said that many times as women we feel we need a man. And, the truth of the matter is, we do need a man. But we need a good man. A bad man is not worth the trouble. It's all right to struggle with a brother to work together to make a better future, to help him out, but physical abuse can never be tolerated under any circumstances.

I told her that I was her sister and that meant that I would be there to help her. We would raise her baby together. We would raise her strong. We didn't need Leon; he was a hindrance, not a help. I gave her the phone number of a lawyer I knew in her neighborhood. If she had any problems, she was to call him and use my name. He would advise her about restraining orders and any legal matters concerning the baby. I said I probably wouldn't be in touch because I would be so far away, but I expected her to use her common sense. If she returned to Leon, I told her that I would stop speaking to her for good. Even though this was not the truth, I knew the threat would keep her away from him for at least the two months I was away.

My sister dropped me at Mona's apartment. I was taking a chance because I was two and a half hours late. Mona might no longer be there. I decided to stop by anyway, figuring that if I didn't give it a try, she'd take it the wrong way. I asked my sister to wait until she actually saw Mona at the door before driving off, so I wouldn't be stranded without a ride.

Mona opened the door with attitude. I stood at the door exhausted from the day's ordeal. Mona wasn't sympathetic. She cut her eyes at me as though I was some kind of bullshitting con woman. She stood with her hand on her hip and her summer, worsted, white wool V-neck sweater draped over her short cut-off jeans. She was barefooted, well-pedicured, and long-legged. She waited for an explanation. I found myself presenting her with an excuse. "Sorry, Mona. My sister got in some bad trouble with her man. I had to go straighten it out at the last minute. I hope I didn't wreck your dinner."

"Come in," she said snootily, letting the door close on me at its own pace. "Most of the dinner was salads: macaroni salad, potato salad, and health salad. So, of course, they're still fresh. The fish dish is cold. But I can always heat it up."

"Look, Mona," I said sincerely, "I don't want to argue. I didn't mean to offend you. Seriously, under any other circumstances I would have called, but I had a bunch of very important things to take care of unexpectedly and only a few hours to do it in." I was growing impatient with her spoiled ways. She was making me feel as if she was my mother. Or worse yet, my man!

"All right, don't worry about it. I really thought you weren't coming, so I made other plans. But that's not until later tonight. We can chill, talk, eat dinner, and I'll take you home on my way out." Then she sighed, threw her hands up, and said, "Welcome to my little spot."

I looked around her comfortable living room. It had the feeling of a place you wouldn't want to leave often. Something like a den or a cave that an animal who had to hibernate would be comfortable in for an entire season. The floors were parquet, the wood well polished and maintained. A white, fluffy rug lay tossed over part of it. The ceiling had track lighting with bulbs of varying intensity. Some lights were carefully arranged to highlight the black-and-white photographs that decorated the walls. The pictures were much like Mona's personality—physical. One life-size photo was of a pair of perfect women's legs. They were long and soft. The emphasis in the photo was on the muscle structure. The muscles were defined but not hard and masculine, obviously feminine, well-kept and exercised. Another large photo was of a neck, throat, and the beginnings of a chin. It was a woman leaning her head backward. But instead of the usual emphasis on the beauty of the face and lips, it was the trachea that was important. The lights shone on the narrow neck and the muscles that undergirded the chin. Mona's bookcase held carefully arranged scientific texts. They included words I didn't understand like "thermonuclear," and "molecular motion," and "electromagnetic fields." On top of the bookcase was a set of fancy candleholders with half-used candles with hardened wax stuck in the drip position down the sides.

Mona was fortunate. Her apartment was not scorching with the heat of summer. Instead it enjoyed the comfort and control of a central air-conditioning breeze. It was neither stuffy nor too cold. I imagined in the bedroom there must have been an incense stick burning because the air had a sweet smell. It wasn't overpowering, like a newly purchased deodorized air freshener. It lingered lightly in a pleasant way. The dinner table was made of glass, polished and decorated with the niceties that are usually collected by a person who intends to stay, as opposed to one just passing through. The plates were arranged as were the bowls, some made of glass, some appropriately wooden.

I looked at Mona. I could see there was no reason to feel bad that she had left school for a year. She was obviously doing quite well for herself. In fact, from the looks of things, she was doing much better than me. She had a fly geometric haircut that looked perfect as usual. Her opened closet door revealed high-quality linens, silks, and wools. She was always high-fashion. She had always been willing to work as hard as necessary to maintain that lifestyle and appearance.

"So," I said. "What's been going on with you, girl? Looks like you're doing fine."

"Yeah, well, after our freshman year I got a summer job at Bell Laboratories. I did so well that they allowed me to come back during our school breaks. I was surprised at the pay I was making because it was more than I had ever raked in. So, I got in good with my supervisor, Gerald. I hung around late, learned things that the other interns didn't know. Then I got around to popping the question: 'What if I take a year-long hiatus from school? Can I land a full-time position?' Gerald said he'd gladly give me his recommendation. He told me that I'd have to leave and reenter school in good academic standing because Bell required all of their employees to be upwardly mobile and scientifically proficient and updated. So anyway, to make a long story short, I'm getting paid well. And I even worked it out so I can return in September, with Bell financing part of my education." She smiled.

She seemed genuinely satisfied and proud of her accomplishments. I was also impressed. She walked to the refrigerator and pulled out a bowl of big purple grapes. She

placed them on the table and said, "Here, have some before dinner. So, girl, I know you're really happy about going to Africa
tomorrow. This must be your lifetime dream!"

"I'm definitely hyped up," I said. "I think I'm gonna
come back much deeper. I'll probably see and learn so many
things I never knew."

She started laughing and said, "Oh, God! Could the
world take it if you got any deeper?"

"What do you mean by that?" I asked.

"Well, you're already the deepest person I know. I may
not be on campus, but I still read the campus news. You're
involved in everything. You're out front, vocal, and concerned.
Don't you think we're kind of young for you to be so worried
about the whole world?"

"Well, Mona," I said, "you're a hard worker. You do
what you have to do. I'm sure you didn't get this beautiful
apartment from kicking back, taking it light."

"I guess the difference is, I do what I do for myself, for
my own enjoyment and benefit. You, on the other hand, put
yourself out there for other people. You hardly ever worry
about yourself, how you feel, or the things that you need."
Mona looked me in the eye and then looked at my clothing as
if she were comparing hers and mine. Or maybe she was suggesting that by helping others I was somehow shortchanging
myself.

"Well, girl, you got it going on," I said. "But not
everybody is interested in the same thing. I mean I look at you
and I say, 'Mona's beautiful as usual.' Nobody can mess with
you on that level. But, at the same time, clothes and beauty and

all that is not my priority. Not when all this crazy stuff is going on in the world."

She rolled her eyes and said, "See! That's exactly what I mean. There's always going to be a bunch of stuff going on in the world, this country, and our community. But why do you have to be involved in it? If every individual took care of their own business, the world wouldn't need people like you to carry everybody else's weight on their shoulders." Then she smiled and added, "I mean, I admire you. The things that you stand for are cool. But I know niggas! They're basically selfish. If you got in some sort of trouble, they wouldn't give a damn. They wouldn't even lift a finger to help you. So why do you feel responsible for other people's lives?"

" 'Cause, Mona, there's a reason for everything. There's a reason why our community is disorganized and in last place. But not everybody knows and understands why. Then you get some people, black college students and professionals who get the opportunity to find out why, through their studies, and what do they do? They isolate themselves, abandon their responsibilities. That's no way to break the cycle. If you know something you should feel obligated to teach it to our people so we can move forward."

"So anyway," she said. She was bored and wanted to change the subject. "What happened with your sister?"

"Well, she had a baby daughter with some brother who couldn't handle the responsibility. So I'm trying to help her put her life back on track so she can take charge of herself again."

Mona laughed heartily. Then she stood up and blurted out, "You have such a nice poetic way of putting things: 'A brother who couldn't handle his responsibilities'! That one sentence represents most of the black men in this country and you just say it so nice and matter-of-factly. What did he do? Did he beat the shit out of her? 'Cause that's what usually happens, you know."

My emotions had been building inside of me. Just remembering what Leon did to my sister made me want to cry and strike out at the same time. Mona's biting sarcasm was inexplicable to me. I couldn't understand if she was sincerely trying to make a point, or if she was trying to hurt me by rubbing something painful in my face. I wasn't sure if she was trying to help or if she was compensating and covering up some pain or bitterness of her own. Wanting to skip the torture the topic represented for me I played it down. So I said, "It wasn't a regular thing, like an everyday beating or anything. It was more like one major incident that kept getting worse and worse. He's outta there now anyway. I made sure of that. So that's the good news."

"Yeah, it's that 'one major incident' that can kill something inside of you, though. It's not like it has to happen to you every day for it to leave a deep scar," Mona said sadly.

Seeing this as a verbal entrance into Mona's world, I decided to take my cue and begin to unravel 'the Mona mystery.' After all, even when we were tight we'd have fun but below her surface optimism and joy, I thought I sensed a real unhappiness. There was an uneasiness within her that came out as a bitter anti-male sentiment, leading to a thoroughgoing cynicism toward life. She wasn't alone. There seemed to be a growing number of college girls who shared this outlook.

Many, like Mona, had embraced a gay lifestyle. "So is that what happened to you?" I asked.

"What do you mean 'happened' to me?"

"Abuse," I said. "Physical abuse by a black man?"

"You know what's sickening to me," she said, "the idea that something had to have 'happened' to me for me to be gay! That is what you're talking about, isn't it, when you ask what 'happened' to me?"

"I guess it is," I said. "But it's a little more than the fact that you're gay. It's the immediate opposition you have toward any male-female relationships. It's the quiet anger, the quiet dislike of men. I can only assume that it's related to something that 'happened' to you."

"There you go again, jumping to the defense of 'the brothers'! Just because I don't like the fact that men routinely abuse women, beat them, rape them, lead them on, play with their heads, doesn't mean that I'm guilty of not liking them. What it means is they're guilty of being abusive! Period! Let's put the blame where it belongs."

"Listen, Mona, I've met all kinds of men and I've never been beaten, raped, or molested by any of them. But I also believe that good and evil exist in the world and that white supremacy is the primary force that has shaped the mind-set of both our African men and women, creating a people who are not living the way we would naturally and culturally live. Instead we're just reacting and reflecting other people's pressures on us. I also believe that sometimes we, as women who don't take the time to understand our history and its impact on the behavior of our people, make bad choices unknowingly, and then we suffer the consequences of the poor choices we make."

She roared with dismissive laughter. "Yeah, what do you call what that asshole Nathan did to you? He may not have slapped the stuffing out of you but he did a hell of a butcher's job on your mind. That's mental abuse. I heard you lost thirty pounds and had to drop two courses behind that fool! I could've told you what time it was with him from the jump. But there's one thing I know about women like you who talk all that black stuff: You need to be face to face with the evil that men do before you become believers. I think it's a shame, but it seems like women would rather wait until after they get their asses kicked than listen to their girlfriends who were right there by their sides from the beginning and through the whole thing!"

"So are you saying Nathan abused me because he was a sexually confused male?"

"I'm saying Nathan abused you with his deceit and you know he did! He lied to you just like they all do. They lie, promise you things they know damn well they can't deliver, manipulate your thoughts, and toss your head around like it's some kind of spaldeen."

"But Nathan didn't do that because he's a man and men are naturally abusive. He did it because he was misled at a young and impressionable age. Besides, it would seem like you would understand the whole idea of keeping your sexual identity a secret, because you did it so well when you were in college! When were you, a woman and my good friend, gonna let me in on the big secret?"

Mona paused. I knew I was stabbing her with my words but I was trying to get her to stop being so self-righteous, as though black men were responsible for all that's bad with the world and black women were guiltless, harmless victims.

"Whatever!" she responded, casting my words aside. "The bottom line is that women are more compassionate, more feeling. We have a deeper connection with one another than we could ever have with them. I don't hate men. Hell, I have a brother. I love him, too. But as far as a man goes, I don't want to share anything beyond a surface-level, limited nonphysical friendship. I know when I'm talking to a woman she understands what I feel because she feels the same thing. We all menstruate. We all have cramps. Most of us have been hurt by men. And we have a deeper understanding of love, sensuality, and sensitivity."

As I listened to Mona's words, I tried to decipher her logic. It was true that she had been there for me all through the affair with Nathan. And it was true that I had foolishly ignored some of her good advice. I also agreed with her conviction that women had an inherently deep connection with and understanding of one another. After all, women all experienced the same bodily functions, so it stood to reason that we would be highly likely to be more understanding of each other's emotional lives. But I didn't see why that meant two women should end up in bed together. I didn't understand what this had to do with sexual desire. Perhaps, at this point, I should have said, to hell with all of this freaky stuff and left, but I wanted to understand every aspect of black life, even those I found personally disagreeable. Besides, I wanted to challenge Mona. For me to give up on the conversation would have given her the upper hand. She'd have conveniently dismissed me as "homophobic." I felt some gays used this term to silence people who didn't share their opinions and to excuse themselves from being questioned, criticized, or challenged. Then, in a clever twist of words, they would try to leave you with the impression that the only issue was your "fear" of them and not their questionable behavior or attitudes.

"So, what do you do?" I asked.

"What do you mean?" She smiled invitingly.

"I mean, explain it to me," I said in an open-minded way.

"I'll be happy to, but after dinner. Right now, I'm gonna put the food together for you. I know you must be starving. Besides, this may be your last great meal of the summer!"

Mona got up and went to her stereo. She turned on some Tracy Chapman album and my spirit tossed uncomfortably. Chapman's music had a tendency to depress me. Somehow it sounded like "victim music." It wasn't necessarily her lyrics, because I really didn't know them. Rather, it was the emotion created by the music itself. I preferred empowering music— whether rap, gospel, rhythm and blues, or jazz, it didn't much matter so long as it made your soul feel good, strong, and aggressive. I watched her as she moved around the kitchen. She was still a mystery to me. She had ducked my question about her past and whatever it was that led her to the decisions she had made in her life. Mona was clever, unquestionably intelligent. She revealed no remorse about her lifestyle. I was convinced she harbored a hidden pain. And I was sure that she shared her insecurities with herself and her lover in her quiet moments. Yes, she was beautiful. She had the type of beauty that would make any black man surrender his heart and wallet.

She didn't fit any of the stereotypes of a "butch." She was feminine and soft all over. Her movements were fluid, not staccato, girlish, not boyish. I wondered how she let other gay women know that she was down with the "gay life."

"Come and get it," she called, having taken the trouble to make everything look better than a table in a fancy restaurant. Just as I started to say my dinner prayers, the telephone rang. Mona wasn't praying. She never did. At least not in my presence. But I didn't make a judgment about that. It was her choice. She got up to answer the phone as I continued praying, "Oh God, thank you for this food . . ."

"Hello," Mona said in a sexy voice.

". . . Thank you for the nourishment."

"Not again. Don't even try it," Mona said. She sounded disappointed.

". . . Thank you for your love, protection, and most of all your guidance."

"No, that's what you said last time. Whatever you have to do, cancel it because I'm coming anyway. I'll be over at eleven-thirty. That should be good enough." Mona slammed down the phone.

". . . Amen." I finished my prayer. I looked at Mona casually as if I hadn't heard her telephone conversation. I watched as she plastered a smile on her face, took a deep breath, and headed back to the dinner table, trying to look calm. I asked her to put on some other music, trying to lighten the mood. She put on Whitney Houston, sat down to eat, and said, "I know you don't drink, but I'm gonna have a glass of wine. You're not gonna bug out on me or give me a lecture, are you?"

"I never have. I won't start now."

She gulped down the drink and seemed to relax. She took a deep breath and said, "So, how do we do it? Well, the first thing for me is the attraction. I see a woman and I look at her face to feel her out. I want to feel her life, her experience, what she's been through. Once I feel the mood in her, the sentiment, I connect with it. Now, I'm not gonna lie. Her physical appearance is at least half of the attraction. She has to have clean hair and a firm body. You know, like she works out, but not fanatically. I like things like clavicles. You know the bone right here. . . ." She took her French-manicured fingernails and ran them from the top of the shoulder to the bottom of her neckline. "You see how defined that is? That's what I like. I like breasts because they're real points of pleasure. A lot of men don't know how to suck a breast, but I'm good at it because I know what I want to feel when it's happening to me."

Mona seemed fascinated and turned on by her own candid talk. She must have realized how graphic she was being because she quickly said, "Oh! I hope I'm not embarrassing you. You did ask."

I urged her to continue. I wanted my imagination to wander with hers, to test myself. I wanted to test my real, unprotected, nonpolitical, undenied feelings.

"Anyway," she said, "the breasts should never be flat. The stomach should never be flabby. Because that ruins the whole picture. The next thing has got to be flexibility. Nobody wants it stiff. Making love should be physical, like a dance or a piece of artwork."

As I sat at the dinner table I tried to imagine sex with a woman. I tried to clear my mind of all prior prejudice and just focus in on the idea of sex with a woman. I could see that it would be gentle and soft. Having my breasts sucked properly would definitely turn me on. But then, what next? The image of two vaginas, two sets of pubic hair rubbing together did nothing for me. It meant nothing sexually and meant nothing in terms of creating life. Kisses, on the other hand, were always sensual to me. They prepared my body for all that was to follow. Kisses intensified the sensitivity so a touch would mean so much more. But how disappointed, I imagined, I would be to receive a warm sensual kiss and have my body ignited, only to have my vagina stimulated by a small finger or an aggravating plastic or rubber vibrator. I had to assume it would be aggravating because I found even the thin rubber of a condom a nuisance. And, although I still used them, it decreased the feeling substantially. I couldn't stomach a fake penis, no matter how it was disguised or explained away. Plus, for me, the hardness, the suction, the power and strength and gentle roughness of a man was a continual turn-on.

"Massages are the best," Mona continued. "Because they relax you. Now somebody like you would need a good massage to help you loosen up all those points of tension."

"You got any tea?" I interrupted.

"Yeah, but I don't have any doughnuts." She laughed, remembering our freshman feasts.

"Believe me, I don't want any doughnuts. I'm watching my weight."

"You're doing a good job. You look pretty good. All you have to do is tighten up here and here," she said, pinching my waistline. "But you're kind of different. A woman would be attracted to you not for the normal reasons. Not that you're not pretty, 'cause you are. But because you have a power. You have a quiet power and a lot of strength. It almost feels like you can influence anyone to do anything. But the good thing is you don't use that power a lot. Some people would abuse it. Your presence alone makes people want to question themselves." Then she paused, turned around, and smiled. "I guess somebody would have to be pretty powerful to get you to question yourself?" She brought the tea to the table. It was herbal tea—that was the best for me. But I also noticed that it was "Sleepytime," a blend I had never tasted.

"Oh, are you trying to knock me out so that I'll miss my plane?" I said jokingly.

"No, girl, this will just relax you. I told you—you have to learn to relax. Don't worry, I'll get you home tonight without a doubt."

So I sipped my tea and Mona continued to entertain me. She didn't need any props. She performed her entire drama with just her body alone.

Soon she checked her watch and in a panic said, "Oh! I gotta get moving, girl. I got a date. I'm gonna jump in the shower. You chill on the couch and I'll be right out. Then I'll drop you home. You look tired anyway."

I laid down on the couch while Mona ran around pulling out fresh fashions for her date. The careful attention she paid to each detail of the outfit she pulled out reminded me of myself when I was getting ready to see a brother I had a crazy feeling for. After she picked out her clothes, she proceeded to wiggle out of the ones she had on, letting them drop casually to the floor. She seemed really focused on all of her movements. I tried to figure out if she was doing the same thing we heterosexual women did when trying to entice a man. That is, sometimes we showed a man our body while pretending that we didn't know he could see it. Maybe this was her way, too, of "upping the ante." Perhaps she wanted me to "see the goods" as her final effort in persuading me to enter her world.

I questioned myself. How, exactly, did I feel being in the apartment with an admitted and committed lesbian whom I used to share a dormitory with? Was I hiding anything? So I tested myself, too. I allowed my eyes to explore her body. There was no doubt that Mona was graciously structured. Her own breasts were as full as she said she required of her lovers. Her lips were thick and her dark skin rich. She was an African queen. But, sexually, I felt nothing. There was no desire in my heart or between my legs to bring my aesthetic admiration of Mona's obvious charms to a sexual level.

After Mona showered, the phone rang. I yelled, asking her if she wanted me to get up to get it. She abruptly said, "No, thanks!" She jumped out of the shower, grabbing a towel but barely using it to cover herself. Facing the other direction, I pretended not to be interested in the call. But I listened anyway.

"How is it that you put this work before you put me?" she asked the caller. "But I haven't seen you in damn near a week." She was trying to lower her voice so I couldn't hear. "Yeah, but you said you were gonna finish that three days ago." There was a pause. "Fuck that, girl! I'm not stupid, you know.

It doesn't take that long to do a board," she said, raising her voice. "No, I think you're playing games with me. Sure, and all the while you and Tanya were working on this together. Right! You know I would have come if I knew. That's why you tried to discourage me."

Mona, now incredibly pissed off, picked up the phone and went into her bedroom and slammed the door. Her voice was now muffled. As I lay there on her living-room couch thinking about how her conversation could've been me talking to any man I was having a relationship with, I dozed off into a light sleep. I dreamed I was in Coney Island, an amusement park I had gone to once or twice in my childhood. I was in the funhouse, the place with the mirrors that could make a fat girl appear to be skinny or a short girl appear to be tall. They could take the most attractive face and mangle the reflection so that the face would be unrecognizable. I wasn't alone. I thought I could see a girl who resembled Mona. At that moment, I woke up. My body jolted and I opened my eyes. Mona was sitting on the edge of the couch in her silk panties and camisole. She had one hand in my hair massaging my head and one placed on the right side of my breast. My eyes opened wide. I gasped and she motioned for me to relax and quickly said, "Girl, I can make you feel good. Better than you ever felt before. And I promise no pain at the end."

I grabbed both of Mona's hands off me and held them firmly so she would be certain of my disapproval. I scolded her saying, "Mona, I love you and I dig you. And we can still be friends. But, no, we can't have a relationship 'cause I'm not a lesbian."

"You're just scared. I'll teach you how. I know you've been hurt by these men, just like me. I'll show you how to relax."

"From the looks of things, Mona, you've been hurt by some guy from the past. Since you don't confide in me that will always be a mystery to me. But somehow you've allowed that experience to turn you off to all men. But sleeping with a woman does not guarantee you anything. Women, too, can be power-hungry exploiters. Women, too, can be two-timing low-down cheats. Women, too, can be emotionally abusive and insensitive. I mean, damn, Mona. I been stood up. Me by a man. You by a woman. I been lied to. You been lied to. I been lonely, you been lonely. But guess what? It doesn't matter how good you can make me feel, Mona. When I think about it, I imagine there are a lot of things that can make me feel good. Maybe you could bring me some level of sexual pleasure. So could a lot of people and a lot of things. That doesn't make it right, though."

Mona, who was usually a tower of strength and opinion, had tears in her eyes. I didn't know if her ego was hurt because I didn't want to participate or if she was touched in some way by what I said. Then she let loose her anger and shouted, " 'Right'! 'right'! Who's to say what's wrong, what's right, and who should be doing what? Who's in charge anyway?"

"Mona, fuck being hysterical. Let's look at this thing rationally. What are you gonna do? Move in with a woman? Marry a woman? Where do you see yourself twenty years from now? What will you be doing? You talked about the deep connection and feeling of being a woman. Well, one of the deepest feelings a woman can experience is giving birth, the creation of life. Sex between two women cannot bring about life. It's impossible because it wasn't meant to be."

"There are plenty of alternatives," she shot back. "Get with it. There's artificial insemination, adoption, all types of options."

"Okay, let's look at it like this. If everyone were to adopt the gay lifestyle, what would that bring about?"

"What do you mean?"

"Look at it like a mathematical equation. If everyone were to adopt the gay lifestyle, the end result would be the death of the entire community because the so-called gay lifestyle cannot produce life. Two men can't make a baby any more than two women can. Secondly, if a gay community were, for the sake of its survival, to turn to artificial insemination, what would you produce?"

She stood there sternly as if I were stupid. She uttered one word, "Children."

"What kind of children? A whole community of children who didn't know either their biological mother or father. A whole network of entangled genetics. You'll have a child whose feelings and characteristics you may not understand and can't explain because, above and beyond some comments on an application, you won't know where those characteristics and feelings came from. You'll have children to whom you'll have to explain that for the pleasure of being with another woman, you were so selfish that you brought him or her into a world where the Bible, the Quran, the Torah, and the community says his same-sex parents are wrong. What church will they go to? Or what will you teach them spiritually? Will you teach them to love God but to disrespect what God lays down as laws? I don't know, Mona, the whole thing seems like an extension of confusion to me."

Mona grew uncontrollable. "You're always talking bullshit. That's what I hate about you. You can never relax. You never open up. God and community, black this, white that. It's all bullshit. I'm from Brooklyn! Don't none of that shit work anyway."

"Mona, all I have to offer you is sisterhood. Real sisterhood. The kind I offer to my own blood sisters. It's what makes me able to work hard and sacrifice to keep another woman from feeling that same pain I felt or the pain of our ancestors. But what it isn't for me is sexual. That's a wrong turn. It's an irrational response to a very complex question. You should understand what that means. If you want to understand Brooklyn and the many confused dark people, you should realize how it has scarred the men and the women to the point where we've even forgotten how to love one another. But what I can't do is do what other people are doing just because they figured out a way to make it look right."

The gulf between us was too big to bridge. The evening would end badly. I continued to feel that Mona's embrace of a lesbian life was due more to inner weakness and her victimization as a black woman than out of any genetic compulsion. Mona was closed and wounded. She wasn't interested in dealing with any criticism of herself. She wasn't interested in change. Nor was she interested in viewing herself as part of a larger struggle or larger community of African people. Her entire focus was on self and pleasure. And even though she had chosen lesbianism for herself, she still was not happy. Nor could I be shaken from my belief that homosexuality, while perhaps offering some individuals relief from their pain, was nevertheless a way of avoiding our people's need to build strong, life-giving, and enduring family structures—structures, rooted in our original African culture, that would stand the many stresses to which our people are daily subjected.

six

Chance

"Now listen to what I'm saying, baby. Now, c'mon, dry up your tears."

These were the first words that hit my ears after stepping off the bus from my university in New Jersey to the Port Authority Bus Terminal in New York City at Forty-second Street. The guy who was talking looked to be in his early forties, but the girl he was talking to was about twelve years old, dressed up as an older woman. The girl was dark-skinned and dirty. Her short red pants were more like panties. They were so tight that most of the material was lost somewhere in her crack leaving her butt cheeks half exposed. They were red, and dirty, too. Her halter top, which would more accurately be described as a bra, was purple. Her legs were long and ashy. Somewhere beneath the crust and funk someone might describe them as "pretty, young, and athletic."

"Now who took plain Vanessa and gave her a new look and a new name?" The older man stood over her confidently as she sat looking up at him from the bench. He wore his hair in long greasy jheri kurls. He talked to her smooth through jagged-edge teeth as though he had recited these lines a thousand times before.

The girl looked up at him as if he were her savior, and said, "You did, Try-Love."

"Now when I turned Vanessa into Queen Khadijah, didn't I introduce you to a life of royalty? Didn't I fatten up your pockets?" He asked the questions gently as though he really wanted her to think about it. He took the time and patience to position himself to sound and look sincere. Then he took his dried-up long finger with the two-inch fingernail and wiped away one of her tears.

"Didn't I . . . ?" He asked again softly.

"Yes, you did," she responded, seemingly convinced that this guy whom she called "Try-Love" had put her in a better position by putting money in her pockets. And then added, without much confidence, "But I just can't tonight. I'm not feeling it." Such grown-up words for such a young girl, I thought. But though she was young, she looked used. Her body hadn't even gone through puberty and already it had begun to sag in several places. He put his face closer to hers, his big wide nose covered with pus bumps and blackheads, and said, "Queen, what did I tell you to do when you were having a bad day?" She smiled, gently exposing her dirty teeth. "You said to 'try love.'"

"Now what's my name?"

"Try-Love," she said affectionately.

"And who's the only one who really loves and protects you?"

"You are, Try-Love," she answered.

"Now let me tell you what I'm gonna do for you." He reached into his pocket and pulled out a money clip with a thick stack of fifty- and hundred-dollar bills.

"Try-Love's gonna take Queen Khadijah to Tad's Steaks for her favorite meal. We gon' git filet mignon and baked potato drippin' with butter and cream." He ran his long red tongue over his black lip as if he could already taste the meal. "But before that, Try-Love's gonna take you up to see Lorraine so you can get your hair did." She smiled like he had just given her keys to her own new Rolls-Royce. "And afterwards, if the Queen still loves me—and I hope she does—she's gonna do what makes me happy. She's gonna charm these dudes with her beauty, make 'em feel real good with that young body and those juicy lips. Then she's gonna bring those green bills back to Daddy so he can personally show her his appreciation. Now, what's my name, Queen?"

"Try-Love," she said proudly. He grabbed her butt cheek and flashed a smile, asking her like a gentleman, "Well then, shall we?" He extended his arm and she tucked hers in his. And to my amazement they walked off together, both looking satisfied and ready.

Now I had seen pimps and whores before. But I didn't remember whores being twelve years old. I had seen women work the strip for a pimp and seen the shit get smacked out of them if they would not. But with this pimp there was no violence, only the illusion of real love and real concern. In fact, there were also illusions of royalty, loyalty, and protection. He had actually convinced this girl that he had made her a queen when she really looked like she had just crawled out of the gutter. She had such evident trust and belief in him that even the smell of her own stinking underarms could not awaken her to her reality. He had convinced her that by giving him all of her money, that she worked for, he was somehow making her rich! The cruelest joke of all, however, was the way he could in the same breath tell her to sleep with various strange men, and then tell her that he loved her and she could return home to "Try-Love," where she would be "protected." How could he have so thoroughly convinced her that he was protecting her when it was actually he who was putting her in danger in the first place? The more I thought about it, the angrier I became. But I soon realized that I could not be angry—after all, she was a child and I had read somewhere that children were innocent. But you would think that if she had seen so much in her young, short life, that she wouldn't be so stupid.

I left the Port Authority and hit the street moving swiftly, not wanting to miss my appointment with the Reverend Benjamin F. Chavis, Jr. He was the director of the Commission for Racial Justice, which was a civil rights agency of the United Church of Christ. I had met him earlier at a students' rally at college. Impressed by what he said were my leadership skills and political insights, he wanted to offer me a job. I was reluctant to come to his office to discuss such an offer because Chavis was a relatively young minister and I had heard enough about what a lot of them really wanted! Moreover, my experience had led me to believe that the majority of churches today were not willing to take uncompromising leadership roles in the struggle for justice. But it was my hunger, poverty, and the confidence of knowing that even if the interview turned out to be a bust, I would never barter my beliefs or be manipulated by him or anyone else, that prompted me to accept his invitation to come to New York and give the interview a shot.

I was surprised to see after arriving at "the Commission" that it was a legitimate establishment, at least judging by its appearance. I had half suspected that the so-called Commission might be housed in some semi-abandoned building with a one-light-bulb office, an illiterate half-naked secretary, and a slipshod preacher sitting in a chalkboard cubicle. Instead, I found a clean, large staff in a more-than-decent Madison Avenue building, bright lights and people professionally dressed, looking serious about their work.

The secretary signaled to me that it was my time to see Chavis. I entered a spacious office that was lined with plaques, trophies, and certificates, all made out to the Reverend Benjamin Chavis for "outstanding service and dedication" to the African community. The interview seemed to go well as I listened to this man who had been at one point or another, it seemed, a member of every black organization that had ever existed. The range was impressive, from a moderate group like Martin Luther King's Southern Christian Leadership Conference to the radical movers and shakers of the Black Panther Party with a whole lot in between. He had served four and a half years in prison as one of America's many political prisoners and emerged with a divinity degree from Duke University. He was a chemist, a doctor of philosophy, and a well-known preacher among those people and clergy who had spent their lives challenging the racial and economic injustices of America. We talked about many things: police brutality, apartheid, African liberation movements throughout the world; we shared a critique of some of the past black leaders and organizations and their efforts to reorganize our people. As we talked, we became more comfortable with each other. I was sure that he wasn't just some phony preacher trying to use people's pain as a path to their panties. He seemed sure that I wasn't just some fast-talking, tight-pants-wearing student leader out to advance only my own ego and career.

He had asked me to meet with him, he said, because he was interested in initiating a nationwide African youth and student movement organized around issues of justice. Somehow he had sensed that I was the person for the job. He told me how desperately the movement needed some new blood to inject new life and new direction into our cause as black people. He added that, unlike many of the leaders that were on the scene now, he was not afraid of surrounding himself with equally dedicated, intelligent, and aggressive young people, because he was convinced that if we were going to survive, we would need the contributions of both wise elders and energetic, sincere, well-studied young people. I agreed. I thought that the generation gap in the African movement was a severe problem and had to be bridged. I told him that young people had little faith in our so-called civil-rights leaders. Too many of them seemed to be selfish, materialistic hustlers disconnected from our present-day realities. He retorted that while this perception was partly true there were, he said, some "good elders and workers," nonetheless. He added that I should remember that as far as many of the elders were concerned, today's youth were a bunch of misguided heathens who were unwilling to sacrifice anything and hell-bent on creating the worst image of African people in our entire history.

So the objective of the job, in addition to the creation of a nationwide student and youth movement, was to help close the many gaps that existed in our community: gaps between young and old, between young people who attended college and young people who did not, between the under, lower, and middle classes. I was to try to bring together African youth from Africa, the Caribbean, and America. I accepted the challenge Chavis offered me with the stipulation that the church would not try to pacify me or confine me with its sometimes artificial limitations.

I would spend the entire next year at the Commission researching the conditions of our people in various parts of the nation. I had to look at urban, suburban, and rural youth. I established contact with the many student leaders and organizers on campuses from every region. I drew on many of the people I had come to know from organizing at college. I coupled this information with the resources of the Commission, which included computers, newspapers, journals from all over the world, telephones, printing presses, and all of the weight and access that can be gained through being connected to a large institution. While I was satisfied that I was making progress in bringing many student organizers from around the country together in a dialogue that needed to happen, I was concerned about how I would now include in a productive way those brothers and sisters who were not in college or college-bound who had been and would be more affected by racism and white supremacy in America. This, I knew, would not be an easy task.

After all, a lot of the black college students thought of themselves as being better than the brothers and sisters from the streets. Even though many of the college students had themselves come out of the same conditions and communities, they had no interest in being reminded of that fact or confronted up close with the harsh realities of extreme poverty, racism, and confusion. Not when they had the chance to hide out in what seemed the semisecure world of the college dorm.

For their part, the youth in the streets were suspicious of the college students, most of whom seemed to take pride in being part of "the system" and accepting and cooperating with white authority figures, white lies, and white ways of doing things. If accused of "acting white, talking white, and thinking white," most black college students would reject the charge, saying that they were not being "white," they were just doing what was right—as though the words white and right were one and the same.

The most divisive factor was the plain fact that street kids could feel that college students thought they were better than them, that college students somehow had all the answers. This attitude of superiority, when it met with the sense of inferiority felt by those who were undereducated, presented a clash that sometimes became violent. The college students who talked the most about being concerned about their community always pointed to this tension as the reason they could not do any practical work with these young people. It was the same reason they used after graduation to abandon these neighborhoods and the problems that came along with them. So I had an idea. We would require all college students who were interested in joining the nationwide organization we were founding to develop a specific project in their local community in order to qualify for membership. I would place pressure on them and challenge the depth of their commitment and level of sincerity by suggesting that if they were not involved in community work, then they were just talking—better yet, faking it. The challenge I presented to students across the country, however, would soon confront me as well.

It had been a year of walking from either Penn Station or the Forty-second Street bus depot, through the business section, where my office was located on Madison Avenue. The fact that African-Americans were not part in any significant way of the day-to-day business transactions that represented power was obvious even to a casual stroller. Every day the scenes that I saw appalled me as I realized that even though I was from New York, there had been a qualitative change for the worse even in the few years since I had lived there. Desperation seemed more like the accepted norm for blacks and it gripped not only the adults and the young adults but the children as well. Where once there had been some small, if feeble, attempt in early years by adults to protect the young, it now seemed that even black adults considered children fair prey in their evil games. Children were no longer children, just smaller versions of adults. They had to learn immediately how to fend for themselves. The environment in which these children had to grow up was unremittingly harsh. The children would make up the first generation to witness and experience the complete death of love between black folks. Love between children and children, between parents and children, between some neighbors and some children was what made racism and poverty bearable when I was growing up. But today, I could see every day as I walked to work how the processes and practices of institutionalized white racism and the way those whites in power had designed, organized, and maintained the lifestyle of urban Africans, had created a pressure cooker in which blacks could no longer survive. It was nearly impossible to see through the steam and stress. We had now accepted the view that we ourselves were the cause of the conditions we found ourselves trapped in. History didn't count. We were to blame for our predicament. Like desperate rats in a cage, we began to fold under the pressure of imprisonment—eating each other, consuming our children with no hesitation or afterthought.

It was during this year that I met Tusani—a young girl living in what the New York City government was pleased to call a "welfare hotel." These hotels were former luxury hotels mostly located in midtown Manhattan that the city had converted into emergency "temporary" housing for homeless families. The catch was that a family of four or five persons or more lived in one hotel room at the same time for an unlimited period of time at the same nightly price that the former luxury hotel would charge a guest. Thus, the landlords of these hotels were receiving a monthly rent of up to thirty-five hundred dollars per family, per room. This lucrative collusion between the city government and the landlords had become so large, profitable, and political that even though for less money the city could have built a separate house for each family, they allowed the scandal to continue. Homeless families meanwhile were trapped in single rooms where there was no stove or kitchen, no hot pots or cooking allowed, no hotel services, and no privacy. This resulted in creating, right in the middle of big-money Manhattan, a ghetto with fifty times the concentrated despair of the projects. The difference in effect was like a drunk who drinks wine coolers and a drunk who drinks a case of Bacardi 151.

Nita was Tusani's mother. When I met her she was outside one of the welfare hotels yelling at the Manhattan borough president, a prominent black politician, who was holding a press conference to discuss the negative effect the homeless were having on business in the area. Nita was one of the mothers the politician had stopped to use as some sort of prop before the cameras. He pointed her out to the press because she was carrying a six-pack of beer. He said that she should be buying milk for her children but instead she was using welfare money to get drunk. Without the slightest bit of embarrassment, Nita turned to the politician and the cameras and shouted, "All I know is I paid a lot more fucking money for this beer down here 'cause these goddamn Jews and Koreans raise the prices 'cause they know niggas ain't got no other store to go to and no way to get there!" Impressed by her spunk, I went over to her and introduced myself. I laughed and told her I thought it was funny the way she flipped the situation on the fake black politician. We talked and she told me about the welfare hotels, the drugs, the prostitution, the physical abuse, the building code violations, and the murders that went on inside. She added that she had an eleven-year-old daughter named Tusani whom she wished I could meet. It would have to be another time: She was in the hospital with hepatitis caught from smoking crack. She gave me the hospital's address and her daughter's room number and said maybe I could help out.

I ordered a box of cookies and had them sent to the hospital under Tusani's name. I began immediately making calls collecting information on the welfare hotels. To my amazement, in Nita's building, according to the statistics, there were about 450 families and 3,000 children. Around the corner was another welfare hotel of similar size. The hotels I discovered were not only in all of New York's five boroughs, they were in existence across the country. Almost everyone who lived in them was black or Latino. Sitting in my office the numbers and data raced around my head. I grew more and more disgusted as I realized the calamity these numbers revealed: We would lose almost every young person raised in this environment. When I added up the numbers of such hotels and the estimated number of children being raised in them, I was staggered. It was no exaggeration to conclude that some 50,000 young minds were at risk. The system that had placed our people in such places was wicked. There was no other term for it. That system, I became convinced, operated with the full design, control, organization, and permission of the whites in charge. It benefited thousands of white families who lived in the suburbs and would swear to God that they weren't racist and had never done a mean or harmful thing to a black person.

Suddenly a young girl, standing at my office doorway, jolted me out of my thoughts and anger. She appeared in my office unannounced. She was petite, just under five feet tall. She was a dark-chocolate girl with big brown eyes. The whites of her eyes, however, were yellow. Her hair was damaged. It looked like it was half permed, half afro with knots around the edges, which clustered around her neck. Some sections were an inch long, some sections were two inches long. She was wearing a big shirt a couple sizes too big for her and baggy jeans. She held her head tilted downward as though looking straight ahead took too much energy. She was dirty and smelled of urine. But, despite all of this, she was beautiful, a fact I was sure she did not know.

"I'm Tusani," she said softly. "My mother said you sent the cookies, thanks."

"Come in," I said. She sat down, still looking down. "How do you feel?" I asked.

"I'm okay."

"Your mother told me about the hepatitis. When did you get out?"

"Yeah, sometimes my mother has a big mouth and she lies, too." Her big, yellow-brown eyes searched the walls examining my pictures of Public Enemy, Malcolm X, Martin Luther King, Jr., the Soweto uprising, and KRS1. She was in no way aggressive or smart-mouthed. Quite the opposite: she was soft-spoken and utterly lacking in self-confidence.

"I thought you was an old lady," she said with a half smile. "How old is you? Seventeen? Eighteen?"

"No, I'm twenty-one."

"And you work in a church?"

"I work for black people," I said. "'Cause we need all the help we can get. And I work for a black man."

"You have something against white people?"

"A lot," I said flatly. "Don't you?"

"They never did nothing to me. I have nothing against them." She paused, and then added, "I have a white girlfriend in the school I used to go to before they kicked me out. She has a real nice house and every toy. Oh, and I know this white politician lady that took my whole family on a trip to Washington to speak about the hotel thing. I haven't seen her since but she sent me a game for Christmas."

I asked, "Do you like the hotel?"

"I hate it. They never clean it up and the pipes is busted—that's how I got sick."

"How?"

"'Cause the dirty pipes was busted and they was leaking into the pan my mother snuck in the hotel to cook with. She was giving us water out of the pan and the stuff from the pipes was in the water and made me sick. That's how I ended up in the hospital."

Confused by her version of how she got sick and her mother's claim that Tusani was a crackhead, I asked, "What about the crack?"

"The crack was in the pipe," she said.

"No, what about you smoking crack?"

"Who?! I see my mother's been lying to you, too. She tells everybody that I smoke crack."

"Why?"

"Because she's jealous of me. I don't smoke no crack. It's her. She shoots so much junk in her veins we ain't even got no food to eat."

"What is she jealous of?"

"Sometimes my boyfriend buys me things and she thinks just because he buys things for me, he should buy them for her, too."

My heart was in my socks. I had thought she was naive because she knew nothing about the history of our people, but here she was eleven years old with a boyfriend. I knew her mother was a drinker, but now I had learned she was a drug addict, too. I asked her why she thought Nita had asked me to see her.

"She wants to use you. She's slick. She uses everybody to get what she wants. You'll see. She has something up her sleeve."

"Where does your boyfriend live?"

"In Harlem."

"How old is he?"

"Seventeen."

I didn't want to look shocked but I was. I had grown up in what was called "the underclass" and now I wondered if it was possible that there was another so-called class under the underclass. "Does your boyfriend go to school?"

"No, they tryna put him in jail."

"For what?"

"For raping his little sister. But he didn't do it though. It was the little girl's father who raped her. Shorty wasn't even there the day she said she was raped 'cause he was with me."

"Who does the little girl say raped her?"

"She said Shorty did it but she four years old and she's confused. She just scared of her father so she blamed it on Shorty. But Shorty know the father did it."

"How does he know?"

"Shorty know the father raped her 'cause his father raped him when he was little. You like rap music?" she asked, apropos of nothing at all.

I said I did.

"Do you have any pictures of Big Daddy Kane or Rakim?"

"Where are you going today?" I asked, feeling a need to leave the building to get some fresh air.

"Nowhere. I can't go back to school 'cause they put me out for too many absences."

"Come on, you come to lunch with me."

Tusani gave me a walking tour of the neighborhood. I listened intently as she pointed out things I had overlooked even though I had walked through the same neighborhood many times. The difference was she knew the faces in the doorways and on the street corners. She knew their various histories as well. I asked her what she liked to eat. She took me to an expensive deli next to Macy's, telling me she had always wanted to go inside. In its windows the deli had huge pictures of fruits, danishes, and specialized candies. I asked her why she wanted to go there. She said it was where she went when she was "really starving." I was puzzled: I thought she had never been inside—besides, it was terribly expensive. "No, I don't go inside," she said, "I just stand here, look at the pictures, and imagine the food is in my stomach." She started laughing. "Then I drink a big glass of water and pretend." We went inside, and ate lunch. I told Tusani to ask her mother if it would be all right if I took her out again tomorrow.

The next day I took Tusani downtown to get some new jeans and a new sweater. She picked out a big fluffy purple one with a large gold "T" embroidered in the middle. Then I took her uptown to get her hair washed and braided. I could tell she felt like a new person. Her smile widened and she even held her head up. I told her she was beautiful and she looked at me suspiciously. Maybe no one had ever told her that before. She asked me if we could stop by Shorty's house for a minute. I was reluctant but I was curious to see exactly what I was dealing with.

Shorty's apartment was on 132nd Street between Malcolm X Boulevard and Fifth Avenue. Appearing to be abandoned, the building was nevertheless home to many people. We entered Shorty's living room. The television was on but only half the picture was clear, the other half had static running through it. Yet, two children sat on the floor watching as though the picture was perfectly normal. A woman I took to be their mother was glued to the TV as well—it seemed her favorite soap opera was on. The small boy who opened the door invited me to sit down. I looked at the couch with its springs popping out, yellow foam screaming for freedom, dried chicken bones between the soiled cushions, and said I'd rather stand. As I stood in the corner watching this scene I noticed something I had never seen in all my days in the projects. The toilet bowl was in a corner of the living room but did not appear to be connected to any plumbing system. When Shorty emerged from a back room he had on jeans, no shirt, and a rag on his head. I looked in his eyes and I could tell at once that he was unbalanced. He was also sweating profusely, which seemed odd for such a cool day.

"So you the lady who bought my baby girl the cookies," he said. "Yeah, it's about time somebody be on our side. Most people just wanna jump down our throats and tell us what do. But me and my baby is going strong. Ain't that right, 'T'?"

She smiled at him warmly. My eyes bounced back and forth between this demented seventeen-year-old boy who acted as though a sexual relationship with an eleven-year-old was completely normal. I turned slightly toward the mother who looked like her mind had long since left her and wondered why none of the children in the home were in school. I imagined that the little girl sitting on the floor sucking her thumb was the one who had been raped, and I wondered why they would permit her and her accused rapist to remain together in the same household even though the case was still not settled. Shouldn't the mother be concerned about this? Feeling I had had enough, I lied to Shorty, saying, "Nice meeting you." I told Tusani I needed to get her back home because I had another appointment. So Shorty grabbed her, gave her a kiss which she returned affectionately, and we left to take the subway back to midtown.

Visiting Shorty had been an eye-opener. While I knew that working with children like Tusani would be a difficult and serious undertaking, I could see now that this would not be a simple case of saying, "Here, read the *Autobiography of Malcolm X.*" There were so many layers of oppression to penetrate before I could even begin to deal with basic historical lessons and link them to their present-day significance. I would first have to observe and be clever enough to realize, much as I had learned living in the projects, that most people like Tusani did not tell the whole truth because it was either too painful or too incriminating. I would then have to establish clearly and beyond doubt that it was love that was motivating my interest in these children—otherwise I would be suspected of harboring hidden agendas of my own, or of others. Giving love would be easy for me because I felt I had so much love for my people, but I knew it would be difficult for the children to accept my love because it was an alien and unfamiliar emotion to most of them. I'd also have to show that I was in it for the long haul, because, as in my own childhood, they were used to most people just passing through and taking whatever they wanted. Perhaps then I could begin to address the problems of hunger, illiteracy, and the lack of basic survival tools.

"So I guess you don't like him?" Tusani said, staring into my eyes.

"What makes you say that?"

"Because you didn't say anything at the house and you haven't said anything since we was there."

"Do you love him?" I asked.

"I'm used to him. He takes care of me. Yeah, and I love him, too."

"Do you ever think about how much older he is than you?"

"Yeah, we talked about it at first but he says even though I'm young, I'm ready. He says that I'm a lot smarter than most of the older girls he know."

"And what do you say?"

"I been through a lot. I guess I am grown up. I hope you don't think I'm some little girl 'cause I take care of my sister Charelle and my little brother Ray. And sometimes I have to take care of my mother, too."

"And what about your father?" I asked, knowing damn well that it was a taboo question in my childhood and in hers, too.

"He's coming home today," she said with a big smile. "He just finished a five-year bid upstate."

"For what?"

"Selling drugs. But he didn't wanna do it but when he came home from doing time before, nobody would give him a job or a second chance. He was tryna be good but we was starving and he said he wasn't gonna let his kids go out like that so he started selling. He was real large for a minute. My mother had a mink coat and I had a new bike and he had a diamond pinky ring. Then he got busted. But his mother still got some of the money hidden somewhere so when he gets home we gonna get paid!"

It was our stop. The train came to a screeching halt and we walked to the Martinique welfare hotel. This was my first time inside the dimly lit lobby. On the left and right side of the entrance were makeshift security booths constructed with wood and bulletproof glass. The security guards were all black and Latino, young, and very large in their physical build. They stood guard wearing no-nonsense screw faces as though the hotel were a prison. Soon as I hit the entrance a big black guard with obvious muscles and cornrows approached me and asked for my identification. I asked, "For what?" but he didn't back down at all, stating confidently, "Procedure." I showed him my ID and he said, "Are you a relative?" I said no, while at the same time Tusani said yes. He laughed sarcastically and said, "Well, which one is it? Get it straight before you get to the lobby area." Tusani rolled her eyes, sucked her teeth, and said, "She's a distant cousin!" He shot back at her, "Yeah, right." Then he placed his arm around my shoulder and said, "Let me talk to you." He pulled me to the side and said, "Listen, to get inside you have to be a relative or on the list. But since you so damn cute and you ass is so damn big I'm a let you go this time." He smiled and waited for my reaction. I grabbed my ID from his hand and said, "Yeah, thanks." As Tusani and I walked past him, I heard him mutter under his breath, "Fucking bitch."

As we approached the elevators at the end of what passed for a lobby, there were lots of children running around screaming, playing, and poking fun at one another. One little boy, about six years old, was bullying another little boy no older than about four. The words that came out of his mouth shocked me for the second time that memorable day.

"Ah-ha, I seen your mother sucking Boo-Boo's dick last night for a crack."

"You a liar motherfucker. That was your mother."

The guard came by and said, "Both of you little bastards shut the fuck up 'cause both of your mothers have sucked my dick!" Tusani was leaning on the elevator button; we had been waiting more than ten minutes. After turning and seeing the look on my face, she said, "That's Boo-Boo, he's stupid, you have to excuse him. Anyway, he do sell crack and so do most of the guards around here. When your mother runs out of money to pay for her habit, dependin' on how they feeling that day, they'll take 'favors' instead."

Finally the elevator arrived. Upstairs Nita's door was closed. Tusani knocked and I heard Nita's voice screeching within. Tusani yelled, "It's me, Ma. I'm with the girl from the church." Nita opened the door a crack and stuck her skinny black face in the space. She looked at me and flashed a fake half smile. Then she looked at Tusani, opened her eyes wide, and said, "Come in here, Tusani." She let Tusani in and gestured for me to wait. Through the closed door I heard Nita get angry.

"Where the fuck did you get all that shit from?" she said, referring, I supposed, to Tusani's new clothes. I heard Tusani's voice trying to whisper her response.

"She bought it for me."

"Did you ask her for it?"

"No, I didn't ask her for nothin'. She just bought it for me." Then I heard a smack and a noise which was probably Tusani falling to the floor.

"Bitch! Don't you get smart with me! I'll knock all your damn teeth down your throat."

I heard Tusani breathing loud and began to feel stupid and guilty because she had already told me about her mother's jealous rages, which I hadn't bothered to take very seriously. Suddenly, the door was snatched open. Nita stood there wide-eyed and mean-faced, looking nothing like the woman I had met outside the other day. She had one hand on her hip with her neck working overtime as she proceeded to put me in my place: "Look. Let me tell you what the problem is. You go out and buy Tusani all this shit. Then I gotta deal with her little fucked-up attitude when she thinks she's cute up in here. You don't know Tusani. You just met her. She's a smart-ass little tricky bitch."

"Ma! . . ." Tusani attempted to interrupt.

"How the hell is you gonna talk when I'm already talking? See, that's what I mean. She forgets who the hell's in charge around here."

I realized then that I really didn't know Nita or Tusani. I was just trying to help out in some way that would eventually make a difference. That's what I thought Nita had asked me to do in the first place. Now this woman standing before me seemed completely crazed, even mentally disturbed. I decided right there that whatever Tusani had done in her eleven years of life, it did not warrant the abusive treatment, rage, and what seemed like hatred that her mother was heaping upon her. Seeing the concern in my face, however, did not stop Nita's show.

"Now what is I'm supposed to do when Charelle and Ray-Ray get back home and they ain't got shit and you bought Tusani all of this shit?" She turned to Tusani and said, "How much did that goddamn sweater cost?"

"Sixty-eight dollars," Tusani reluctantly murmured. Nita flew off the handle with renewed energy.

"Sixty-eight dollars! Sixty-eight goddamn dollars. I could have fed my whole family for two weeks with sixty-eight dollars but instead you wearing sixty-eight dollars on your back? Take it off. Take it off right now and give it back."

Tusani, with eyes filled with tears that refused to fall, as though she had been through this torture many times before, took the sweater off and handed it to her mother. She stood silent in the middle of the cluttered floor clad in just her dirty, yellow, used-to-be-white bra and her new jeans. Her mother came over to me, turned the sweater right side out and gave it to me.

"I want you to remember one thing. Tusani is black. She ain't nothin' but a black nigga. She ain't no princess bitch. She's a nigga just like everybody else around here and she was born to suffer. She don't need no special treatment and she sure don't deserve none. Now, you take this and you can go."

I turned around and fled that filthy madhouse as quickly as possible with tears in my heart. Like a mantra, I kept thinking, 450 families in one building, 3,000 children in one building. Five welfare hotels in my immediate area alone. Welfare hotels in every borough and every major city. Herded into these urban hellholes, African children were doomed. It was a recipe for the extinction of my people. It was a *de facto* genocide. I pledged that I would do my part to resist this fate.

As time went by, I got to know not only Tusani, but many of her friends, and other children, too. Eventually I came to know about seventy children fairly well. Many had worse lives than Tusani, some about the same, and some a little better. Tusani and I meanwhile grew very close, as though we were blood sisters by birth. I offered her everything that I had spiritually, intellectually, mentally, and materially.

"Project Hotel," at my urging, was adopted by the national student organization I was working with, and we used it as an example of work that should be done by every concerned student in every local community. It was also a way for me to lead by example as I demonstrated that I was as willing to work as I was to give directions or what some might consider orders. As I brought other students in my region into Project Hotel, we began to share our love, trust, friendship, and understanding.

My long-range goal was to found an African youth survival camp. I had discovered with the help of Reverend Chavis that the United Church of Christ owned a facility in North Carolina that they underutilized. It had once been a black university and when it closed the church had purchased it lock, stock, and barrel. It had classrooms, a cafeteria, a church, an auditorium, an Olympic-size pool, many acres of surrounding land, plants, flowers, and trees. I believed that if I could take about one hundred kids for the summer months to this facility—removing them from the intense pressure of their inner-city lives—we could make some progress in teaching not only basic reading, writing, and arithmetic, but also how to think, how to survive family life, how to make decisions, and even some politics and history, health and hygiene, and whatever else they might need to escape their earmarked destiny.

I spoke to Reverend Chavis and he agreed the camp was a good idea. The church, however, did not have enough money to fully fund it. He said that if I could raise the money to rent the facility, maintain the children, and pay all related costs, he would ensure my job as a youth director for the Commission at a salary of about $12,000 a year. I was happy to accept the challenge. I was committed to serving God and my people not so much by words but through my own deeds. So I went back to college, transferred myself from full-time to part-time status, and found an apartment in Harlem with the help of some friends. I wasn't particularly worried about my changed status as a student. As I observed from my older friends who had graduated with their various degrees, there was no rush to finish, no reward pending, and few fulfilling jobs available to black graduates anyway.

It was on the platform at the subway station that I met him. He was a brother I would see at the station almost every day on my way to work. He was beautiful. His hair was very short, black, and wavy, always perfectly cut with lines and the latest design or at least the most permissible for any employee at any firm in the midtown Manhattan business district. He wore a clean, white, well-pressed business shirt with an undershirt underneath that any curious woman could see gripped his powerful arms and muscular physique. He was tall with a small athletic waist and always dressed in the requisite pair of slacks. His, however, were of high quality, in the best taste, and well-tailored, unlike many men who wore the cheap tight polyester type. I would see him staring at me regularly from across the platform as he bopped his head to whatever jams he had playing in his Walkman. Then we would lose sight of each other when we would be obscured by the morning rush. This went on for weeks.

One morning when I didn't see him I thought about how long it had been since I'd been with a man. My girlfriends were always reminding and teasing me just how long it had been. But I knew myself better than they knew me. Love was as serious to me as life itself. A deep and dangerous emotion. I couldn't share my sweat with man after man night after night and coldly dismiss and dismantle him the way my girlfriends could. Quite the opposite. My mind would explore and search the man's mind and would link up as though we were one mind. We would join the compatible and would fight to resolve the areas that were incompatible. My heart would merge with his and it would be as though there was only one heart pumping blood through both of us. My body would lock into his body and learn its exact contours so that only he could elicit the most passionate and unrestricted hot, sexual, and sensual experience. Yes, love was deadly all right and I preferred not to play with it. So I tucked it away, which was not hard since I was so picky and extreme, and so few men really turned me on. After all, by this time I had come to know men from all over the country in businesses, schools, and churches. I knew them because I worked with them. But none of them interested me deeply enough.

I did not know if I was right, but I was looking for strength, masculinity, depth, conversation, compassion. I also wanted excitement. I wanted no ass-kissing yes-man or effeminate executive. (Not effeminate because he was an executive but perhaps because those were the ones that white folks felt comfortable promoting.) Perhaps I wanted too much. I wanted the calm and the storm, the polish and the roughness, the intelligence without the conceit, the compassion without the exploitation, the handsome without the player.

Yeah, right. The result: I was consumed with work and without a man. Now don't get me wrong. I saw beautiful men on my block in Harlem every day and I admired their physical beauty. But I could not see that they were productive. Nothing turned me off more than knowing all the work that needed to be done in our community, and then seeing a physically beautiful masterpiece made in the image of God sitting on a stoop when I left for work early in the morning and still there when I got back at eight, nine, or ten o'clock at night. So I chose to pass on the many offers I received and accepted looking and fantasizing as my appetizer during my long dry spell between men.

While at work one day I received two dozen long-stemmed red roses. I searched through the flowers and found the card. It was from a brother I had met at a conference I attended in New Jersey. His name was Owen and he wondered if I would have "lunch or dinner" with him. His invitation was unusual because mostly the men that I met at political events were interested in me when they first saw me but after they heard me speak their interest would disappear. So I decided I would see what this brother was about at a nice public lunchtime date. I took out the business card he enclosed in the envelope and gave him a call that night.

"What's up, Owen? Thanks for the flowers, I was shocked."

"Small gesture for such a beautiful woman," he responded. It was a corny come-on. He sounded like an old man and yet I knew he was only in his mid-twenties. Then he continued, "Yeah, I was doing some research in your part of town and I see there's a black-owned restaurant that we could go to. *The New York Times* gives Mr. Leo's four stars. So how about it?" My first impulse was to say no. I knew, however, that I had been under too much stress and needed to relax. I also knew that Mr. Leo's was too expensive for me to afford on my own budget, so I agreed to meet Owen on Monday for lunch.

Monday came and so did Owen. He called me from his car phone saying he was parked in front of my office and I should come down. I wondered why he didn't just park his car since the restaurant was around the corner. When I got downstairs and saw his BMW I figured he had wanted to impress me with his car. He whisked me around the corner at top speed, then pulled into the lot and let me out while he parked. While he was performing—tipping the parking attendant before the man had even provided any service—another brother stepped up to me standing on the sidewalk. He flashed a bright smile showing his pearly white teeth. It was the brother from the train station. "What are you doing out with that sucker?"

I smiled back and lied, "It's business."

"Why don't you duck out on him and come have a slice of pizza with me?" By this time Owen was upon us. He stuck out his hand to the brother and said, "Owen Stillman, nice to meet you." The brother didn't return the shake but acknowledged Owen through a nod of the head. He turned to me, smiled again, and said, "Maybe next time." He placed his Walkman back in position and headed down the street to the pizza place. My eyes followed him by demand and not on purpose as he moved slowly, confidently, and rhythmically, with a certain obvious masculinity that I saw lacking in so many brothers who for the sake of not offending their white employers held their asses tight and straight.

At lunch Owen, during the course of our conversation, told me he was a Republican. He said he felt that the Democratic party had taken advantage of black people because it took for granted that blacks would automatically vote Democratic. He said this lessened the power of blacks at the party's "negotiating table." That was mostly why, he said, he had decided to "go Republican." He had heard my voice on the radio and caught me on a television talk show or two and he said, "I think what you're doing with the kids is great!" He added, "I'm not sure how much success you'll have because usually when somebody is raised in a negative environment, it's hard for them to rid themselves of that deprived state of mind."

I smiled and said, "Yes, well, I guess somebody's got to give it a sincere and qualified try—otherwise young entrepreneurs like yourself will have your businesses destroyed by this army of neglected young African people. And I don't know when was the last time you checked, but there happens to be more of them than of you."

"Are you saying that these homeless hotel kids represent the average black youth in America? Because if you are, I strongly disagree."

"I'm saying the difference between the youth in the hotels and the youth in the projects and urban centers around the country is small. The destruction of the minds of both groups of youth is severe and needs to be dealt with in a very serious way since our family structures are no longer fulfilling that need. And if you want to get right down to it, the consciousness level in the suburbs is extremely low as well. You guys are just better trained on how to behave!"

"It's so hard to have these discussions with Democrats," he said sarcastically, "because they always become emotional rather then concentrate on the issue." He chuckled, "Besides, you live in Harlem, which is one of these 'urban centers,' and a lot of great African-Americans have come from Harlem."

"It's a shame, Owen, that you can't understand that I'm talking about the rule and not the exception to the rule. I'm interested in the majority of our children and creating a curriculum that makes success a normal thing. I'm not looking for one or two African-American superstars!" Then I curled up my lips, twisted my neck and said, "And for your information, I am not a Democrat."

"Oh yeah, what are you then?"

"I'm an African woman interested in creating some financially and culturally independent institutions for our children where we can set our own standards and agenda."

"Fat chance!" he responded. "Hello, this is your wake-up call! You'd better hook up with the big boys 'cause like they say, 'You've got to be in it to win it.' There is no such thing as financial independence in today's economy. You gotta pick a team and play by the rules and advance up the ranks. You gotta know who the real players are." Then he leaned over and smiled paternalistically and said, "Listen, honey, I know you're all caught up with these homeless children, rappers, and poverty programs, but you're too beautiful, way too intelligent, and you deserve to be operating at a much higher level. The Republican party could really prosper if we had a great mind like yours in our ranks. Not to mention that if I had you for a wife to stand behind me, I could make some real powerful inroads."

That's where lunch ended for me. I tried not to typecast certain brothers. I tried to give them and us a chance, but Owen was exactly what I thought he would be: another ass-kissing black fool who really thought that he could be a power player in the Republican party. Too naive and unsuspecting to know he was probably nothing more than a token or prop. So limited in his vision that he didn't believe black people could achieve anything independently and so unaware of his history that he thought the reason why we were losing battles as African people was because we had chosen the wrong political party. Experience had taught me to maintain courteous relations, so I politely dismissed myself as having another appointment and I stepped.

When I got back to my office I thought about Owen's words. Out of habit, I was careful not to dismiss somebody's words without examining the entire content. There was one thing Owen had said that I definitely agreed with. I suppose I just didn't like the way he had phrased it. That was the notion that the American government ought not to be given a free hand to make decisions that affected African people in America and throughout the world. We needed to have influence and power. We needed to participate. But I did not believe that by joining one of the two major parties we would be allowed access to the reins of power or decision-making. I was convinced that white people would change the rules to their benefit and protection and would kill before they would allow any real "power sharing." After all, they were the designers of what was for all intents and purposes their game. Plus, most blacks were so weak-minded that when they joined these mainstream parties they could not stay focused on their agenda, interests, or needs, and instead became consumed with servicing somebody else's needs in order to advance their own individual careers. That's why I was interested in children. Because I thought that if we could create a vehicle that educated black youth to be knowledgeable, proud, aggressive, intelligent, and rooted in protecting the interests of African people, then and only then perhaps we might make genuine progress. But if we were to continue the patterns that we were following, we would most certainly be destroyed and dominated in the worst way.

The next day for lunch my budget brought me to the pizza store. And so as not to be full of it, I might as well admit that I was hoping to see the brother from the train station. When I walked in I saw him sitting in the back but I pretended I did not. I ordered and got my slice of pizza and sat down to eat. I opened my notebook and began reading over my notes on the proposed curriculum for the camp.

"Looking for me?" He was standing over me as I took a bite out of my slice.

"Eating pizza," I said coyly. He sat down with his plate and I started writing. To my surprise he didn't say anything. He just stared at me. I continued to write. He had a big smile plastered on his face. Finally, I put down my pen and said, "So, what are you staring at?"

"You, of course."

"What for?"

"Because you're gonna be mine. It's just a matter of time."

I laughed and said, "Oh, yeah, what makes you think so?"

"Because I'm a winner and I get what I want. I'm patient. I don't make dumb moves and I've been watching you."

I laughed again, and said, "So does this winner have a name?"

"My name is Terrance but my friends call me Chance."

"That's interesting. What does that mean?"

"It means I'm willing to take chances that other men won't. A lot of brothers don't have guts, no heart. So they just walk the same thin line every day." He began shaking the oregano bottle over his slice. "Me, on the other hand, I make plans and then I move."

"What kind of plans?"

"I work nine to five. I'm into my music and I save my money for smart investments. That's what it's all about anyway. If you follow their rules, you'll never get ahead."

"Where do you work?" I asked.

"At the accounting firm around the corner."

"Big-time executive?" I asked with a smile, suspecting that he was just as regular as the rest of us.

"No, billing department, but that's beside the point," he said with no embarrassment. "Because I'm gonna win." Then he flashed that smile again. "You have some long eyelashes and big beautiful eyes. Did anybody ever tell you that?"

"Maybe."

"Damn, you're beautiful and I'm gonna have you. But it's no rush." He began to get up, having finished his pizza. "Here, let me walk you back to your office and you can give me your number."

On the way around the corner, I watched him move with the confidence and rhythm of a tiger. I smelled his cologne and it was manly and seductive. His precise homeboy haircut turned me on. His skin was the color of maple syrup, and it glistened in the sun. When we were in front of my office building, I handed him one of my cards with the church number on it. He smiled and his soft mustache expanded over his fleshy lips.

"Don't try to play me, girl. If I call this number, will I get you?"

"You may not 'get me,' but you'll reach me." I smiled, feeling I had caught him good.

"Oh, I'll get you," he said, walking away.

That afternoon I felt relieved. My days and nights were so work-filled, and the lives of the children and challenges of the students, plus trying to keep my head above water in my few classes, weighed me down. Chance seemed a breath of fresh air. The best thing about him was that he was different. He had a job but he wasn't a kiss-ass. Plus, he seemed to have some talents and plans of his own. Best of all, he didn't act like I was some overpowering intimidating woman. In fact, he minimized my importance, which excited me.

Later that night I had a meeting with Bill Stephney, the vice president of Def Jam Recording. The idea was to tell him about our work with the children, show him the rough draft of the curriculum, and get him to commit some of his hip-hop artists to perform at a benefit concert for the camp. Meeting with him was a pleasure and would have an important impact on me. He was a college graduate, very well spoken, a down-to-earth and concerned, feeling brother. He wore regular street clothes to work even though he was second in command over a multimillion-dollar firm. He didn't talk down to people or act like a big shot. He told me he was glad I asked for his help because he felt that it was important that we build networks. He thought that rap music would be completely taken over by the mainstream because our people failed to work together, were ignorant of the methods of making money, and were scared to take risks and execute plans. From his Greenwich Village office we rode the subway to the Prince George and Martinique hotels and I gave him a personal tour of the wretched conditions. I admitted that the camp was a modest start that wouldn't begin to reach all of the children, but it would be an important beginning. He told me that I had absolutely nothing to prove to him. He had heard me on the radio, remembered the work I had done in support of the anti-apartheid movement, and had been proud of me for some time. He would be "honored" to work together.

That night I ran my bathwater in my small one-bedroom apartment. I was lucky to have some privacy because usually by the time I would get home one of the children would have found his or her way to my doorstep. As I soaked my tired body, my mind drifted as I thought about Owen, Chance, and Bill Stephney, three different kinds of men. I didn't care for the Republican, so I dismissed that thought. Bill was too important a business associate, so I dismissed that thought. As for Chance, he seemed too good to be true.

Three days later, on Friday, my telephone rang. It was Chance.

"Come downstairs, I'm waiting for you," he said authoritatively.

"Okay," I said, surprising myself. When I got downstairs he had a big smile on his face. "We're going up the street to the Chinese restaurant," he announced. Somehow it was a relief for me not to have to make even that small decision.

At lunch, Chance asked what seemed like a hundred questions. Where are you from? What do you do? Where do you hang out? The conversation flowed freely until he learned that I was what he called a "college girl." He said "A lot of college women think they know everything but a lot of simple, obvious, and commonsense things they can't figure out."

"Like what," I asked. "What can't we figure out?"

"How to love a man right. How to loosen up and enjoy life. How to stand by your man and enjoy life without always competing with him like you got something to prove!"

I said, "Yeah, well, I'm different."

"Oh, are you a pro or something?" he asked with a smile.

"No, it's just that I'm real regular. I don't come from money or from the middle or upper class. Any hard time you've had, I can match. Although I don't think hard times are anything to brag about."

He smiled.

"And I have a deep love for black men so I don't have to compete with them. But if they fall short of being a man, that's their problem, not mine, and they shouldn't put that on me like some brothers do."

"Oh, baby, you tryna hurt me?" he said, faking like he was shot or something.

"It wouldn't hurt unless it were true," I said confidently.

"Well, beautiful, you don't have to worry. I don't have no problems in the manhood department. I make the moves. That's why you're here, right? I mean I know you must be tired of those 'ducks' you been going out with. Like homeboy I saw you with the other day." He started laughing.

"I told you that was business," I said.

"Let me tell you something about men, sweetness." His voice was smooth and confident. "Any man who sits across the table with a brown-sugar tender like you, with those kiss-me eyes and suck-me lips, wants some pussy! I don't care if he's showing you engineering plans for the next rocket to the moon! Them thighs and that ass gone get his blood pumping!"

I started laughing loud. It had been a long time since somebody talked raw and plain to me, and I liked it. No fronting, no politics, just plain old regular conversation.

"What's so funny?" he asked.

"You're crazy," I said, still laughing.

"Anyway, my point is I can look you in your eyes and see that either nobody's loving you, or somebody ain't loving you right. But I'm not surprised because there are a whole lot of weak cowards around here. But I'll do you right."

"Promises, promises," I said, looking him in the eye.

"What did I tell you the other day?" he asked while I sat there with a blank face. "I'm a win-nah! And I can win!"

Chance walked me back to my office. He placed his hand on my back, sending a sensation up my spine, and said, "Next week I'm coming upstairs to check things out. You women have to be watched. A man got to know how many roosters are in the barn." I batted my eyes and went upstairs.

Monday I called Bill Stephney. I needed to find out the exact procedure for making this concert happen. He was pleasant and said that with his 100 percent support, which I had, I should not have any problem. He needed time to ask the artists. After that, it would be up to the particular artist's attitude, schedule, and what point he or she was at in his or her career. For instance, if an artist was booked to perform a paid date in New York already around the time I wanted to do the benefit, then that would preclude his participation. He told me to let him handle the artists; I should take care of all the administrative responsibilities, including developing and financing the production budget. That meant arranging the concert hall rental fee, lights, equipment, transportation, advertisement, et cetera. That would keep me busy while he worked on the artists. He also gave me the name of his assistant since he was often traveling in other parts of the country.

Meanwhile, I met with the students in my region from the nationwide student youth organization. We gave each other updates on our various community projects. Oddly enough, when I mentioned the progress I had made on the camp curriculum and my plans for a benefit rap concert, students who had given every reason why they couldn't work on Project Hotel suddenly became interested in signing up. I made it clear that they could not work on the concert if they weren't willing to work with the children. We put together a list of additional fund-raising ideas and delegated responsibilities to various students to explore them. Our morale was high, and we had a good core of serious and committed hard workers.

I soon received a call from Owen, who wanted to go out. I had been seeing Chance and talking to him on the phone so I really wasn't interested in going anywhere with Owen. He, probably anticipating my rejection, said he had a check for me for the children, a token of his "commitment." He also said he had a list of potential fund-raising sources. He added that if I could control my temper I might make some headway with some of the people on the list who, while I might find them politically repulsive, were basically "concerned black folk." He asked if he could come up on Friday and bring the check and the list and maybe have a drink. I told him that as I did not drink, I'd have to pass on that invitation but that humbly, yes, I needed all the help I could get. I would wait for him in my office Friday evening so he could drop the information and the check off. He sighed as though he did not get what he really wanted but somehow he sensed that this was one of those "take it or leave it" deals. Friday evening came and I sat waiting for my Republican for two and a half hours. At 10:30 P.M., I left my office—pissed.

The following week Chance and I spoke. It was nice getting to know him slowly. I felt more secure this way. Instead of having him just jump in my bed, we got to kick it around for a while, talk, laugh, or go to the park. I knew the slower we took in coming together, the closer our attachment would be. I had already started to depend on him as my release. He helped me to let go and I found myself comfortable with him taking over and directing everything when I was in his presence. In every other area of my life, I was the director of everything and everyone. To be sure, Chance was possessive, but somehow this wasn't scary to me. It made me feel loved. He wanted to know where I was going, when I was going, and how long I was going to be. He wanted telephone numbers so he could check up on me and to "make sure I was safe."

The next week I fell sick with some kind of flu. I had a fever and the whole nine yards. But, me being me, I decided that I had to go to Washington to deliver a presentation I had promised to make. Just as I was packing to leave the office, Chance called and wanted to know what I had going on. He asked me what was wrong—my voice sounded extra sexy and raspy—I told him I was sick but I was about to leave for Washington but not to worry: I had taken some cold tablets and had my bottle of Nyquil on hand. He wanted to know who was going with me. It was no big deal, I said, I was traveling by myself but the Metroliner would place me right by my hotel, so I would be safe. I would go straight to bed when I arrived and be prepared for my presentation early the following morning. No way could he allow me to travel alone, he said, especially since I sounded so bad. He asked why I hadn't told him in advance. I told him I was doing so much that I had allowed it to slip my mind and I just realized it myself when I checked my calendar late last night. He told me to sit myself down. He had to make some calls and then he would be right there because he was coming with me.

Sitting on the chair waiting on Chance, my thoughts flickered through my head at a feverishly slow pace. I wondered if Chance thought he was slick. I wondered if he thought he was going to maneuver me into giving him some in that Washington hotel room. I felt uncomfortable allowing him to come. But I also felt uncomfortable telling him not to come. One thing was sure, though. I was too sick and beat-down to hump that night. I was hot, but not for him. I took my temperature. It was a hundred and one.

One hour later, he came through the door of my office ready to go with his one change of clothes on a hanger. We went to Penn Station where he bought his ticket. We boarded the Metroliner and I promptly fell asleep for the two-and-a-half-hour ride right in his arms. In the hotel room I kept my clothes on and laid down on the bed. I was woozy from the Nyquil and Tylenol combination I had taken trying to flush out the sickness before my morning presentation. As my eyes closed, I remember feeling Chance rubbing my face gently. As I drifted into sleep, I thought I could feel Chance lean over and kiss me on the cheek and tell me that he loved me.

The next morning, I opened my eyes and found my whole body on fire. It wasn't fever this time. I was curled up on the bed and Chance was curled up and glued to me. He had somehow fitted his body solidly against mine, fitting into every curve and groove I had to offer. My nipples were hard and my whole body was consumed with desire. Chance had his arm around me and his hand rested in between my breasts. I lay still for about ten minutes luxuriating in the good feeling. Then I peeled my body away from his and hit the shower. He continued to sleep soundly. As I got dressed, Chance awoke.

We went to the presentation. Chance sat in the back and watched me. I could tell my delivery just made him that much more mine, as he was obviously taken with my performance. I thought to myself afterward, Good, maybe he'll see that I'm not some shallow college girl, as he prefers to put it. Maybe he'll realize that there's much more to me.

Later that night, once I was back in New York, home alone in the comfort of my lonely bed, it hit me. I was falling in love, missing Chance, wanting him near me. As I lay there I saw images of him in my mind and it was as if he could read my mind, because just then the phone rang. In my best bedroom voice, I said pleadingly, "I miss you." He said, "I know. I'm feeling it, too. I miss you." He agreed that we needed to talk about "things." We set a date for Monday evening after work.

Monday morning I received a brief letter from the Republican. It read:

"Darling. Here's my check in the amount of $200 as a donation to Project Hotel. Spend it wisely. Also, I've enclosed the list I promised you of potential financiers. By the way, I came last Friday night as promised. I ran into that guy from the parking lot in the lobby of your building. He said you were his 'woman' and I'd better leave you alone. Now, I like you a lot. But since I don't know how you feel about me, I wasn't sure if you were worth dying for. Take my advice, dear, watch the company you keep. Love, Owen."

I read the note three times. I wanted to understand my feelings and reaction to what Chance must have said and done to him. The truth was my feelings were mixed. On the one hand, I felt Chance had intruded because I told him my relationship with Owen was business. On the other hand, I admired that he had sense enough to know that Owen wanted much more than that. But then again, I wasn't Chance's "woman." But who was I fooling? I had been seeing Chance, and he had every reason to believe, based on the way we clicked together, that I would be his. Then I began to laugh at the absurd image of Owen actually allowing Chance to scare and outsmart him. If he was that easy to deter, then maybe he needed to go back to South Jersey where he came from. I thought: Chance must really like me if he took it that far. He was obviously serious and aggressive—two traits that I had always admired. Besides, I was sure Owen had exaggerated when he wrote that business about me being "worth dying for." Chance would never kill anybody. I let it all go and decided that I felt good that at least with Chance I'd be protected. After all, he had said that he would never allow anything to happen to me.

That evening I greeted Chance with a stern look. He smiled as though there was no way he would allow me to get him bent out of shape.

"What's the mean look for, beautiful? Aren't you happy to see me?"

"What are you, down with the black mafia?" I asked jokingly. He began to laugh.

"You must've heard from that 'duck.' Yeah, I told him to go find another pond to swim in."

"And how do you know what business I had with him?" I asked. Chance laughed again and said, "Whatever you had in mind wasn't what he had in mind. Later for him. Let's talk about me and you." He took his hand and put it through my hair. Then he took my hand in his and said, "I want you for me. Mine alone. You and I, nobody else, no interruptions. So what's the answer? Is you his? Or is you my baby?" He smiled again, knowing that his smile was my weakness.

"Chance, I'm into you. I'm in deeper than I should be because I don't know enough about you."

He threw his hands in the air and said, "Ask me. Go ahead, ask me anything you want to know. No excuses."

"Well, I've never been to your house."

He said, "I've never been to your house."

I said, "You said the most important person in the world to you was your mother and you haven't introduced me to your mother."

"And I never met your mother."

"I don't know any of your friends."

"And I don't know your friends either."

"Yeah, but you've seen the kids I work with and that's where I spend most of my time."

"Yeah, and some of those guys you call your 'kids' look pretty damn old to me!"

"What religion are you?" I asked.

"My mother's a devout Christian. But I don't believe in religion the way I see people practicing it. I believe every man is born with a Bible and a Quran inscribed in his heart. Every man knows the difference between right and wrong. Every man chooses which way he wants to go. We don't have to be led like sheep by preachers. We all know what we're supposed to do. Listen, if you want to meet my mom it's no problem. I'll take you to see her. . . . You know I live in the Bronx, right, Castle Hill Projects. It's a dangerous area. But I'll bring you there and you'll be safe. What else?"

"I need your home number. You always call me and I never call you."

"I'll give you the number, no problem. But I'm gonna call you so much you won't have time to use it." He smiled and said, "C'mon baby, what's next? I'm shooting down everything you coming with."

He was playing with me, mocking me. I was so taken by how cute he was, I wanted to say yes, but I was afraid. I had been hurt too much already. Everything seemed okay but I wasn't sure. He didn't rush me but I felt rushed anyway. So I said, "I'll tell you on Friday."

He said, "Aaah, come on! Today's Monday! What you want me to do—bite all my nails off?"

I said, "What are you worried about? You're a win-nah! Right?"

"There you go. Damn right. That's who I am." He resumed his cool demeanor.

I told Chance that on Wednesday night I would be cooking for some of the kids from the project and some of the students. I wanted him to come. Then he could see where I lived and meet some of my friends.

He said, "So, you can cook, too? I git a gold mine."

I said, "You just tell me what you want and I'll have it ready for you."

"I want the kids and the students to disappear and you can cook me some nice fried chicken and some biscuits. In the morning I want a cheese omelette with home fries and toast."

"Slow down, Chance. There are going to be people at my house Wednesday night. This is my work. This is what I do and love. And I want you to meet the rest of them."

"All right, check it out. I'll do it this time for you. But you'll learn that I gotta come first. I gotta be number one. Me and you need to get together alone."

Wednesday night everybody had a ball cramped up in my little Harlem apartment. Chance, as I could have predicted, was the life of the party. The smallest kids jumped all over him. The young girls admired him. And he taught the older boys how to box. As for my girlfriends, they said if I didn't scoop him up fast they would be happy to take him outta my hands. It was plain to see that he charmed everyone the same way he charmed me. This moved me closer to him because I liked the fact that they all liked him. One little badass girl from the hotel said, "I didn't know you liked dudes like that."

I said, "Dudes like what?"

"You know, the cool ones." She said Chance could rhyme. He could fight, and he was "real cute, too."

"What kind of guy did you think I liked?" I asked.

"You know, the kind like Brother Charles who reads books all the time and wears dirty sneakers." She started laughing.

The night ended with Chance riding the train back downtown with the boys and then going back home to the Bronx.

The next day, Chance came by my office with two of his friends—Blinky and Gary. He described Gary as his music partner, a good singer and songwriter. Blinky was his cousin. Neither looked like the same kind of guy Chance was. They were real quiet. One of them was so frail he looked as though a twenty-five-pound dumbbell would be too much for him to lift. They were devoid of the kind of charm and style that Chance naturally exuded. At least they were courteous. But they looked at me as though they didn't trust me. That was fine with me because I didn't trust them either. Before they left, Chance called me back into my office, gave me a kiss good-bye, and said, "Don't pay them no mind. They're followers. I'm the leader. They'll do whatever I say. And if I like you, they'll have no choice but to like you, too."

That night I lay in my bed and made plans. I decided to tell Chance "yes." I was scared to lose his attention. It wasn't his fault that I was hesitant because of my past relationships. Plus, I knew it wasn't every day that you found a brother who thought the world of you and was so attentive. I did worry about his possessiveness though. Even though it brought a warm feeling to my heart, it wasn't practical. For instance, I looked at my calendar and for the next four weekends I would be tied up organizing the African Youth Survival Camp. One of those weekends would be spent in North Carolina taking inventory. I couldn't see asking him to pay his own way down; I didn't think he could afford it. The Church of Christ was picking up my expenses. Of one thing I was certain, the rule my mother taught me: "Don't allow men to stop you from doing what you must do because men do what they want to anyway."

The telephone rang, interrupting my thoughts; it was my girlfriend Sofia, a Muslim student at college with me. We used to discuss politics and religion. She was calling to let me know that Ramadan would start Friday night. She wanted to know if I would be fasting in solidarity with their community like I normally did. Of course I would. I had been so busy in recent days that I was grateful for her reminder. Ever since I had met Nathan my first year of college I had fasted during Ramadan. I found that the fast cleansed my system, helped clear my thinking, and helped me to avoid confusion. Plus, by concentrating on my prayers I felt I received increased blessings and spiritual rewards. I somehow didn't think Chance would understand any of this and concluded I'd have to consider postponing my fast. But, in the end, I decided to fast anyway.

Friday night Chance arrived at my apartment. I cooked him a good meal. He ate and smiled at me the whole time. I was eating only a bowl of vegetables because after sunset when you were allowed to break your fast you still were not supposed to eat like a pig. He wondered why I was eating so little. He said he hoped I wasn't trying to be cute because he was there. I simply said, "No, I'm fasting for Ramadan."

"Who's Adam?" he said, laughing.

"I said Ramadan. It's a religious holiday for Muslims."

"Are you a Muslim?"

"No, I just do it in spiritual solidarity. It lasts about thirty days and you don't take liquids or solid food until sunset each day. It helps you to . . ."

"It helps you to wanna eat a goddamn cow!"

"No, really. It's an important thing that I do every year. For the duration of the fast I can't have any sex." I slipped that point in fast. That's when he really laughed.

He went over to the couch, sat down, and said, "That's what's wrong with you college girls. You think too much. Now, don't stress me. I been waiting a long time for you. The last thing I need is this 'who's a damn' celebration." He extended his hand to me. I reached out and took it. He walked me into my bedroom, pushed me up against the wall, and said, "Now, don't you want to kiss me? Don't you want to feel me? Come on. No more hiding."

I felt his hard body press against mine reminding me of the night we had spent in Washington, D.C. My whole body ignited and he gave me the softest, sweetest kiss imaginable. My mind went blank. His hands firmly gripped my breasts— pumping them gently. The blood accelerated through my veins. He slid his hand down the front of my body and up under my skirt. All I could feel was warmth, moisture, and fingers caressing my insides. Soon I was stretched out across the bed getting what I had missed for the past year. Soaking wet, exhausted, we fell asleep.

I could feel myself dreaming. I was somewhere in the wilderness, lost and scared. I took one step to the left and stepped on a hidden but huge black cobra. It reared its ugly head and sank its fangs into my right leg. I woke up screaming. Chance grabbed me. "What's the matter, baby?" I told him about my nightmare. He stroked my hair and chuckled, "It's all right, girl. It was just a sign." "A sign of what?" I asked. He said, "If you step on me, I'll bite you." He began kissing my face and easing my fear. Just then, I heard the doorbell ringing. I got up and went to the door. It was Tusani. I told her to wait a moment. I told Chance to get dressed and let her in while I showered and got dressed myself. When I came out, they were joking and talking together like old friends. Tusani turned and gave me a grown-up smile absent of innocence. Her look seemed to say, "I'm glad you finally got yours!" Chance pulled me into the bathroom and said he was gonna leave. He could tell Tusani had to talk to me. Then he joked and said I should be glad he was leaving because he was gonna get up and whip me in a game of chess anyway.

Tusani and I sat down to talk. Clearly she had something on her mind. But, as usual, she was very good at holding everything inside until she was ready to let it go. She started off light, smiling and joking. I looked at her with love and pride because in the year that I had come to know her both her inner and physical beauty had emerged. It was hard to consider her a child. She seemed as experienced as any of my girlfriends if not more so. She said, "I'm glad you found somebody that makes you smile. I can tell you like him a lot."

"How can you tell?" I asked.

"Because when he around, you be so carefree, and you know how you usually are: real serious! He's a crazy cutie, though, and a real ladies' man. You'd better watch him. I'm not saying nothing bad. I could tell he likes you too, but you gotta watch these men. Do he have a job?"

"Yes, he works at a company around the corner from my office."

"That's good. So you get to see him every day?"

"Yeah, when I'm not too busy."

"Better not be too busy. Does he have any kids?"

"No!" I said, as if it would be a disaster if he did.

"Why you say it like that? How old is he anyway?"

"Twenty-six."

"Where he from?"

"The Bronx, Castle Hill Projects."

"Oh! Then he definitely has at least one kid! A nigga that fine! I mean, it ain't no big thing or nothin' but you should ask him. Don't wait for him to tell you, 'cause they never do."

I started to feel uncomfortable with the idea of my student becoming my teacher. I was uncomfortable with receiving a lesson on life that I probably should already have known. I changed the subject. But she caught my attitude, and said, "It's just that you real nice. I don't have to tell you how there ain't that many nice people left. Especially not around here. So, if somebody meet you, they hear the tough talking that you do so they might back down for a minute. But then they find out the truth."

"What's the truth?" I asked, not sure if I wanted to hear the answer. She held her arms out as far as they could possibly go, smiled, and then said, "That your heart is this big!"

"So what's up with you, Tusani?" I asked, changing the subject. "It's Friday night and instead of being with Shorty you're here. So what's up?"

"That's just it. They locked him up." Her eyes were sad.

"He's in jail?"

"No, he's in the crazy house! He's on mental lockdown."

I held my face blank. I felt Shorty needed to be somewhere he could be helped. Not that I thought he would be helped where he was, but at least he wouldn't harm any more little girls or, God forbid, eventually Tusani.

She said, "I know you didn't like him. So you don't have to act like you're sad or anything. I just wanted you to know what happened."

"So, how do you feel?" I pressed.

"Like I'm going crazy. Shorty took care of me. You know I use to always be at his house. Now I'ma have to be stuck around my mother."

"Well, you can always come here. You still got your key, right?"

She felt her pockets, saying, "I thought I brought my key with me. I don't know where it went."

"You couldn't have brought it. Because if you did you wouldn't have rung the bell."

"Are you kidding? I still would've rang the bell. For all I know you could've been doing the hootchie coochie!" She fell out, laughing.

I said, "All right, Tusani!"

She said, "What's wrong? You do do the hootchie coochie like everybody else, don't you?"

On Monday Chance came to my office as soon after five o'clock as he could get around the corner. He was hyped up and real close up on my ass.

"Give me some tongue," he said with his sexy smile.

"This is my office," I protested, trying to cool him out until later. He closed my office door and locked it. He edged his way around my desk and said, "When your man says give me some, you give me some." He stood over me. I got up out of my chair and he proceeded to chase me around my chair and then back around my small office. When I couldn't get away, he pushed me up against the wall, grabbed my titties, and started tonguing me down. I slid to the floor. He sat on top of my lap with his legs stretched out on either side of me.

"You'd better be careful," I said, "you might make a baby."

"What's wrong with making a baby?" he asked.

"Nothing, have you ever made one?"

His face turned serious, "Oh, so this was a set-up."

"What?"

"Don't play dumb with me. You wanted to ask me if I had any kids anyway. So you just decided to slide it in right there."

"Well, do you?"

"Yes, I have a son."

My heart dropped but I didn't let him see.

"How old is he?" I asked.

"He's eight and a half months old."

"Oh, my God!" I said. "He was just born."

Chance picked up his jacket and headed toward the door.

"Where are you going?" I asked.

"Listen, I know what time it is. It's over. It's over 'cause you a college girl. You college girls don't like niggas that have kids 'cause y'all gotta start off with a clean slate. Fresh. With a proper family, right? And a proper husband, right? And a white picket fence, huh?"

"No, wait!" I said. "It's not that. It's just that babies come through mothers. If your son is only eight and a half months old, you must have a girlfriend. And you been pumping my head up with all this 'It's gonna be me and you. Just us and we can win.' For how many months now, Chance? For four months you been telling me this."

"It is you and me! I'm not with her. I don't even love her. I love my son. But I don't love her. She's a project girl. She's got no sense. She's lazy. She don't do nothing for herself. She's nothing like you. She definitely can't be trusted. I didn't even know at first if the kid was mine 'cause she was playing games with this other kid because he was some big-time drug dealer. So I said I'd lay low, see if the kid is mine. 'Cause I didn't want to be fucked up like my pops. And if it's mine, I'd take care of my responsibility."

"I don't know," I said slowly.

"Listen: I love you, girl. You different than all these whores. I don't know why one of these crazy niggas out here ain't married you yet. They was stupid to let me meet you. 'Cause you mine now." Then he looked me in my eyes and said, "You are still mine, right?"

"I don't know. I gotta think. 'Cause you didn't even tell me. When were you gonna tell me?"

"I wanted to get in good with you first. I didn't want to lose you. He's just a baby. He's harmless. I'll bring him to your apartment. You do like babies, don't you?"

"Who, me? Come on. I love all my people. Especially the children. Maybe that's my problem. Too much love." I paused to think and then asked, "So who does the baby live with, anyway?"

"The baby lives with her in her parents' house."

"So you gotta go to her house to see him?"

"Yeah, but it ain't nothing. Look, don't think she wants me. 'Cause she don't. She leave the baby with her moms and goes out. I call the moms and she tell me when I can come see him. They let me check him for a couple of hours in their presence and then I'm out. She don't even be there. She's out doing whatever she does best."

I said, "I don't know. I gotta think about this."

He said, "All right, baby. Well, you let me know. But I'm telling you, me and you. . . . We can win. I can feel it."

By the end of the week I couldn't take it anymore. Late one night I talked to my girlfriend Jasmine on the phone, who told me I was making a big thing out of nothing. I asked her how she could call a human life nothing. She said that all these guys like Chance had babies. He's sweating you, chasing you, calling you, she said. "You'd better jump on it while it's hot!" I felt the whole situation might cause me more headaches than I needed. She said I would have headaches anyway if I left him because I was in love. She went on to say I might as well feel good even though the situation was not perfect. I asked her if she would take me in her car to Castle Hill to see him. I was miserable and couldn't wait any longer. She asked if I thought it was safe to be roaming around the projects. I told her I was filled with curiosity and had to go there. She shouted, "You've never even been there before?" I told her not to make an issue out of it because I had my own apartment. Chance, I explained, lived with his mother. We both worked in Manhattan so he "chills at my place." She said, "I'm coming now."

We arrived at Castle Hill at about midnight. Just like my memories of the projects, people were still up milling about outside like it was 8:00 P.M. I knew the number of Chance's building, but I couldn't remember his apartment number, or if he had told me at all. But I told Jasmine I wasn't leaving until I found him. She giggled, and in a carefree way said, "Okay, so we'll call him." She faced the building and, at the top of her lungs, she screamed, "Chance! Where are you? Chance! Somebody looking for you, Chance, where you at?" I joined in and we called some more. Just then, out of the corner, like a rat, appeared Blinky. He put his finger up to his mouth and said, "Shhh. Shhh. What are you doing?"

"Where's Chance?" I asked.

"Do he know you here?"

"Where's he at?" I pushed.

"Did you tell him you were coming here?"

"No. But I need to see him right now," I said firmly.

"You'd better stay right here. I'll go and get him. His moms is real religious and it's way too late for you to go knocking on his door."

"Well, how come it's all right for you to go knocking at his door?"

"Look, I'm family. Me and Chance been together since I was yo high. You just chill right here."

I waited patiently while Jasmine took out her bright red lipstick and wrote all over the bench: THAT'S RIGHT, CHANCE. I WANT YOU BACK! After a long while, Chance emerged out of the darkness looking good, strong, and light on his small feet. Before I could say anything, he grabbed me. He started kissing me all over my face, and said, "College girl! What you doing all the way out here at this time of night?" Then he flashed the smile that dislodged my senses and said, "You must really love me!"

"I do," I said, forgetting that Jasmine was even there. "I want you back. I'm sorry. I can handle it. Just me and you, right?"

"That's right, baby, 'cause we can win!" Then he grabbed my hand and asked how I had come to Castle Hill. I pointed to Jasmine's car and he said, "Let's go. I'm in there."

With me in one hand and his Nike overnight bag in the other, we got in the car and Jasmine dropped us in Harlem, where we quickly made up for lost time.

The next few weeks I was zooming around on a cloud. I was so gone that I had to sit down and make a real effort to concentrate in order to remember what I had to do concerning my work. I had lots of meetings and many responsibilities, including the education and love of, and attention to, the children. They liked Chance a lot. They even claimed I looked prettier every day that I was with him. I was so hyped up I introduced him to my mother. She wasn't enthusiastic at all, but I paid no attention. I waited patiently to meet his mother but he told me that she had been very sick. He said the doctors were not sure of the diagnosis but they thought that it was cancer. I imagined that she and I would get along when we finally met because she was always courteous to me when I called his apartment. He told me not to mention the illness to her because it was a sensitive and emotional issue. I agreed that I wouldn't, and spent my time comforting him instead.

Chance and I tried to do as much together as we could. It was difficult sometimes with my work schedule and his studio schedule. But, every now and then, he would accompany me on some business trips. On those occasions I would do only the work required of me. I wouldn't go sightseeing or touring. I'd just spend time in the hotel room with Chance, discovering more and more about him. One thing I found out was that he had served a year in jail for vandalizing vending machines when he was younger. I was not surprised; most black men had some type of run-in with the law at some point or another, whether they were innocent or guilty.

The work toward the summer camp was progressing. I had completed the curriculum. I had designed the budget. Bill Stephney confirmed the appearance of Public Enemy, LL Cool J, Heavy D, Big Daddy Kane, Stetsasonic, MC Lyte, and other rappers. With this lineup, I went to Reverend Chavis and convinced him to lend our Project $20,000 to be returned on the night of the concert after ticket sales which, I believed, were certain to sell out. I used the money to rent the Apollo Theater, run radio advertisements, make posters, print flyers, arrange transportation, provide food, and underwrite production costs for the artists' equipment. I was pumped up, and Chance shared my enthusiasm. He asked if he could perform in the show to help advance his music career. This was his big chance, he explained, because everybody in the industry would be there. He was sure that once they heard him and saw his show, they would love him. It seemed so important to him that I agreed. Plus, I figured it couldn't possibly hurt.

It was so important to him that I decided to help out. I told him there were four different groups requesting to open the show. If he wanted he could audition next week before a panel of four judges from our youth organization. He smiled and asked, "Are you one of the judges?" I laughed and said, "Of course not, but don't worry 'cause you're a winner!"

Chance's cologne filled the small space provided for the audition. Some of the children snuck in to see the competition, but really to root for Chance and his band. Each of the groups performed as though this audition was their shot at entering the multimillion-dollar hip-hop industry. They were all perfectly groomed and dressed as though this was the actual night. I admired all of the energy and especially the originality and style that was displayed. But I was poised to see Chance walk away with first place.

I was shocked when Chance and his two sidekicks, Gary and Blinky, took center floor. He never mentioned that Blinky was part of his group. And, based on his "performance," Blinky should never have been. He had no talent, couldn't rap, sing, or even dance. He was so out of sync with the act that the children cracked up and fell out. Even the judges had to muffle their laughter as they couldn't help but conclude this was a comedy skit. As Blinky went left while Chance and Gary went right, their big break went straight down the toilet. Chance would not be performing at the huge Apollo concert. His group had blown the audition. The whole thing depressed him. He was not used to losing.

The concert was a major success. We earned over $60,000. It all went straight to the church. In a single evening, I repaid my debt, insured the camp, and created a pool of money from which we could sponsor at least five more different types of events to fulfill the camp budget. Everybody was buzzing since it had not been at all certain that we would be able to operate the camp. The rappers felt good that they got an opportunity to meet the children the money was for. I felt good because I had begun, if only in a modest way, to provide for the children's futures.

Chance did not show up for the concert. Nor did he show up for our date afterward. I waited nervously in my apartment, flipping from one television channel to another, pacing the floor. I was worried. The phone rang about 10:00 P.M. and it was Chance's singer friend, Gary. He said Chance had been picked up and arrested. The charge was murder. I was speechless.

"Are you there?" Gary asked.

"Murder," I muttered. Who? Who did they say he murdered?

"Chance doesn't even know who. Chance don't know nothing about the whole thing. He just wanted me to call you so you wouldn't worry."

"Wouldn't worry? You call me about a murder charge so I wouldn't worry? Where is he? Where is Chance? I want to see him."

"He's at the precinct around our way. But you never know. They might have sent him to central booking or he might have appeared before the judge already."

"When did this happen?" Gary's phone beeped for call waiting. He asked me to hold on. When he came back, he said, "That was Chance. He said make sure you don't call his mother, because she's sick, and he doesn't want to worry her because it might make her condition worse. He needs ten thousand dollars bail so I guess he'll be in there for a while." His tone was matter-of-fact.

Immediately after Gary's call, I started calling Jasmine, Kim, Dina—every "friend" I ever had, asking them for money. By early morning I had gathered $4,000 in commitments to be collected later that day. I was frustrated because I knew that I would not be able to get the kind of money that Chance needed. Still, I thought if I came up with a portion maybe Chance's family and friends could come up with the rest. I started looking around my apartment at the various items I could sell. I was willing to fight for Chance because I knew damn well he didn't murder anybody because he was too sweet. Jasmine came and picked me up, driving me around after the bank opened to deposit the money I had collected. I decided I would find Chance, talk to him, tell him how much money I had, and ask his advice. Jasmine had a million questions but I asked her not to talk for the sake of my twisted nerves. Try as we might, we could not find Chance. I checked the precinct, central booking, precincts next to the precinct I originally thought he was in. Nor could I contact Blinky or Gary. Frustrated and crying, I returned to my apartment and collapsed in a chair while Jasmine fell asleep on the floor.

Hours passed. I was frantic and feeling helpless. Then, at 6:00 P.M., Chance's calm, smooth, sexy, and confident voice was on the other end of my telephone bringing joy and relief to my heart. I was so excited, I started asking a zillion questions. He couldn't get a word in edgewise.

"Slow down, sweetness," he said. "Listen. It was all a big mistake. See, there's some cops around my way who have it out for me 'cause they don't like the way I walk and talk and the respect I carry with me. So, whenever something goes down around this way, they automatically come and pick me up just to harass me. You know how it is. So the other night they started asking me about some kid that got murdered. I told them I didn't know nothing. But they weren't trying to hear it so they ran me in. But they had nothing on me so eventually they had to let me go, so you know they were pissed off."

A big smile creased my face. I was relieved that Chance was home. I was more relieved that what I thought all along was true: Chance would never hurt anybody. He wasn't that kind of guy. He said he was coming right over and I longed to hold him in my arms once again.

That night I cried. I told Chance how happy I was to have him back and how much I loved him. Like a proud little girl, I tried to impress him with the fact that I didn't lose my cool throughout the entire scare. I added that I had managed to collect four thousand dollars from all of my friends. I confessed that half of it was my entire savings since I had started working. He sat up in the bed with a smile that brightened the room and said, "Baby, you did all of that for me?"

"I'm an activist," I said proudly. "I don't sit by and watch. I make things happen. Did you think I would let somebody just come and take my man away?"

"What did you do with the money? I hope you're not gonna keep it here in the apartment?"

"What do you think—I'm stupid? I gave it to Jasmine. She left before you got here. She'll take it back to all my friends that lent it to me. I'm just glad you're home."

The following weekend I had to go to Los Angeles to speak at UCLA at the invitation of the campus African student group. I didn't want to go but something inside of me, probably my mother's voice from my early childhood, reminded me that I should not place a man before my educational commitments. So off I went.

When I returned, I was met by an empty apartment. My belongings were all gone. Television gone. VCR gone. Stereo gone. Jewelry gone. My personal items tossed about. I stood in the middle of the floor, horrified. Not at the notion that my material possessions had been taken from me, but at the fact that my little home had been invaded. In a panic I called Chance. He told me he would be right there. He ordered me to go out and sit on the stoop and wait for him where everybody could see me, so he'd be sure that nothing would happen to me.

When he arrived he assured me that he would take care of everything. He advised me not to panic or "mess with the police." There were ways these things could be resolved on the street. Then he proceeded to lecture me about my "damned independence." He told me that all women need protection. Yet I, he went on, thought I could walk all around and move all around the country and be all right. He said the reason why my apartment was robbed was because the men in the neighborhood "don't see no man living here taking care of you, protecting you." I was considered open and vulnerable. Then he asked me if I could follow directions. I smiled and said, "If I think they're good directions." He told me to go sleep over at my girlfriend Jasmine's house. He would take me there. Then he said I should meet him for lunch tomorrow at the little deli next to his job in midtown. I agreed.

The next day Chance was smiling as usual. He handed me an envelope with three hundred dollars in it and told me to go buy another television. Meanwhile, he would take care of everything else. I didn't want to take his money because I knew he was saving it for his investments. I told him the television and the VCR were mostly for the kids and we would all be leaving in a month and a half to go to the camp anyway. He told me that, once again, I wasn't following directions. So I took it. Then he said, "The next thing is we are going to get married."

I just about blasted through the roof with excitement. I couldn't believe it. I never imagined it would happen to me this way. After I finished bugging out, smiling, gasping, I said, "When, where, what about your mother? I haven't even met her yet."

"That's your job," he said. "You pick the place, date, and the whole nine yards. You tell me when and I'll be there. As for my mother, let me break the news to her. Then you and her can talk."

"But when, this year, next year, when?" I said, my head swirling.

"I don't want to wait. You need somebody to take care of you. You need protection. So let's just do it. Go ahead and send out the invitations. I'll bring the ring on Friday and some money, too. As for my mother, she loves me. And once I tell her that I love you, she'll love you because I love you." He smiled and added, "There's one catch: You have to learn to follow the rules if you're gonna be my wife."

"And what rules are those?" I asked with laughter in my heart.

"You do what I say. I'm the husband. You take the lead from me. I don't like you running all around the streets being involved in all the stuff you're involved in. I don't like you traveling, because it's too dangerous. Plus, you're surrounded by too many men all the time. If you need to meet with men, you need me to go with you or me to go instead of you. We'll get a bigger apartment until we save for a house and you'll move your office in there so I can watch you."

I began to laugh so hard I nearly fell out of the restaurant booth. I laughed so hard my sides started to ache. I laughed so hard tears came to my eyes. I glanced at Chance's face; it was stern and angry. He wanted to know what I was laughing at, and reminded me that he didn't like to be mocked. This, he said, was "serious."

"How could you know me so well, who I am, what I stand for, what I believe in, the work I do, how much I love African people, then turn around and attempt to turn me into some little speechless housewife who takes orders from you because you're a man? That's funny!" I exclaimed, still laughing. "How could you take the female with the biggest mouth and the most to say and try to lock her up in a house? You're so funny! I mean, I love you. But you must be some kind of a comedian or something." I was still convulsed in laughter.

"Look, do you want to be my wife or not?"

"Of course I do. But that doesn't mean I want to lose myself. What do you mean 'no traveling'? I've already been to England and France. I studied in Spain. I've been to Portugal, Finland, the Soviet Union, Zimbabwe, Zambia, South Africa. Now you're asking me to go in reverse. That's impossible."

"Oh, I see this is not gonna work." His tone was indignant.

"Oh, is this the 'win-nah' speaking?" I mocked him.

"You just don't understand," he said, lowering and shaking his head.

"Understand what?"

"How it has to be." He said, "Listen. I'll meet you tonight after your class. We'll talk then."

After class I waited for Chance. He did not show up. This time, I did not panic because I knew I had thoroughly annoyed him at lunch. After all, he felt he was conferring the greatest honor—marriage—on me. So I headed home. I hoped that I wasn't sending him the wrong signals. I wanted to marry him. I loved him. I was completely flattered by his offer. I didn't want to seem ungrateful. My own girlfriends had long teased me for being old-fashioned for doing things like cooking meals from scratch, remaining sexually loyal, and considering having umpteen babies because I loved children. Chance was the first person ever that thought I was too liberal, stubborn, and independent.

Days passed with no Chance. I grew angry because I felt he was being foolish, acting like a child. I buried my emotions by plunging into work. I wasn't going to call him. After all, he was the one who had stood me up. As the camp departure date grew closer and closer, I had to run out, purchase books in bulk, comparison shop for sports equipment and other items. Not to my surprise, there were also some parents who had not taken their children for their required physicals. So, in addition to giving their children six weeks in a free sleepaway camp, I also had to escort some of them to the doctors to get medical histories and clearances.

Friday was supposed to be ring day. I got no ring. I saw no Chance. I broke down and called his house. His mother answered and said he wasn't home. She added, "You know how you young folk are. You stay out and don't call. I don't know where he is, but when he gets in, I'll tell him to call."

At about midnight I was home in my bed. The doorbell rang. I got up figuring Tusani needed a place to stay and had lost her key again. I looked through the peephole; it was Chance. I opened the door and his big physique came strutting through in the dark shadows of my small living room.

"Hey, baby," I said. "Where you been?" He didn't respond. I leaned over and turned on my small night-light so I could see better. There he stood in jeans, sneakers, and a Polo shirt. I was surprised because I was used to seeing him in his work clothes. He was looking rugged and that turned me on. Just then the light caught a shimmering glimpse of his gold chain. In his moist mouth were what seemed like five gold teeth, one with a diamond planted right in the middle. Then, finally, he spoke. "Sit down." So I sat. He walked over to the window, pulled back the curtain, and looked out onto the street. "I gotta hurry up. My boys are parked downstairs and we got crazy work to put in tonight. Listen. Me and you. It ain't gonna work out 'cause we come from two different worlds. I don't know what I was thinking by messing with you in the first place."

I sighed and thought to myself, Not this bullshit again.

He continued: "You might as well know. I'm a drug dealer. A stone-cold street soldier. You, you're some kind of a princess or savior or something, I don't know." He took out his beeper and his stack of neatly packed tens, twenties, and fifties, and said, "These are my 'investments.' I just thought you should know. I didn't want you worrying your pretty little head off. I know how much 'work' you have to do."

I stood up with tears in my eyes and got angry. "So, you think after all that we've been through you can just walk through my door just like that and dismiss me as though I was one of your 'workers'? Well, I ain't going for it. You think that I'm so thin-skinned that I'm gonna say 'Later for you then'? Well, that ain't it. Where's my damn ring? You're supposed to be my husband, the win-nah!"

Chance smiled and said, "You still wanna marry me? Oh, baby. I didn't think you was that tough and . . ."

I interrupted, "Don't give me that college girl shit either. We can get married but you just have to change. That's what life's about anyway. Of course you have to stop selling drugs. It's against everything that I believe in, everything! But that's not impossible. You're talented, handsome, God knows you're a good talker. You can do something else. Some other legal, profitable business. We can work on it together if you could stop trying to stuff me in a closet and make me some powerless silly little girl. I can help you."

Chance was quiet. His face looked solemn and skeptical. He looked into my eyes and said, "My spots are in white neighborhoods. It's not like I'm selling drugs to the blacks."

"Then you'd better quit anyway 'cause whitey ain't gonna let no little nigga sell drugs to his kids in his place and stay alive. Only we allow people to do that. Listen, Chance. It may be money, even big money, but it's short-term. We can build for the long haul. You said you loved me. Love is supposed to give you the strength to overcome all weaknesses." I paused. "So what's it gonna be? Are you gonna give the drugs up? Or are you gonna give me up?" I stood there resolved, with my hands on my hips.

Chance thought for what seemed like minutes on end. Then he flashed his smile and said, "All right, baby. I'll do it. But I can't do it overnight. I have partners. I don't want to burn down no bridges, make no extra enemies. These are my boys who been down with me since the beginning, through thick and thin. Can you give me a week?" I nodded with approval.

"Meet me on Friday at Sbarro's. I'll bring the ring and we in there." He smiled as he got up and walked out into the night.

Alone, I sat on my couch, thinking. I had appeared strong and in control in front of Chance. But I was inwardly confused and mad at myself for not having seen what was going on. Somehow I just couldn't get this "man thing" right. I thought Chance was different. I was weak for him. I was so seduced by his sexiness that I think I was more attracted to the attraction than the actual sex. I loved the masculine way that he presented himself. The way that he walked. The way that he talked and smelled. I knew that when I was with him, I was protected. I was sure that any person or group that confronted him in a beef would be whipped. I loved how warm his hands felt all the time. The way he reminded me all day that I was beautiful. I loved how he treated me as an individual woman, not as a political entity or "black leader." He had a knack for pushing the right buttons.

The next morning when Chance called he sounded smooth and excited. He said his "boys" wanted to meet me. They had told him I must be a "bad bitch" if I had convinced him to close up shop. He said he'd bring them by one night. He told me not to worry. He loved me and would see me on Friday.

I arrived at Sbarro's on Friday excited enough to burst. I had gone to get a manicure earlier to prepare for my ring. I stepped into the restaurant early and was surprised to see Chance sitting in the back, waiting. I looked in his eyes expecting him to return my loving gaze, but all I saw was uneasiness and worry. I rushed to the booth and said, "Hey, baby, what's wrong?"

"Royce is dead."

"Who?"

"Royce, my man, my ace." I had never heard that name before. Chance looked dead serious. Then he continued, "We was chilling in the diner the other night talking about who was gonna take over my end of the business. Me, Royce, and the boys. There were some other niggas in the booth across from us. So the nigga on the other side kept beaming on Royce. You know, like he wanted beef or something. So Royce jumped up and said, 'What, motherfucker?! You want some of this?' So the kid nodded to his boys, laughed, and they left. I told Royce right then and there he should've done the kid 'cause I don't like to do too much talking. Plus, if we see the kid again and he catch us off guard, we'll be at the disadvantage. But Royce said, 'Naw, man, I'll let it go this time.' Then we left. When we hit the parking lot we got in Dwayne's side and the next thing you know on the passenger side, 'Blam, Blam, Blam.' Royce was dead. Three to the head."

Chance paused for some time, and then broke the silence. "Baby, I didn't bring the ring. You probably won't need it now anyway 'cause you're looking at a dead man."

With tears streaming down my face, I said, "What do you mean?"

"You wouldn't understand, baby. It's the law of the streets. They hit my man, now I gotta hit them. Don't try to argue or reason with me. You wouldn't understand. It's on. The war is on."

"But what about us?"

"I can't do what I promised. I can't stop selling 'cause I need the money to set things up. I still love you, but we gonna have to lay low for a while. This is how we gonna play it. I can't come to your place 'cause I don't want to lead them to you. These motherfuckers would love to knock off my girl. I don't want you to come around my way 'cause it's too dangerous. If they know I'm weak for you, they'll use it against me. Whatever you do, don't call my mother, 'cause the worrying would kill her. I'm gonna have to throw twenty-four-hour surveillance and protection on her anyway."

"Are you gonna tell her what happened?" I asked stupidly.

"Of course not. Knowing would put her in more danger because she would get nervous and start bugging out. If I throw the protection and surveillance on her she'll go about her normal activity and she won't have to know nothing. . . . Listen, don't call my job, 'cause I'm gonna have to tell them something for the days I'm missing. I can't lose the job because that's my cover and my mother went through hell to hook it up for me. I'll call you as much as I can. But when I call, no crying. If you make me go soft they'll get me. I'll lose my concentration and they'll take me out. You got it?"

"For how long? I don't understand," I asked.

"You'd never understand these things. The war lasts till it's over. You think after I hit them back they gonna stop? Hell no! They gonna come after me. So it'll go on till we get tired. But to let it all go would be suicide. Not only that. I can't let my man Royce go out like that."

I walked back to work in a daze. I could see Chance had made up his mind. It would be useless to fight him. He didn't want to hear it. I convinced myself that it was all out of my hands. The bottom line was that I had thirty days till the bus pulled out of New York for the African Youth Survival Camp in North Carolina. That was my priority. The facility was paid for. The equipment and supplies were purchased. The healthy menus were squared away. The black-owned bus company had been paid. The curriculum was in order. All I had to do was to finish training the counselors. I had started nightly classes. Perhaps they would keep my mind off the madness in my personal life.

Forty-eight hours later, Chance called at about 2 A.M. I was in a deep sleep. Chance spoke briefly before hanging up, muttering something about still loving me and that he "got one of them." I tried to get back to sleep, but it was impossible.

A few days later, Chance called again. He wanted to know if I could meet him with three thousand dollars. I was shocked at the request and immediately asked him what happened to all of his money. He said he couldn't talk much on the phone but he had "put it to very good use." The proof was that he was still alive. I told him that I wasn't willing to contribute to anything that involved drugs. I added that the money would be my total savings plus some borrowed. That's when he said if it wasn't a matter of his mother, he wouldn't have asked. He had run out of protection money for his mother, he said, paying guys to watch her around the clock was more expensive than he thought. He said that if she were killed because of him he would never be able to forgive himself. He feared his enemies were so ruthless that they'd rather kill his mother and let him suffer alive knowing that he was the cause of her death. So I told Chance I would do my best to get him the money. I made arrangements to meet him away from my house and office. When he picked up the cash he asked me not to cry. He said he would forever be grateful and he would repay me soon. On the verge of a nervous breakdown, filled with anxiety, I whispered "I love you" as he walked away.

The next week Chance called again. I asked how his son was and if he had seen him. He reminded me that I had promised I wouldn't ask emotional questions. It was bad for his head. Then he answered that he hadn't seen his son, which was heavy on his heart. But if he came out of this thing alive, why, me and him and his son would have our day together. He asked if I was giving up on him or if I still loved him. I told him I didn't love what he did. But I did love him. He promised that it would all be over soon. He said I didn't have to worry about the drug thing anymore because when all was said and done, he'd be out of business anyway. Wars destroy business, he said. And since he had me, there would be no sense in setting back up. We could just get together and start our own business like I had suggested.

The third week came and went and I did not hear from Chance. The stress was tearing at me. I would try to go to sleep and would wake up tortured by scenes of shootouts, blood and death and destruction. I'd lay awake wondering what it would take to stop the cycle of death in our community. I'd think about how important the summer camp was for younger brothers who otherwise would grow up to face the same drab realities that men like Chance lived. I did not want this future for them. I realized my work with the children was my only source of relief.

It was now three days before I was due to depart for the camp. It had been a month since I had seen Chance, and two weeks since I had last heard from him. Worry had given way to anger. Just then the phone rang. I picked it up. It was Blinky.

"Yeah, Chance told me to tell you . . ."

"I don't care what Chance told you to tell me," I blurted out. "Chance knows damn well that in three days I leave the state for the next six weeks. He knows how much I care for him and he couldn't even come and see about me. I don't want to hear from you, Blink. You ain't my man; Chance is! You tell him I said to hell with him. You tell him I said to give me back my damn three thousand dollars, too." I slammed down the telephone.

The day before departure, a Sunday, I sat in my office on Madison Avenue because that's where Blinky said Chance would meet me when he had called back. I was so disgusted with Chance, his war, my love for him, that I refused to wash. I was trying to convince myself that I didn't care for him anymore. I just wanted my money back. So I would greet him with dirty underarms, and the same clothes from the night before. I would have no sex appeal for him. I would arrange to collect my money. I would change my telephone number so he could never call me again. Then the knock came to the side door. It was Chance with a proud yet angered face and Gary and Blinky standing there looking stupid.

I looked at Chance. Chance looked back at me. We both seemed emotionless and angry so we didn't say anything to each other. Chance, Blinky, and Gary sat in the reception area and since nobody was saying anything I wasn't gonna say anything either. That's when Blinky couldn't take it anymore. He got up and said, "Well, aren't you two gonna say something? If you're not gonna say nothing, what did I set up the meeting for?" Finally, Chance got up and pointed toward my office. I got up and went in. He followed me, closed the door, and we stood motionless for a minute or so. I broke the ice. "How could you do this to me?"

"Do what? Do what to you?" he said angrily. "Have you ever seen a man killed? Do you know what it's like to have your friend's guts spilled out all over your face? Do you know what it's like to lose half of your best friends and have the other half turn their backs on you because they're scared little bitches?" Then the tears welled up in his eyes. "Do you? Well, if you don't, then shut up. Nobody did anything to you. If anything, I kept you alive. I knew you wanted to see me. What do you think, I'm stupid or something? Do you think I don't know you want to see me? But what's a deeper love? Is it to satisfy myself by coming to see you, only to see your guts spilled all over the sidewalk the next day for some bullshit that you don't even believe in? What's a deeper love? For me to involve you in something after all the work you've done in the community and have your name go down the drain because you were killed in a 'drug-related incident'? You tell me what should I have done? Do you want to see me dead? Do you? Do you want me so choked up with love that I can't even shoot straight? So lost in love that my spot gets raided while I sit there fantasizing about you?"

My hardness melted away as the veil dropped from my heart. My eyes turned into seas of comfort. Chance continued, "You knew I missed you. You knew I wanted to see you. What fool in his right mind would leave a beautiful, thick, chocolate, voluptuous woman like you unattended? I know the sharks are waiting to take what's mine!"

I spoke softly. "Nobody has touched me. I followed your directions. I did everything you asked me to do. I didn't violate one word."

"Then what are you standing all the way over there for? Come and get what's yours." I walked toward him slowly. I was self-conscious because I was not clean. When I got up close to him I made an excuse for myself: "I was up all night so I have not showered." He said, "Shhh. Give me what I've been waiting for." And in the small confines of my office we made the best use of the space. We talked for another hour until interrupted by Blinky's impatient demand to go. Chance yelled through the closed door, "Get away from the door, man. I'll be out when I'm done." He turned to me and said, "So what's this about your money? That's always what it boils down to with all of you women."

"What about it?" I stupidly responded. "I was just angry. I needed to see you. I still get paid every two weeks, so I'm straight for right now. You can pay me later."

Chance took the telephone number for the camp in North Carolina and promised to call. He said he was kind of glad I was going away because it gave him the opportunity to get his head together. He said he was feeling shell-shocked, like somebody who had been sent away to fight and had been in the trenches too long. He said he would spend the time relaxing his nerves and forcing the images of blood and death out of his mind. He added that if I weren't going away, he, in his present state of mind, would be of no use to me anyway.

Whatever Chance was, a drug dealer, a gangster, a murderer, my mind's eye simply refused to see him that way. When I looked at him I saw only what he could be, not what he was. And day after day those two images fought in my mind. I left with the children for North Carolina for our six-week educational journey. To my surprise, Chance was to call me every day of that trip during my one and only break at lunch.

Whoever said that black people were strong because we had survived over four hundred years of oppression was both right and wrong. Yes, we had survived in that we were physically still here. But the damage that we incurred psychologically was deep-seated and hard to overturn. The damage we received spiritually was even more debilitating. Each day that I worked alongside the counselors and Reverend Chavis with the children at the African Youth Survival Camp, I was shocked at the magnitude of damage that was done. There were layers upon layers of sickness that had to be peeled away before we got to ground zero. Yes, we had produced some prize scholars, scientists, singers, musicians, engineers, architects, and lawyers. But the vast majority of us were stuck. Yes, white supremacy had done its job as the children, counselors, and older adults dealt with our scars in different ways and attempted to heal one another. But by the end of six weeks, there were many breakthroughs, some outright successes, and some failures. It was important that the camp had happened. I could not have learned better lessons at any college or by reading any book.

When I returned to New York I was so exhausted I checked into a hotel for four days and gave no one the telephone number besides my boss, Reverend Chavis. At the end of the four days, I met Chance for lunch. We talked and laughed and hugged. He confided that he wanted to slow everything down, the way it was in the beginning. I didn't mind. After all, I wasn't prepared to rush into a marriage, but my love for him was very much alive. I thought about how, far from breaking us up completely, our crisis seemed to increase our passion and connection.

Things went fine for the next three weeks. Times seemed just like old times. Then my world turned upside down. I was home in my apartment. The telephone rang. There was what seemed to be a small voice on the other end that was either whispering or just difficult to hear. The voice said, "Hello, I'm sorry. I'm sorry for calling. But is Terrance there?"

"I think you have the wrong number," I said.

"No, wait a minute. Chance, is Chance there?"

"No, he's not here right now, can I help you?"

"I'm sorry, this is Angela. It's an emergency or I wouldn't have called. The baby is sick and I need to speak to Chance."

"Angela?"

"I'm his wife."

I gasped for air but there wasn't any left in the room. There was only heat as the walls closed in on my existence. My head felt light and I fell onto the couch. Only the girl's voice revived me as it faded in and out, in and out. "Where did you get this number?" I asked slowly.

"From a sheet of paper I found in his pocket a long time ago. He would kill me if he knew I was calling, because he always tells me not to interfere in his business dealings, but it is an emergency."

"Well, Angela, you don't have to be sorry, because I'm sorry. For the past year and some time I have been Chance's girlfriend. We were supposed to get married two months ago but I've been away."

"What?" She screamed as her little voice turned into an indignant cry. "Wait a minute. Wait a minute. Here he come now. I hear the key in the door. Terrance, come in here!" Then I heard what was definitely Chance's smooth voice. The tears filled up in my eyes, hot tears. I heard him say, "What's wrong, baby? What you all worked up about?" Just as if he were talking to me. Then, in a dramatic switch the little small voice that seemed timid and harmless, shouted, "This bitch claims you been fucking her for the past year."

"Who?" He grabbed the phone from her. "Hello," he said innocently.

Sniffling and bewildered, I said, "What's up, Chance, it's me. How could you do this to me? How could you be so low and so evil?" Then I heard some wrestling. The phone dropped down on the floor and bounced.

"You never said you were gonna fuck her! That's not what we agreed on when we heard her on the radio. You said you was gonna get the record deal and the goddamn money! You didn't say shit about sex. Now who the fuck does she think she is talking 'bout you, her goddamn man? You better get on the phone and tell her. Tell her. Tell her we're married. We've been married. We got one daughter and one on the way. We live in Co-op City and we're happy. Tell her so she can get off of your dick." Then I heard someone pick the phone back up and it was her again.

"He doesn't love you. He was just fucking you for the money. It was just business. Tell her, go ahead, tell her." Then I heard a hand wrap around the receiver trying to conceal their conversation. I strained and I could still hear. It was Chance saying, "Will you stop? You're messing up everything. You mad now. But if you tell her what's up you gonna be madder later when the money run out. C'mon. I got her right where we need her." Then I heard them wrestle again and she said, "Fuck that. I don't care. Fucking was never part of the deal. Marriage! She's bugging all the way out. Now you tell her."

Chance got on the phone. In the role reversal of the century, this confident masculine bastion who gave all the directions and called all the shots sounded like a trained puppy dog. He said faintly, "Hello." I squeezed out of what was now my small voice, "Yes?" and with no hesitation at all he said, "I don't love you and I never did."

Click.

seven

Derek

My beeper went off. The loud noise echoed around my semi-empty apartment. I threw open my closet and put on the first pair of sneakers that fell out. My hair was a wreck. I couldn't worry about that, though. I no longer had a phone in my apartment. I would have to find a pay phone on the street. The elevator was too slow coming. So I ran down eleven flights of stairs. When I got outside, I picked up pay phone after pay phone. Some were missing wires. Some were missing the dial tone. Some were missing the mouthpiece. After running eight blocks I finally found one working on 126th Street. I called back.

"What took you so long?" he answered.

"I couldn't find a phone that works," I replied huffing and puffing.

"Don't give me that bullshit!" He paused. "Why are you breathing like that?"

"Because I was running."

"Who are you with?"

"I'm alone."

"So you expect me to believe it took you twenty minutes to get back to me because you couldn't find a phone?"

"That's what really happened," I said with tears in my eyes and mucus building up in my throat.

"You're full of shit, girl. You better stop playing with my head. You think you're too damn smart."

Then he hung up. Just like that. I started walking back to my apartment. I was glad it was dark. That way nobody could see me cry. Looking lonely and vulnerable was just not safe. My thoughts were a jumble. I wondered what I would have to do to prove to him that I was true. It seemed he was always jealous, obsessive even. He questioned everything I did. Even when I went to work. If I could just gain his trust, I thought. After all, I did pick him up right off the corner. He was on the pay phone looking manly and dapper. With one hand he cradled the phone; with the other he held a leash at the other end of which was a pit bull. I didn't mind. If you lived in New York you needed some kind of protection. It was better than carrying a gun. He looked healthy. His eyes and skin were clear. His body was strong. I could tell he was drug-free. He was dressed hip-hop style. He wore expensive, studious-looking, wire-rim glasses. I decided that here was one of those one-in-a-

hundred opportunities. If I played cute and didn't say anything, I probably would never bump into him again.

I pulled over in my van and got out. I wiggled my way
over and tapped him on the shoulder. "I like you, can I get your
number?" My confidence was booming. So were my hips. I put
one hand on my waist and I smiled bright. He looked me over.
Then he hung up abruptly. He smiled and said, "You must be
joking, right?" I said, "Do I look like I'm joking?"

Later on, because we had met this way, he said he
couldn't take me seriously. Who else but a slut, he asked, would
pick up a man, bold, like that? He said he figured I did it so
well that I must have done it a dozen times before. But he was
wrong. I was no slut. I was lonely. It had been a year since
Chance and I had broken up. Since then, I had had no man, no
sex, no good male-female conversation. It had begun to sink in
that no Prince Charming was coming. If I wanted a man, I had
to go out there and stalk him down.

The fact that I was now working in the entertainment
industry didn't help my man problem. To be sure, I had had a
tryst with a famous hip-hop star. He was deep, soulful, and even
spiritual. But if I learned one thing it was: Never mess with an
entertainer. They were in love with only their careers. They were
also loved, lusted after, and literally hunted by hundreds of
women. What these women were willing to do to accommodate
these entertainers distorted their self-perception. They started
believing that they were larger than life. Then they developed
obstacle courses and hoops that you would have to jump over
and through to prove that you were different than the other two
hundred women who had called and hunted them this week. I

got tired of the visits at three and four o'clock in the morning when he got out of the studio. He said if I couldn't stay awake for him, it meant that I really didn't want to see him. Therefore, he concluded, I didn't really deserve his attention. After several weeks of trying to rearrange my sleeping habits, playing loud music, leaving windows open so I wouldn't fall asleep, I looked at the bags under my eyes and decided that he and I would do better to just remain friends. It worked out perfectly. The fact that I hadn't given him any pussy meant that he still retained his respect for me. When we became friends he put away the hoops and abandoned the tricks. We became tight.

That's what gave me the nerve to push up on the handsome brother on the corner. I figured he was an everyday guy who might not be conceited. Maybe he'd have some humility about himself. But it was hard. I tried to have a regular relationship but he refused to trust me. I talked his ears off trying to convince him that I was a strong, decent woman. I shared my views with him. I showed him my community work. I let him drive my van. I lent him money, which he always paid back. I helped him enroll in community college. I even showed him how to start his own little clothing business to keep him off the streets. But the more I did for him, the less he trusted me. So I decided right there on 135th Street, in front of Lenox Terrace, my apartment building, that I would hop in my van and go see him. I would tell him how I felt about him. I would beg him to understand and trust me. Then we would make love and I would pop the question. Maybe he should move in with me? That way we could grow together. He would learn to trust. He could watch me, listen in on my phone calls, do whatever he wanted to feel more secure about us.

I knew I was taking a gamble. He had told me never to come by his apartment without calling first. We had argued about that. I said that if I was truly his girl, I should be able to come over any time I wanted. He said as long as he was living with his mother, even though he paid half of the rent, I should respect their house rules. His mother, he explained, had a boyfriend. She got pissed when too many people invaded her "space," especially women. Even if the woman was coming to see her "precious son," you still just "never know about women," she'd say. For the past three months I had respected her rules. Tonight was special, though, because I was hurting inside. Never before had any man thought of me as a whore. Never before did I have to prove that my reputation was clean. But I couldn't blame him. After all, we didn't grow up together. He had no way of knowing how, who, and what I was. So off I went.

I held my breath as I headed up the stairs of his Brooklyn building. The stench reminded me of the Bronx. I knocked at the door and he answered, "I thought I told you not to come by without calling?"

"I'm sorry. I just wanted to clear up our misunderstanding. Is your mother home? I'm sure she'll understand. It's just one of those things."

He rolled his eyes up in his head and exhaled. That's when a little five-foot-tall girl with the face of a troll came to the door holding what looked like a butcher's knife. Instead of fear, I felt disbelief and curiosity. She opened up her mouth and a voice scratched out, "So you the uptown bitch who's been trying to buy my man's love? Think your ass is hot 'cause you work at some big record company. Well, fuck you, Salt 'n' Pepa,

Mony-Love, 357, and all the rest of you lowlife whores. And if you bring your ass back around here again, I'll slit your goddamn throat."

I turned to him and looked him in the eye. He shrugged his shoulders as if to say he had nothing to do with it, she and I should fight it out. I remembered my mother's advice: "When you see trouble move in the opposite direction." But I was pissed off. I was mad that he was acting like he never told me that he was not dating anyone else. Mad that he was full of shit. His story about respecting his mother's "space" was garbage. I was mad that she was mad at me and not him. But what really plucked my nerves was her suggesting that I was some rich bitch from uptown who was so shallow that I had to buy love.

It was true that I helped him out sometimes. But it was also true that he always paid me back. What was wrong with that? So I rolled my neck, twisted up my lips, and said, "I don't feel sorry for you just because you're ugly. And I don't feel bad about the fact that I'm pretty. I didn't know that he was sleeping with you. Then again, nobody did 'cause you're so damn ugly he hides you in his house underneath the bed!"

Well, to make a long story short, she chased me with that butcher knife that night. I ran. He caught her before she could catch me. He restrained her while she shouted every foul name she could think of. Back in my van, I laughed hysterically. It wasn't until I got back to Harlem that it sunk in that I had put my own life on the line just so I could dig into her nerves.

I was hurt. But I was not crushed. It had been impossible for anyone to crush me ever since Chance had rolled over my soul with a Mack truck. In fact, I had decided that being in love was senseless for African men and women in America, that racism had made us all too crazy to handle the power of love. Love, after all, was an emotion that was a gift from God. We all had moved so far away from God that for us to try to deal with love was like letting babies play with steak knives. The only result would be blood and pain.

But I was human. I had needs, sexual, intellectual, and spiritual. So I locked my heart behind a steel door. I surrounded that door with barbed wire and posted security guards everywhere. I settled for the phrase: "I have feelings for him." That was good enough. When I found a guy attractive with an interesting or intriguing mind and a knack for serious conversation, I checked to see that he was healthy and drug-free. Then I considered whether I wanted to develop simple feelings for him. That way I didn't have to worry about having myself reduced to nothing. That's what had happened when Chance left. It was a costly kind of pain. I had to completely move out of my apartment. I left all of my few belongings because everything reminded me of him. In my new place I put nothing but a blackboard and a bed. The bed to sleep on, the blackboard to write down a list of what I had to do each day in terms of work and projects. And, boy, did I need that blackboard, because my spirit was wounded, comatose even. The only way I could function was mechanically. I'd get up in the morning, sit on the edge of my bed, and tell myself: "Number one, stand up. Number two, take a shower," and so on.

When I first moved in, I had a telephone and an answering machine. I sat motionless as people called. I pretended not to hear. I did my work, though. Not to do it would have left me hating myself. It also would have given me too much time to think about what Chance had done to me and how I had hated and loved him at the same time. Eventually even the phone was unbearable. I had it disconnected. But before I did, I called one of my best friends, a South African sister, whom I loved and respected. I asked her to rent a car for me for the weekend. I would drive around aimlessly every night from midnight until the sun came up. I was so emotionally scarred by Chance that I couldn't face the night alone, sitting or lying in one position. In fact, I rarely slept at all. The problem was I couldn't give the car back. To be stranded would mean surrendering to the night. That was too frightening to me. So instead I kept the car. I ran up the bill. I collected parking tickets and caused the breakup of a friendship with a special and brilliant friend. Eventually, when I finished driving around in a funk, I returned the car and paid the bill.

Meanwhile, my job as a youth director had come to an end. The Commission for Racial Justice and the United Church of Christ closed down and relocated in Cleveland, Ohio. They offered me a transfer but I declined. The timing was perfect because the welfare hotels where I did my work with the children also closed down. The children and their families were redistributed into so-called apartments where racism and poverty could work on them from yet another angle.

I got a new job as vice president of a small, independent, black record company that was distributed by a major label. My work on the benefit concert had brought me to the attention of people in a position to hire. It was a good, paying job. Moreover, it taught me the useful skill of how to "make stars." How to take an idea from my brain, put it on paper, and through a step-by-step process bring it to life. It taught me the value of mass marketing, public relations, commercialism, and finance. I learned the power of creating and controlling images. I knew that if I could create characters and artists through radio, television, and film, who represented the values that I worked for, I could actually reach more children than it was possible to reach individual by individual.

My community service work continued in the form of lecturing in prisons. This was challenging, since I considered myself to be politically strong yet emotionally fragile. The first time I visited a prison the reality slapped me in the face as I was searched, interviewed, escorted down cold corridors, and startled by loud clicking and clanging locks. The doors were massive and impenetrable, making a mockery of all of the phony prison escape movies. Nobody was getting out of there without permission. As I walked to the podium to deliver my talk, I heard thunderous applause. When I looked up, I saw several hundred black men assembled and seated. When my eyes connected with them, they stood up. As my eyes danced, I felt I had found a hidden treasure. Wall-to-wall beautiful, built, ancient-souled black men. Men more valuable than gold or any material item. Men who were undoubtedly loved, desired, missed, and definitely needed by our community outside. I attempted to look into each of their eyes. It was impossible to accomplish. Even though I knew many of them had maimed, raped, and even murdered, I saw nothing but souls who wanted to be loved, minds that wanted to learn, and men who would have flourished in another land, in another time. I wanted to hug them all. This, of course, was forbidden. Instead, I cried. I told them how beautiful they were to me. Then I gave the most powerful, informative, and life-changing talk I was capable of.

Afterward, I developed a writing and telephone relationship with an incarcerated brother named Dresz. He was beautiful, too. When I got around to asking him what he was in for, he said, "Murder." He had killed another black brother when he was fourteen. They were at a party, and what he thought was his "manhood" was threatened. So he took a life. He said he regretted it. He believed he deserved to be in prison. But did he? Yes, he had killed, and killing was definitely wrong. But who or what had twisted the minds of so many of our young boys? What educational institution had taught him, or failed to teach him, the meaning of manhood? Who had taught him the violence and surrounded him with frustration? Who had sold our men the weapons of death and destruction? The answer, as far as I was concerned, was simple: white people in power who wanted to preserve their privileged position in this sick society.

The more I talked to Dresz, the closer he grew toward me. I yelled at myself for being so stupid. Didn't I know he would get attached? The fact was, for all my good intentions, I was frightened of entering into a relationship with a man who was in prison. It was impossible to fully comprehend the fact that when you asked a brother when he was getting out, and his release date was so incredibly far away, he simply said, "Not for a long time." I also had images of him being raped and beaten by other male inmates. The thought of a disease like AIDS was frightening. The thought of a sexual relationship with a possible voluntary or involuntary bisexual or homosexual was not only unthinkable for me, it was undesirable. So I cut off our communication. I figured it was the least painful way.

As I grappled with my own loneliness and inability to find a man who was good and true and deep, I came to see that my problem was not mine alone. Millions of sisters faced it as well. Question: Where were the African men in America? Answer: in prison, under court supervision, gays in love with each other, mental institutions where they were diagnosed not as victims of white supremacy but under some other fancy label, in college being educated and emasculated simultaneously, or successful and therefore involved with or married to another woman already.

It occurred to me, based on everything I had experienced, that we African women were, actually, all sharing our men. But most of us turned a blind eye to that fact. After all, wasn't it the deceit, trickery, and manipulation men engaged in that put a knife in our lungs? Wasn't it the everyday deceit that took our breath away and assassinated our spirit? The thought that you were loving a person who you thought you knew but obviously didn't? So I decided that I was willing to share a man with another willing sister as long as it was honest. That way perhaps I could escape and even eliminate the lying and the pain. Perhaps I could organize the relationship, like a chore or a job. I could make it functional.

When I mentioned these thoughts of openly sharing my man (or someone else's man) to other women I knew, they thought I was crazy. Never have I seen such neck rolling, lip twisting, finger pointing, and attitude. One woman at my job even went to tears. Why? I wondered. Almost every single woman I knew had been sharing a man with or without her knowledge. The majority of them, once they discovered their man was cheating, still never left him. Instead, they argued with him. What they were really asking for, it seemed to me, was for the man to hide what he was doing. They wanted him to keep it out of their way so they wouldn't have to deal with it. Some of these same girlfriends had themselves gone out with married men. Some were married and knew their husbands were having affairs. Who was crazy? Me, or them?

About six months after starting work at the record company, I found myself in a music store pricing some equipment. The store was crowded. Suddenly, I felt someone tapping me on the shoulder. He asked if I really was who he thought I was. I looked at him. He was very light-skinned, well-built and of medium height. He had brown kinky hair. He smiled, and said his name was Derek. I felt nothing. "Why do you ask?" I said.

"Because I heard you speak once. I think you have a real talent." Being a complete sucker for a compliment, I blushed and asked, "What kind of a talent?" I was starved for attention. He said, "Well, your voice is beautiful. When I hear it, it touches my soul. I've listened to you. You come across so clear, so honest."

"Are you trying to butter me up?" I asked. He smiled and said, "No. I'm dead serious."

I recalled my relationship with Chance. I became serious and stern. I said, "Look, if you're looking for a record deal, then just ask me for my business card and make an appointment. You don't have to flatter me. That's not my style."

"See, that's what I mean," he said. "It's all honesty with you. Your voice comes from deep down in your gut. When I listen close, I can tell that you feel every word that you say. No, I'm not looking for a record deal, but I think it's interesting that I ran into you. I think your voice would sound rough over some music."

Now he had me thinking. He was a courteous and unpretentious guy. That was rare for the record business. I wasn't attracted to him but I was interested in what he had to say. He continued, "I think your voice and what you have to say to our people needs to be heard. If we took pieces of your speeches and put them on top of some hard beats, I think we would have a hit."

I was fascinated by the idea of mixing political-historical speeches over hip-hop beats. It seemed like a step in the right direction toward the media projects I was interested in creating. Derek said he would produce the music if I would do the lyrics. If we got a deal, I'd pay him for his work and keep the largest bulk of the money for myself. He would go his way; I would go mine. He explained that we would both benefit: He would get a break as a producer, I would get to explore a new and powerful arena as a performing artist. I figured I had nothing to lose. He promised to bring me a tape with some of his original music on it. If I liked it, we had a deal.

Derek and I got together. I listened to his music. It was good. We agreed to take no more than six weeks to complete the project. He would bring his equipment to my apartment. We would work after work, Monday through Thursday from early evening until almost midnight. As we worked, we learned a lot about each other. As we attempted to develop concept, content, and theme, we would talk over many topics and points of view. With his help, I learned how to properly breathe and relax. Derek was perceptive. He noticed how difficult it was for me to open up and let loose. He said that if I was going to be creative I had to let go of my fear of experimentation. He characterized me as the sort of person who was comfortable doing the things that I was already good at. The real test, he explained, was being able to try something new in which I had no pre-established confidence.

After a week or so I realized how comfortable I was becoming with the routine of Derek's coming over to my place. I still felt no sexual attraction whatsoever. He was much shorter than I like my men. Plus, his very light skin did not appeal to my sense of beauty. However, he was intelligent, friendly, warm, and sensitive. I admired these qualities. After a while, I came to crave our conversations. Having him in my apartment regularly made me feel safe. Around the third week of our working together, we discovered that we had been overambitious about our finishing the tape in six weeks. We decided we would continue to meet for as long as it took until we were both satisfied with the result.

One night my youngest sister stopped by. She was shopping on 125th Street and found herself in the neighborhood. When she saw all of Derek's equipment in my living room, she laughed and asked me what I thought I was doing. When I told her I was doing an album, she exclaimed, "Not my sister doing an album! Does he realize how corny you are? What are you gonna do? Talk some African mumbo-jumbo on a record?"

I shot her one of my serious stares. She stopped teasing me. She stayed for a while. But her presence made me tense. Her comment made me fear that all of the nonthinking black kids would be critical of my efforts because, after all, records were for dancing and good times, not thinking and education. Derek pulled me into the kitchen. He suggested that when we worked, we work alone. He said he noticed that the "vibe changed" when other people entered the room. I agreed. I told my sister I had to get down to work and needed some privacy. She giggled and said, "If I had a cutie like him in my apartment, I'd need some privacy so I could get down, too!"

I told her it's not what she thought. She smiled and said, "Maybe it's not for you. You always were stuck up and picky. But he's definitely in love with you." She put her coat on. As she exited, she told me I could pass him off to her if I didn't want him. I sneered at her and reminded her that she liked every light-skinned guy with curly hair without even so much as knowing what he was about.

Eventually Derek and I began to talk about relationships. Derek thought it was hard to have genuine relationships because black men felt so inadequate. I told him that a good woman should know how to make her man feel good and special so he could overcome any inadequacies. I told him I didn't have a man, that I had had a tragic relationship in the past, that I'd drifted along ever since. He looked shocked. Maybe, he said, I was looking for the wrong kind of guy. He went on to say that any time he mentioned my name to any brother he knew, the brother would say, "Oh, man, she's beautiful." I laughed at the compliment. Unfortunately, I somehow never met any of those brothers. He asked if I was bitter, if it was possible for me to forgive? I told him my love for the black man was so deep and profound that it was not something to be trifled with. When it was, I was slow to heal. I was still open to relationships but I had one requirement—honesty.

I poured my heart into our conversation. I told him how I had a burning hatred for lying and deceitful men. If they were truly men, they would be able to face and handle the truths in their lives—even when those truths hurt. Men who lied and slithered in and out of holes like snakes should get it back tenfold, I felt. Derek mounted, as best he could, a defense. He said brothers would not lie if sisters were more intelligent and realistic. Many sisters, he charged, didn't have what it took to satisfy the multifaceted needs of their men. That's why men cheated. If you tried to teach a sister to grow intellectually or to expand her horizon, she fought you "as though a brother is her enemy." On the other hand, if you left her, she called you a dog. If you stayed with her and dated other women on the side to supplement what she lacked, she tried to kill you. So brothers were in a no-win situation.

I told him there was some truth in what he said. But usually guys chose women who were unintelligent. Then they acted surprised when they discovered their women couldn't think! Guys judged women by the size of their breasts, waist-line, and hips. Then they appeared disappointed when they found out that's all there was. If men dated women who were both intelligent and attractive to them, then they could have real relationships, I argued. This would be the challenge that kept the relationship interesting. But this was precisely what brothers didn't want—a challenge.

Well, we laughed that night. We even kicked around the idea of doing a record on the subject. As Derek was leaving my apartment, he asked me, "So, you're saying that you're the type of sister who, if your man was seeing someone besides you, you'd rather him tell you than hide it?"

I said, "Of course."

"And then what? You kick him out, right?"

"No! I've decided that if a brother can be honest with me, I can share him with another woman. At least that way, I know what I'm getting. I know where he is and how to find him. I'll know her and nobody ends up crying."

He left my house that night with excited eyes.

The following week Derek asked me to the movies. There was a black film festival screening great works of black directors. We went to see Spike Lee's *She's Gotta Have It.* Although I had seen it when it was first released, I went with him anyway and laughed even more. Later we talked about the film. I didn't agree with a woman seeing more than one man at a time the way the girl in the film did. He argued that some sisters would say I was crazy. How could I believe in polygamy and not believe that sisters had the same rights to have more than one man at a time? I argued that the only reason sisters should consider sharing our men was the shortage of black men. There was no shortage of black women. We needed to share in order to keep our families intact, to keep our children connected to a male presence, a father figure. We needed social order and balance, not disintegration and chaos. Sharing men was not about having sex with as many people as you could. It was about finding an alternative lifestyle—a lifestyle that was open, honest, and less painful.

Derek's face turned red. It seemed that every time I opened my mouth, he ate up and loved my every word. For my part, I was becoming fascinated with the idea of somebody being absolutely smitten with me. As time went on, Derek and I talked more and worked less. Finally, one night Derek said, "I want you to be my woman. I want to be the man who meets the challenge."

I smiled and said playfully, "Oh, yeah." I thought about it. I still was not sexually attracted to him. But I was sexually starved. I also thought if you can't be with the one you love, then love the one you're with. After all, Derek was a nice guy. I was a lonely woman. If I said no, would he disappear? If I said yes, would we get along? Could I love him? I wasn't certain. He moved closer to me and said, "Come on, I've spent all of my time with you. You know if you're interested or not."

I decided that he passed my test. He was intelligent, healthy, courteous, and drug-free. I would try to love him as a black man even though I was not in love with him. So I said, "All right, we can give it a shot. But you have to answer a lot of questions first. Do you sleep with other people?"

"Do I sleep with other people?"

"See! That's what I mean. While we were friends, it seemed everything was honest and open. Two seconds after I say 'yes,' you start to act like you're stupid. Answer my question: Do you sleep with other people?"

Derek looked shocked at how rapidly my attitude flipped. He put his hand up to slow me down and said, "Hold up! You can't be screaming on me like that. What's wrong with you?"

I put my temper in check and apologized, "I'm sorry, you know I've been through a lot. I can't take nobody holding out on me and gassing up my head with a lot of lies."

"All right, check it," he said. "I have a girlfriend and I was also talking to this other sister. But ever since you and I starting working together, I haven't seen that much of her."

"Oh, so you have two girls already?" I asked with my hands on my hips.

"No, the other one is not like my girl. She's just, you know . . ."

"You know what?"

"Well . . ." he said.

"Yeah, that's how you'll be describing our relationship to the next girl you meet, right? You'll say I'm not really your girl, I'm just 'you know, well, you know . . .' "

"No, it's not like that with you."

"Yeah, I've heard that before."

"Tell me what it would take for me to have you. Whatever it will take, I'll do it," he said.

My blood boiled with excitement. The idea that there was somebody who liked me so much he was willing to kiss my ass pumped me up. So I smiled and said, "Go tell both of them that you're seeing me, too. If we are all three going to be dating you, we ought to be aware of it. That way I don't have to feel I'm part of a lie."

Derek looked thoughtful. I could see his mind speeding. I guess he was trying to imagine telling the other two women about me. After thinking awhile, he looked me sincerely in the eyes, and said, "There's one problem." Impatiently, I rolled my eyes and said, "If you don't do it, I'm out."

"Slow down. I'm gonna do it. I can talk to you, right?"

"Yeah."

"Well, I'll tell both of them about you. But right now they don't even know about each other. I'll be walking into a minefield. But I'll do it."

"So you've been lying to both of them," I said as though that's all I expected from a man.

"No, not exactly. The second one knows about the first one. The first one doesn't know anything."

"Why's that?" I asked.

"Because she can't handle the truth. She won't go for it."

"Well, she's going for it anyway 'cause you're doing it anyway. It's happening. Why would you want three women, anyway?"

"It's not that I want three women. I had the first one first. I love her but she doesn't understand anything about the history or even the condition of African people. Anytime I tell her anything about our people she says I'm making pitiful excuses for myself and for black folk. I tell her how much I hate my job and how much racism I have to deal with. She says I should thank God I have a job. She can't relate. She thinks racism was only in the past. Black people should forget it and move on. Once I lost a job and was out of work for a long time. I couldn't find any decent work anywhere. She wouldn't even lend a brother some money. Instead she turned me into a slave and enjoyed it. I got to eat and stay at her place sometimes. The trade-off was I had to listen to her belittle me every day when she got up to go to work. The clincher was when she took her savings and went to Aruba with her girlfriends and left me home broke."

I started laughing. I didn't believe any woman would be that selfish. Derek didn't laugh though. I could see the intensity on his face.

"No," he said. "I'm dead serious. I asked her not to go to Aruba. I showed her my business plan and asked her to have faith in me, invest in my idea. She laughed and said she didn't want no part of my schemes. She said she was going to Aruba because she worked hard and deserved every minute of her vacation."

"Where does she work?" I asked.

"She's a nurse."

"What's her name?"

"Her name is Katrina. We call her Trina."

"Why don't you leave her alone if she frustrates you so much?"

"I have a problem leaving people," he said, with a sweet innocence that I rarely saw displayed in men. "My mother left me when I was a child. I guess ever since then I've had a complex about being so cold as to leave someone."

That sentiment touched my guarded heart. After all, hadn't all the men I had ever known found it quite easy to walk away? "Why did your mother leave?" I asked.

"She and my father were having problems. She said he was 'going nowhere' with his life. She called him a dreamer. My father said that a few years after they married he realized they were just two different people, with two different sets of values. I grew up with my father." Then he smiled and added, "My father has two wives."

"Get out of here," I laughed.

"No, for real. They live in Los Angeles. Me and my father are the same."

"What happened to your mom? Where is she?"

"After the divorce, she went and married some success-ful middle-class sucker. Some college professor. My mom said he was a 'real man.' He ended up sexually molesting my sister for five years while my mother pretended she didn't know what was going on. Then he fucked up and molested some girl at the school. It became a public scandal. He couldn't handle the pressure so he shot himself. That's a 'real man' for you, huh?"

I lowered my eyes and thought, black people are so destroyed, it seems like we have nothing sacred left. "So, where's your mom now?"

"She's living in this area trying to pick up the pieces with my sister. She and I don't get along too well. I figure, what woman is so selfish she gets up and leaves her own son for almost twenty years?"

"She sounds like Trina," I said. "How come so many brothers who have complaints about their mothers end up hooking up with some woman who's 'just like Mom'?"

"I told you," he said in a serious voice, "I know her faults but I just can't leave anyone."

We sat quietly for a while. I thought I could make him leave Trina, especially since she was such a witch. Then I could have all the attention. Plus, why should she be allowed to continue to humiliate Derek? Then I remembered that there was still the issue of the "other woman." So I said, "Derek, let me guess. The other girl is the one who licks your wounds and makes you feel good when Trina's being an ass?"

"No. Trina makes me feel good. The other one is somebody who I can talk to. She's intelligent and understanding. She knows everything about our people, our history, and all."

"So what do you need me for?"

"To tell the truth, if I had it in me to leave a person, I would have left both of them and moved in here with you the day I met you in the store. You're everything I want in one woman. No headaches." Then he asked slyly, "You know one of the good things about you?"

"What?" I asked, ready for the butter.

"You're nasty."

"What?"

"Listen . . ." he said. "I know you're good in bed. Your eyes tell it all. It's just that you're proud, real proud. On top of that you're intelligent. That makes it tough and guys would rather not deal with that. But I'm positive about the fire in you."

Well, that was it—the compliment I needed. I asked him again if he was going to tell the other two about me. He promised he would. Then we did "the nasty" right there on my living room floor.

The next morning Derek asked for time to straighten out his relationships with the other two women in his life. He added that since he had spent the night at my place and had not been home at his aunt's where he usually stayed, he would definitely have several fights waiting for him.

We talked every day on the phone. Not about the other two, but about our usual topics and our music project. At the end of the week, he came back over. He said, "Well, I did it. It wasn't fun but I told them."

"What happened?" I asked with excitement in my bones. I couldn't believe he had actually placed his own head in a noose.

"Well, Shequila broke up with me. She said she had been patient. She had asked me to tell Trina about her when we first hooked up. But I refused. So she wanted to know what was so hot about you that now I'm willing to do what I would not do for her. I told her that you're very special to me. She said, 'If she's so damn special then she can have you.' I tried to convince her to stay but she was furious. She said I'm full of shit. I told you every time you tell a sister the truth, she gets mad."

"Damn, you must feel real bad," I said with evident insincerity.

"Not really. Her leaving makes things less complicated. I said I couldn't leave a woman. I didn't say a woman can't leave me."

"What about your girl?" I asked, feeling suddenly strange about using the terminology "your girl."

"She bugged out. She kicked me. She slapped me. She spit on me. She cursed me out. She said what in the hell gave me the nerve to bring some shit like this in her face?"

"So what's up?" I asked, hoping she had left him, too.

"She said she's not sharing and she's not leaving me either." He looked at me.

"So what she's saying is she's going for it but she doesn't want to admit that she's going for it?"

"I don't know. But she knows about you. It's all honest. It's on the table the way you wanted. I even told her you believe in polygamy. I told her you'd be willing to talk to her about it."

"Sure," I said. "Why not?"

Derek and I had fun together. We weren't "in love" lovers. I just didn't feel that way about him. But by now we were tight friends, like partners. I loved being with a man again. I loved going places and not having to look for a date. I enjoyed talking and having Derek understand with little explanation. One thing was strange. Even though I was not in love with him, I still felt uncomfortable knowing that when he left me, he was going to see another woman. I would have to remind myself that I had agreed to share. But something inside of me found it disconcerting and foreign.

A couple of weeks later I received a phone call at about three o'clock in the morning. I had fallen asleep while listening to music. So I picked up the receiver and said, "Hold on. I have to turn the music down." When I returned to the phone I heard a female voice say, "All-night party-woman, whose man are you screwing tonight?"

Fighting off sleep and trying to awaken myself, I mumbled, "What?"

"Don't act like you were sleeping, bitch. I heard the music. You're having a party. Only thing, he's not there with you tonight because he here with me. So whose man you got in there tonight?"

I thought: This must be Trina. Three o'clock in the morning. She must be flipping. I asked her to hold on again. I went to the bathroom and ran a cold washcloth across my face and came back. "Are you still there?" I asked.

"Why are you filling my man's head up with this polygamy bullshit? Can't you get your own man?"

"First of all, let's start at the beginning. I'm not having a party. I'm alone. I fell asleep with the music on. I'm not sleeping with anyone besides Derek. Lastly, 'your man,' as you put it, came to me first. He didn't even mention you existed until after I asked him."

Then I heard her voice shrill, "You're sleeping with her. You're already sleeping with her? Well, what was the sense in acting like you were asking for my permission when you were already fucking her anyway?" I then heard Derek say, "We can talk in the morning. I told you it's too late. I'm tired."

"I know you're nothing but a dirty whore. You slept with him already?"

"I've known him for over three months," I said.

"Ooh, that's a long time." She was hysterical. "You know how long Derek and I have been together? Nine years! Ever since I was fourteen years old!" She was screaming into the telephone.

I heard Derek in the background saying, "No, baby, it's only been seven years." Then they started arguing about which years were legitimate to count. Trina got back on the phone and said, "So tell me about this sharing shit you're talking about. I'm a Christian. Do you believe in God?" she suddenly and angrily asked.

I explained that there was a man shortage in our community. I told her that I believed we were all sharing our men anyway at one point or another. But since we were afraid to admit it to ourselves, we didn't deal with it. I told her that I'd rather deal with it honestly. I added that racism had systematically made it impossible for black men to survive. But since most of us were too naive and too lazy to fight white supremacy while building our communities, we had better get used to the idea of sharing our men.

Trina retorted, "Well, sweetheart, my man can do something else for the community besides fucking you."

For the next two weeks Trina called every night. It did not matter whether Derek was at my apartment or hers. They were crazy, loud, screaming calls. I understood that she was angry. But I told myself that she would have been a lot angrier had Derek and I deceived her and she found out about us a year into our relationship. I also knew I could give him up and return him to her because I did not love him. But if I gave him back she would probably forbid him to continue to work with me. Then I would not only lose a man and a friend, I would lose my music project as well. I knew that she was more entitled to him than I was. After all, she had been with him for all those years.

Besides, I realized that if we were truly practicing polygamy as practiced by some of my Islamic friends, Trina and Derek would have to be married. Plus, I would have had to have received Trina's permission to become the second wife. If she disagreed, it simply could not happen. Also, Derek would have had to have been financially stable along with other rules and regulations governing such multiple relationships. But who was I fooling? I wasn't a Muslim. I simply—and rather conveniently—grafted their philosophy of polygamy onto the social predicament that African people in America found themselves in. It was an honest system of man sharing, I rationalized.

What really bothered me about Trina was how she talked to me. She called me a whore, a slut, a homewrecker, and, as one might expect, was real nasty toward me. I figured for a woman whose man went out on his own and selected another woman, she had a lot of nerve blaming me instead of looking at what she was doing wrong. It was the talking down to me that got my blood boiling. Inwardly, I accepted the challenge to fight over him until one of us won. So I continued to see Derek. We went to movies, museums, festivals, parties, rallies.

But I soon grew tired of Trina's unrelenting harassment—the late-night phone calls, the yelling and screaming.

So the next time my phone rang, I said, "All right, Trina. Congratulations, you won. You get to keep him. Here's the deal: You tell him for me that it's over between us. Tell him, please don't come by my house anymore. You keep him over there with you and everything will be fine."

Then Trina said, "See, I knew you didn't love him. Derek, wake up. She said it's over. I told you she doesn't love you."

I hung up.

Only one week later Derek returned. I couldn't hide the fact that I was happy to see him. I still didn't want to deal with Trina. So I left Derek standing on the steps outside my apartment building. I quickly phoned Trina and said, "What's up, girl? Your man is here. I thought you agreed to keep him away from me?"

Trina wept and said, "I've tried everything. He doesn't listen to me anymore. I don't know what to do."

My heart softened toward her. I told her I'd send Derek back home. She surprisingly thanked me. So I opened my window and yelled down: "Derek! Trina said to come right home." Then I added sarcastically, "She misses you."

He yelled back: "Come on, girl. Stop playing with me. Let me in. I need to see you."

I went downstairs. I looked through the curtain at Derek's smiling, unpretentious face. I let him in. We had fun together, like old times. Then the phone started ringing again. I told Derek that while I liked him, the fighting was getting on my nerves. I was willing to share if Trina were willing, but apparently she wasn't. Therefore, we would have to end our relationship. He looked at me sadly. He agreed that she would always have problems sharing. But he didn't feel he could just leave her out in the cold. It was a real dilemma for him because he had grown to love me. I sympathized but said he should leave and not return. The whole situation was too much trouble. I had Derek leave. But my phone kept ringing. I refused to pick it up. I knew it was Trina because an hour and a half later it stopped—about the length of time it took Derek to drive from my apartment to hers.

For the next week I dodged Derek's calls. By the second week without him—or any man to replace him for that matter—I started bugging out. While I had my community service project on the weekends, during the week I was blue with boredom. I would spend my evenings reading and writing. Occasionally, I would watch reruns of "I Love Lucy" to entertain myself. Soon I started calling all my old girlfriends. I would start with last names that began with the letter A and proceed down to Z. The small talk with them was no compensation though. My boredom grew. I decided I wanted Derek back. So I waited for him to call again, as I knew he would. When he called, I put on my best sexy voice. He asked me what I was doing. I said, "Oh, I just finished exercising." A complete lie. "So now I'm sitting here all covered with sweat trying to slow my body down. Then I'll take a hot steam shower. Later on, I'm gonna start reading this new book I picked up on Malcolm X."

I knew how to push his buttons. I knew I'd catch him one way or another. I figured since he had been stuck with Trina for two weeks, he hadn't enjoyed a good, intelligent conversation. He asked to see me. As I was telling him to come right over, I heard Trina come in, and say, "Why are you whispering into the phone? Damn it, Derek, are you calling her again? I told you she doesn't love you. Who has always been there for you? When you need that bitch, she'll be out somewhere protesting on a picket line."

His voice went even lower as he whispered to me, "I'll be right there."

Our reunion was even better than I imagined. I unplugged the phone to avoid Trina's calls. I decided I was gonna take her man. I was bored and she had refused to cooperate. I asked Derek to move in with me. I knew this had been a sensitive issue with him and Trina. She had refused to let him move into her place until they were married. Derek was pleased with my invitation, but surprised. I told him that, as far as I was concerned, an apartment was just a material thing. I assured him that he could come to my place, escape the turmoil, and relax. He asked about Trina. I told him Trina had had her chance but she blew it playing games. Plus, if he moved in with me it would put pressure on Trina to accept the arrangement. She would finally realize that I was more than a piece of ass or his plaything on the side. He told me that Trina already realized that. She called me names because she was angry. He smiled and said that if Trina and I had met somewhere else without this situation having ever occurred, we would probably have liked each other a lot. It was issues of the heart, he said, that kept sisters at each other's throats. I sat quiet for a moment. Derek was a real gem, I thought. Then he said he wanted to tell Trina that he and I were going to live together. Perhaps that would force her cooperation.

Two nights later, Derek phoned. He had talked with Trina. She wasn't pleased. He said, "She wants to meet you. She figures if we all see each other face to face, I'll be able to choose which one of you I really want."

"Will you be able to choose?" I asked.

"I won't choose. I want you both, and I'm optimistic. Can we come by your place tonight?"

I agreed, but after hanging up the phone shock waves shot through my body. What had I done? Was this girl really coming to my apartment? I had yelled at her on the phone but I had never actually expected to see her face. Was she crazy? Was I? Would she bring a gun, a knife? Was she big or small? Could she fight? Why should we meet at my apartment? Why not someplace more neutral? What did she really want, anyway? I began to panic. Should I fix my hair? Would she try to outdress me? What would Derek do? Would he hug her? Would he kiss me when I opened the door? Where would we sit? Oh, no!

When I opened the door to my apartment, I saw Derek standing there humbly, wearing dress slacks, a nice shirt, and shoes. He looked me squarely in the eye, unafraid and serious. I turned my neck a quarter of an inch and saw a woman I knew must be Trina. She didn't look anything like I had pictured. She was beautiful. I had always assumed that I was prettier than her. I was wrong. She was very dark-skinned with lovely, jet-black hair. She had it nicely combed into a French roll with curls on the side. She had on a light, long black cashmere coat. Her nails were perfectly done in a French manicure. Around her neck dangled a gold chain with a crucifix on it. She had a fine, black leather Coach pocketbook. I cleared my throat and invited her and Derek into the living room. I sat on a chair. Derek sat on the couch. Trina said, "No, thanks, I'll stand up."

"So . . ." I said with confidence, "where do we start?" Derek began by saying, "I'll start. This is a situation that is very painful to me. But I've handled it the best way I know how. That's honestly. But it seems when a man takes a strong and honest stand, there is always opposition, which has led many men to take the easy way out and lie. Now Trina, I love you . . ."

My heart fluttered. I was uncomfortable but I sat like a proud and impassive hostess. I wondered what Trina thought of me. Now that we were inside and her fine coat was open, I could see that she was thin and somewhat flat-chested. I found myself thinking that while her face was pretty, I had the voluptuous body of a woman. Still, she was very feminine in her bearing, the way she stood, the way she held her hands. I had always wanted to appear feminine. Unfortunately, I found that being aggressive, planning rallies, and building schools had left me a little less ladylike than I desired to be. Our hair was the same length. Hers was better groomed. I calmed my fears down by telling myself, of course she looked better: she had plenty of time to work on her appearance because she had no brain.

Meanwhile, Derek was saying: ". . . Trina, you have always been there for me. You're the house that always welcomes me. You know that, and I have told her that, too . . ." Trina stood proudly holding on to her pocketbook and Derek showered her with compliments. Then Derek changed the topic. He was staring at me. "But I also love her. She is everything that I've ever wanted in a woman. She's intelligent, political, and, as you can see, Trina, she's also beautiful like you. What I want to know is if we can work this out? You are two people who I love, at war with one another. It does not make me happy. For some men this would be a hell of an ego trip. I don't think they realize how difficult this is when the issue is love and real concern. But I'm prepared to handle this."

Silence fell on the room. I looked at Trina. Her face was frozen. I imagined that it took all her strength to hold it like that. She refused to speak. So I said, "You don't know me, Trina, and I don't blame you for being upset. Believe me, if I thought there were some better way for us as African women in this country to get by and get along, I'd tell you. But this is the ugly predicament we find ourselves in. As a sister I love you even though the only thing we have ever done is fight. Now, I care for Derek and so do you. I believe we can share fifty-fifty. I'm willing to work it out. I'm willing to get to know you if you're willing to get to know me."

Trina was clenching her teeth. She put her thin hand on her hip and said, "Get up, Derek! Let's go. Get me out of here."

Derek stood up and said, "Trina, we're not finished talking."

Trina walked up to Derek slowly swaying her little behind with her long pretty finger pointing at him, "Derek, you listen to me. I love you. This bitch is crazy. What does she mean 'she cares for you.' I love you. You are coming home with me. You two ask me what I want? What I expect? I want ONE HUNDRED PERCENT, ONE HUNDRED PERCENT! You know why, Derek? Because that's what I gave to you! Do you love me, Derek?"

"I already told you that."

"Well then, put your coat on—we're leaving here. We're going home and we'll pretend that this whole thing never happened. That we never ever laid eyes on this African bitch!"

"Trina, I can't allow you to disrespect her like that. She's a beautiful woman, a real leader. Everyone in our community respects her and you should, too."

Trina twisted up her lips and said, "Derek, this is the last time I'm gonna say it: Let's go home, right now."

I got up from the couch. I was burning up inside but I had a weird kind of respect for Trina's persistence. But I didn't like her calling me a bitch. There was no need for me to fight her physically, we were both too old for that. Besides, I figured I had the advantage anyway. After all, this was her man. He was in love with me. He was standing inside my apartment telling her that he loved me. I had never seen the inside of her apartment! So I said, "Look, Trina: I can see that you're hurting. I don't want to hurt anybody. You and Derek can go. Be happy together. I just want one thing. I'd like to talk to Derek alone before the two of you leave here. Just for five minutes and you-all won't be seeing me anymore."

I really didn't know why I was making this request. I suppose it was because as I watched Derek go about each phase of our relationship being honest, putting himself on the line, and looking out for my feelings and interests, I had come to have a deep respect for him. I wanted to say good-bye. I could see that juggling two women was too much of a strain. But Trina did not care about my problems. She said in a voice that sounded more like a mother than a girlfriend, "Derek, come now." He said, "Here, take the keys and get in the car. I'll be out in five minutes." She stormed out of the living room and down the corridor. I gave Derek a hug, and said, "We tried. It's not gonna work. It will be easier for me to get over this than for her. So I'll bow out, leave it alone."

He looked at me as though the whole thing was tearing him apart. He gave me a kiss. Just as he got the words "good-bye" out of his mouth we heard a loud crash. We went to the window. Trina was in Derek's car trying to drive away. But his car was a stick shift, which she couldn't operate. So she had crashed into a street sign. We ran down the stairs and out the door. There was glass all over the front steps. Apparently she had broken the glass to the outside door of my building. She had the car moving again. It was jerking wildly as she attempted to use the clutch. Within seconds it just shut off. She jumped out of the car and started honking the horn like a madwoman. People from the block came to their windows. Some people came outside. When she saw the audience she started screaming, "She doesn't love you. What did you do to him to turn him against me? You must have sucked his dick. That's right, everybody, she sucked my man's dick. She sucked my man's dick."

By now I was ready to fight. She ran up to the steps where we were standing surrounded by the glass, looking stupefied. She tried to swing her pocketbook at me while she cursed me out loudly. Derek jumped in front of me and grabbed her. He held her, then picked her up. He carried her to the car. She fought him. He had to struggle with her to get her in the seat. Once he got her in, he ran to the driver's side in an attempt to drive away. She jumped out and started charging toward me. Finally, after nearly a half hour of the two of them wrestling, I watched as they drove their dented car down the street and around the corner.

A couple of days later, Derek called to tell me he had spoken with his father and told him the entire story. His father had said that Trina was a spoiled, selfish middle-class manipulator. He had always felt that way about her. Trina was empty-headed and reminded him of his ex-wife. He told Derek he thought that it was great that he had discovered a woman like me, that we had a lot more in common, and an opportunity to challenge each other to grow. He advised Derek to leave Trina and her silly games. If Trina wanted him, Derek's father had added, then she would straighten out her attitude and cooperate.

Derek soon showed up at my place with his belongings. We sat down and talked. He wanted us to live together, but he made it clear that he didn't consider himself to be leaving Trina. He was just waiting for her to settle into the arrangement.

Living together was fun. It was like being back in college. Derek was my roommate. We went everywhere together. He was fascinated with my meetings, lectures, rallies. We even attended one of the entertainment parties that I usually liked to avoid. Trina continued to harass us. She called my apartment so much that I had to keep the phone off the hook most of the time. This was bad for my business and annoying to boot. The more I ignored her, however, the more determined she became. She started calling prominent black leaders in our community, telling them how I as a young leader was misusing my leadership powers and destroying love relationships. She asked them to call me and discipline me for stealing her man of nine years. Eventually, I received a call from a world-renowned elder historian. He told me he had received a call from Trina. He asked me what was going on. I explained the entire situation to him. He asked, "Well, what kind of a young man would date a woman for nine years without marrying her?" I responded, "A dysfunctional one, but that's all the younger generation of women has to choose from." He explained that polygamy was a complicated system. He said that it was only utilized by the African elite out of greed. The preferred African practice was one man, one woman. I told him I also favored one man, one woman, but it just hadn't happened that way for me or any of my girlfriends. He told me that he didn't want to get in my business but that I should be careful because Trina seemed distraught yet determined. It could become dangerous.

In fact, Trina seemed increasingly out of control. She would call my apartment until she finally reached Derek and say she had a flat tire and was stranded. Could Derek come and fix it? She would call and say she had a bad case of the flu and couldn't get to the pharmacy. Could Derek bring her some medicine? She would say that she lost the key to her apartment and was locked out. Could Derek come with the emergency key she gave him? Derek would simply remind me that I had promised that he and Trina could maintain relations. Then he would kiss me and go.

Finally, I made a decision. I was going to tell Derek that he couldn't see Trina anymore. I would explain that if we were in an honest, open relationship where there was no resistance it would be fine to see Trina. Because then we could agree on a structure, a system, a schedule. But since Trina refused to admit she was sharing, she caused disruptions and chaos in our household, creating crisis after crisis. This meant that there was always stress. I was a nervous wreck. I wasn't happy.

Derek said he had never agreed nor intended to leave Trina. He said he would have yet another talk with her. Needless to say I didn't like his response. So I plotted. The next day when he got home from work I was nowhere to be found. I had taken off to my friend the entertainer's house. I had deliberately locked Derek out of our apartment. He didn't have his own key because usually we were together. I knew Derek was jealous of the entertainer. After all, he was a hip-hop star. I stayed at his place until midnight. When I got home, Derek was sitting on the front step. We had our first serious argument. He didn't want me to go over to the entertainer's or any other man's house. He wanted me for himself. I told him that's exactly how I felt, so we should have a one-on-one relationship, no Trina, no entertainers, just the two of us. He didn't want to but he gave in against the threat of me seeing other men.

For the next month, Derek and I held each other hostage to our new agreement. He didn't trust me. I didn't trust him. Because he and Trina were so close, I knew he'd probably try to sneak and see her. He knew if he messed up, I would run right down the block to the entertainer's house.

Derek soon became depressed. He seemed out of focus and disinterested in our relationship. He stopped tongue-kissing me. Then the sex became less and less frequent. When I asked him what was wrong, he would answer "nothing." I started to feel he was just going through the motions. This was no good for me because one of the things that had attracted me to him in the first place was that he was totally fascinated with me. Now that I seemingly had gotten what I wanted, I was still unhappy.

I called one of my girlfriends to discuss the problem. I felt a little guilty because I had not let her in on what was going on. But Sheri was cool. She was the only one of my girlfriends I would ask because she was the most mature and the least likely to kiss my ass. I needed a reality check. Sheri was politically minded, a graduate of Howard University, and a big women's rights type of female. So I took the day off. Sheri and I met at a quiet little Thai restaurant where we could have the privacy we needed and hear ourselves think at the same time. I took a deep breath and told her the whole story, every detail. When I finished, I took a sip from my water glass to beat back the dry-mouth. I looked up and waited for her to say something. It was slow coming. She held up her right hand and spread her fingers wide apart. She knitted her eyebrows together and peered at me while the flame from the little candle on the table danced on her face. Finally, she said, "I thought you told me you were over him?"

"Over who?" I asked, confused by her response.

"Chance!" she said sternly.

"What does Chance have to do with it?" I asked.

"Chance broke your heart. Now the rest of the entire world has to suffer, huh? You're losing it, girl. I've always respected you but I can see that you're losing it. How could you be so cold-hearted to that poor girl Trina?"

"Poor girl!" I raised my voice. "Her man came to me. I didn't come to him. I was just trying to be honest. The sharing thing was a political decision on my part because of the geno-cide, the man-shortage problem."

"Bullshit!" Sheri said. "The sharing thing doesn't make any sense. It's not even logical. It's unlike you to be illogical. You're saying that you know these men out here are dysfunc-tional?"

"Yes," I said with certainty.

"So you're asking a dysfunctional man who cannot properly manage and conduct one successful relationship with one woman, to conduct two relationships with two women? It's impossible. If you can't handle and love and support one, how can you handle and love and support two?"

I sucked my teeth at her. I wanted an honest opinion but now I wanted to take back my story and make her disappear. But it was impossible to shut her up. I should have known. She continued, "You're just on some kind of power trip."

"No, I'm not that kind of person. You know that."

"Then why do you emphasize 'I didn't come to him. He came to me'? I'll tell you why. Because you're used to being in control. Chance not only broke your heart, he destroyed your ego. So you go find what seems to be a nice brother who you can lead around by the nose, and you make puppets out of him and his girlfriend. It's cruel. You don't even love him."

"How do you know?" I asked.

"Because no sister in love is gonna sit down and discuss sharing the love of her life. That's why Trina can't do it. You can do it 'cause it's just some kind of game to you."

"You make this Trina girl sound like some kind of angel. If you knew her maybe you wouldn't be sticking up for her."

"Oh, no, I don't think she's an angel. She doesn't have to be. She sounds to me like a regular sister. The kind you and I want to educate and empower. You act like just because she doesn't know as much as you, she doesn't deserve to have her man to herself. For nine years she was with him. Come on! That's her man no matter how appealing you may be to him."

I started to feel ashamed of myself. But I just couldn't give in, so I searched my mind for good points. "If it wasn't me, Sheri, it would have been some other woman. Even he admits that."

"Yeah, well, he needs to resolve some issues himself. He's either got to find an effective way of sharing information with and educating her, or he's got to leave her and find another woman. What he can't do is show up on your doorstep with all his problems and his little broken-down relationship that he carries around with him like a security blanket. Even if he is a nice person, it's just not fair."

"Sheri, what about me? What do I get? What do I end up with besides back-to-back lonely nights?"

"Girl, you and I will find strong men. But it will take time. They're scarce. But in the meantime, girl, you can't get desperate. Desperate women settle for anything. They lower their standards and all the dogs come wandering in."

That night when Derek came home from work his eyes were sad and distant. I didn't know where to start, but I felt we needed to talk. Before I could even begin, he said he needed to drive his grandmother to his aunt's house. Was that simply a lame excuse to go see Trina? He said it wasn't. I asked him again. He denied it. But I felt it in my bones. I asked him if I could come with him. He reminded me that his grandmother didn't care for me. But I remembered that he had once told me that she and Trina were always tight. Derek, the man who tried to have an honest relationship, lied to me that night. Derek, the man who could never leave a woman, left me and all of his belongings that night and returned to Trina.

It was for the best.

Listen Up!
(Straighten It Out)

What are the roots of problems in today's relationships between African men and women? That question—and the quest for its answer—is the central issue of this book. The question is easy to ask. The answer is hard to find. But the search is essential. Too many of us are in pain; too many of us are lonely. Sex is everywhere while true love falls victim to the turmoil of our fight merely to survive.

Racism is a disease. It affects whites as well as blacks. It may even be a kind of mental illness. But the effect on black people is greater because we are the victims of it. The effect on whites is severe because it deforms their thinking and gives them a distorted picture of the world. But because the economics of racism is inarguably in their favor, most whites learn to live with it, even to deny it.

But we cannot do so. Racism has turned our communities into war zones where we are dying every day. It is black-on-black hate, created by racism and white supremacy, that is killing us. Black people killing black people. Can African male-female relationships survive in America? Not if black-on-black love is dead. Not if we are still too scared to admit there is a problem while our families fall apart. Not if our young men continue to refer to young women as "bitches," or our young women refer to young men as "motherfuckers," or all of us refer to each other as "niggas." It is a sad measure of our profound contempt for each other and of our thoroughgoing self-loathing that we continue to persist in this ugly practice.

Listen up! You've read the book, now it's time for the sermon. My message is simple. Our lives are hard. Here are some rules to love by:

Parents are the most influential people on the planet. Even before a child is born, it receives messages and emotions from the mother who carries it. How the father relates to and treats the mother will be felt by the child even in the womb. For example, if the father leaves the mother and she must endure her nine months of pregnancy alone, the child will also receive messages of depression, anxiety, and abandonment. If the mother hates the father, the child will absorb messages of hate and anger. Make no mistake: Everything the mother does, says, eats, and feels will affect the development of the child, its intelligence, and its emotions.

It is important for all children to have two parents—a mother and a father. The absence of either will affect the child. The consequences may not be apparent for many years. Perhaps not until that child attempts to have a relationship of her or his own. But if she had no experience of a father, then she will have had no sound criteria by which to judge a man she might choose to marry. She may also give too much of herself to a man precisely because she had no father and now values the presence of a man more than she values herself. If a son is raised with no father, he will lack the criteria for understanding what it is to be a man. Instead, he may look toward the guys in the street. Moreover, if a young boy has no father who takes responsibility for his wife and family, then he will grow up to believe that he needn't take such responsibility either. Soon a cycle of abandonment is established. It will be almost impossible to break.

Parents must understand that children are smarter than they think. They see and watch everything. It is bad to be a woman who has a lot of men in and out of her home. It is bad to be a father who has a lot of women in and out of his home. A carousel of lovers causes a child to lose respect for the parent. It also causes a child to get a warped idea of what a true relationship or marriage is. Instead of holding out stability as a worthy goal for a healthy family, such behavior strongly suggests that life is just a sexual merry-go-round. Remember: Children will do as you do, not as you say.

If you live in a dangerous neighborhood, and the majority of Africans in America do, you must take the time to explain each and every detail of your life to your child. It does not matter whether you live in the inner city or in the suburbs.

The facts of life must be discussed, as openly and as candidly as possible. Your child must not be taken by surprise by anything he or she might encounter. Prepare your child to survive.

Do not assume that the public schools will properly educate your children. You must teach your child how to use the library. Make sure your child knows where the local bookstore is. Teach your children to question the things they are taught. Encourage them to search out answers for themselves. Take nothing for granted. The education that you give your children out of school is as important—if not more so—than the education they will receive in school.

Welfare is designed to keep you trapped. We must abandon the notion of welfare as a way of life, or even as a way to survive. At best, welfare is something that may help us in a small way for a short period of time. It is up to you to investigate other social programs, both public and private. Any program that offers genuine job training or helps you to develop employable skills is worth taking seriously. Any program that offers you an opportunity to return to school or to start your own business is worth pursuing. Women on welfare have a unique opportunity to raise their children, to spend time teaching them, to enjoy them in ways denied to most working mothers. Use this precious time wisely.

Dark-skinned people are looked down upon in America—and not only by white people. Many of us are considered—even by ourselves—to be ugly. The dark woman is insulted and often ignored. So is the black man. Our children are often teased mercilessly, often by other children of color who have absorbed the twisted values of white culture. Parents must teach their children to love themselves, to love the color of their skins. Dark is beautiful. Racism and its terrible effects must be understood and overcome so that our children do not internalize the enmity they may well encounter as they grow up.

Pride in the bodies God has given us is extremely important. Especially for women. Men will often tell you there is something physically wrong with you. They may complain about the size of your breasts, the shape of your butt, or the length of your hair. Often such complaints are merely a way for men to divert attention away from themselves and their problems. Your main goal, which you should never forget, is simply to do what is necessary to be healthy and fit. You should resist the temptation to alter your natural self by artificially increasing the size of your breasts, flattening your butt, or reducing the thickness of your lips. Obviously, if you are extremely overweight, you may have a health problem for which you should seek a doctor's advice. In any event, if you meet a man who keeps complaining after you've begun a relationship, perhaps it's time to move on rather than drive yourself crazy trying to change the body that God gave you.

Men who vanish from time to time are probably guilty of doing something wrong. Don't make excuses for them. They will make plenty of excuses for themselves. If you can't independently verify their alibis, if you have the feeling inside that they are lying, go with your gut intuition. Remember: Men will lie. If you let him lie to you with impunity and without consequence, he will do it over and over again. If your man lies to you and you forgive him, give him a very hard time. If he loves you, he will remember the hard time and may not feel it's worth lying to you again. If he does it again, leave. No relationship can survive without mutual respect.

It's important for women to have a healthy definition of themselves. You should not look to the men you meet, or to your girlfriends, for your sense of yourself, your self-esteem, your role as a woman. You should cultivate your mind, spirit, body, heart, and soul. Doing so will make you even more attractive and increase your intelligence. Hard work will be rewarded, oftentimes in ways that can't be foreseen early on. Be compassionate and loving. Keep your mind balanced. Demand respect and courteous treatment. If you act only in a sexual way, you will be treated like a whore. A man may love your sex, but he will probably not love you, respect your mind, or your spirit, heart, or soul. If you only concentrate on matters of the mind, a man may respect your intelligence but he will not consider you a sensual person. If you only devote yourself to questions of the body, a man may well respond to the sexuality you offer up to him, but he is more than likely to abuse you, to take it, and to run. Remember: Even though women say they should be able to wear anything they want, we forget at our peril that we live in an extremely sexual, dangerous, and disrespectful world. You cannot afford to act stupid; society is savage. Act smart: Don't end up crying and hurt.

Men, for their part, must learn how to properly look at a woman. Hollywood and Madison Avenue encourage men only to focus on women as physical objects. Or even particular portions of a woman's anatomy—legs, breasts, ass, and so on. Men must begin to look at every woman whom they intend to have sex with as the potential mother of his child. They must learn to distrust women who give their sex away. Women who do so obviously do not respect themselves. Sex should be beautiful—for both men and women. But it is not something to be indulged in lightly. Like drinking, it can be an addiction. We must exercise discipline over our desires. Sex is fun, but sex is dangerous. Be careful . . . and be prepared.

Women, like men, play games. Many men are locked up in prison today because they took some silly woman seriously. Some women get off on the drama of seeing several men fight over them. Perhaps it fulfills some perverse fantasy. But men make a terrible mistake when they throw their lives away on women who were never really theirs to begin with.

Women should not date a girlfriend's man or ex-man. It will ruin the friendship between you and your girlfriend. Some men enjoy pumping their ego up by having sex with their girlfriend's friends. They create bitter wars between the women. He plays you against her. He tells you negative and ugly things about her. Then he turns around and tells her ugly and negative things about you. Both of you stupidly fight each other thinking you're the one he really wants. The truth: He doesn't want either of you. Probably he even has a third girl stashed somewhere else. He finds it exciting to see the two of you fight over him. Don't do it. He will make a fool out of you.

Don't tell your girlfriends how your man makes you feel in bed. Don't brag about the size of his penis or the way he does it to you. Your girlfriends will become jealous and they will screw your man.

Do not go anywhere with a man you do not know. If you do, you may be hurt, or even killed. Doing so permits a man to regard you as an idiot only to be sexed and thrown out.

Always meet a man in a public place. Find out his telephone number. Find out where he lives. Meet his mother. And his father, if possible. Meet some of his friends. Find out what he wants out of life. Find out if what he wants and what you want are the same things. Find out what he likes to do in his spare time. Find out his talents and skills. Ask him if he reads. Find out where he works if he works. Visit him at his job. If he goes to school, visit him there. In the beginning of your relationship, bring someone along with you to meet him. Insist that he meet your family—your mother and father, your brothers and sisters. Make sure your family knows who he is, where he works, and where he lives. This is critical!

Do not mess with a married man at all, ever, for any reason. It does not matter what he tells you. He may say he's getting a divorce. Wait until he gets one before you go anywhere with him, before you touch him, before you kiss him, even before you have a lot of conversation with him. He will tell you he doesn't love his wife. Or he will tell you he does love his wife, but not the same way he loves you. He will tell you that the two of you can be together forever. He will tell you that he's only with his wife because he loves his children. Then he will say he doesn't love her. He will tell you he hasn't slept with his wife for months. No matter what he tells you, don't go for it. Do not mess with a married man. He will take your sex and go back to his wife. You will end up crying and in pain. Moreover, by messing with a married man you will be helping to destroy a family, an African family, which already is struggling to survive. To steal away with the father of someone else's children is wrong. You would not want it done to you once you get married. Remember: Anything a married man tells you is a lie because, after all, he already promised God that he would honor his marriage. If he lied to God, the preacher, the state, and his wife, he will certainly lie to you.

Do not believe that same-sex love will solve your problems. You can be hurt in any human relationship. Leaving your man because you have experienced pain, only to sleep with another woman will not guarantee that you will be treated more kindly, with greater tenderness, and with more respect. Women are abusers just like men. Confront your inner confusion before you enter into any relationship.

Beware of gangsters and macho men of all kinds. Question a society that prizes and rewards men who are seemingly "tough," but refuse to deal with the responsibilities of leading their families, respecting their wives, teaching their children. A successful black man is someone who has a relationship with his God. Who knows he has boundaries and guidelines to live by. Who tries to live a moral life, a good life, who understands that he must sometimes refuse to do things that are so hurtful that they violate the spiritual principles on which he bases his life. A real man respects his women. A real man claims his children, serves as their father and provider. When a real man has difficulty providing for his family, he will exhaust every ethical and positive means of supporting them. A real man seeks to gain mastery over his inner rage and desires. This means he resists enslavement to crack, alcohol, sex, power, or anything that corrupts the soul. A real man—even in bad times—has life-affirming goals. He makes plans. When some of his plans fail, he refuses to be defeated. He picks up and starts again. His will must be indomitable; his spirit unbroken. This is a lot to ask. But he cannot afford to do less if we are to survive and flourish as a people. He must rise to the challenge of our times.

It is possible to use your power as a woman to take a man who is doing wrong and help him to become a stronger person with a new outlook on life. It is easier to try to help a brother before you give him any sex. Show him alternative routes. If you need information, go to a bookstore. There are books on every topic. If you cannot afford to buy them, go to the library. Help steer him in the right direction. Learn how to be forceful without arrogance, without talking down. You will be surprised how such an approach works. Have patience. We sisters overlook good men in our community every day. Instead, too many of us fall for the dangerous men—men who will break our hearts, and sometimes our bodies. Avoid them like the plague.

When a woman becomes desperate for companionship and love it is obvious to everyone around her. She thinks she's fooling people but she is not. Desperate women can be pretty, unattractive, working women, or college graduates. It does not matter. Loneliness does not discriminate. Nor does desperation. A desperate woman tries anything to get a man. She will start wearing provocative clothes that expose her breasts, butt, legs, thighs, shoulders. She will start dating men who she knows are not compatible, but she will do so anyway just for the company. She may date a man who physically or mentally abuses her. She will refuse to leave him—even though she inwardly knows she should—because she's desperate and scared she'll be alone again and will have to stand on her own two feet. A desperate woman will steal someone else's man and make excuses for it. She will delude herself into believing someone else's man wants her because she is the better choice. The truth is she can't find anyone else and has no confidence that she ever will. Such a woman may try desperate tricks like telling a man she's on birth control when she isn't, and so gets deliberately pregnant. Desperate women are capable of anything. Men: Beware of desperate women!

I believe in God. I believe God is spirit and the power of God lives in the soul of every boy and girl, man and woman. The reason why most of us don't feel we have the power of God inside us is because we are not taught that it is there from childhood. Nor are we taught how to use it. We live our lives wondering why we do not have focus and understanding. We wonder why things are the way they are. Some of us wonder why things and conditions don't change.

Many young people say there is no God, because if there was things wouldn't be as bad as they are. They give up on life. They neglect the power they have within themselves. When things get worse, they say, "See, I told you there wasn't any God." But things will continue to get worse if we don't find a simple way to reach the God in ourselves. God gave us human will. Thus, we have the power to control each and every action we take. God may say, "Do not steal." But people every day decide to steal. That's human will at work. When we make bad decisions, we suffer consequences. Sometimes we blame God for the sins we ourselves committed. We blame God for the conditions we find ourselves in. Or we blame the racist system we live under—and we are not entirely wrong to do so. But God gave us minds with which to think. Remember: No one will save us but ourselves. Neither God nor white people will do so.

But first we must learn to respect ourselves. That is the test we must pass, the promise we must make to each other, the challenge of all of our lives.

Acknowledgments

To be isolated is a hell of a thing. It helps you to appreciate so much more the few warm embraces you experience. My sincere thanks goes first and foremost to God, the mother and father of Creation. I am grateful to all of my people, past and present, who have made a conscious effort to improve life. I want to acknowledge Robert Scheer for his generosity in steering me to Steve Wasserman, my editor and a good human being. I want to thank Steve for having high integrity and keeping my words as I wrote them. Lastly, I thank Times Books and Random House for providing a forum—at a time when nobody else would.

For those of my readers who would like to write me, I invite them to do so directly, at the following address:

Sister Souljah
208 E. 51st St.
Suite 2270
New York, NY 10022

ALSO AVAILABLE FROM

Vintage Books

FATHERALONG
A Meditation on Fathers and Sons, Race and Society
by John Edgar Wideman
"An important, moving, large-spirited book." —*Washington Post Book World*

John Edgar Wideman examines the tragedy of race and the gulf it cleaves
between black fathers and black sons through the lens of his own relations
with his remote father, producing a memoir that belongs alongside the
classics of Richard Wright and Malcolm X.
African-American Studies/Autobiography
0-679-73751-0

THE FIRE NEXT TIME
by James Baldwin
"One of the few genuinely indispensable American writers."
—*Saturday Review*

At once a powerful evocation of his early life in Harlem and a disturbing examination of the consequences of racial injustice—to both the individual
and the body politic—*The Fire Next Time* stands as one of the essential
works of our literature.
Literature/African-American Studies
0-679-74472-X

INVISIBLE MAN
by Ralph Ellison
"The greatest American novel in the second half of the twentieth century
. . . the classic representation of American black experience."
—R. W. B. Lewis

Winner of the National Book Award, *Invisible Man* is the searing portrait of
a black man's search for personal identity in modern American society.
Fiction/Literature
0-679-73276-4

MAKES ME WANNA HOLLER
A Young Black Man in America
by Nathan McCall

"So honest, so well-written, so powerful that it will leave you shaken and educated."   —*USA Today*

In this outspoken and fiercely eloquent memoir, *Washington Post* reporter Nathan McCall tells the story of his passage from the street and prison yard to the newsroom of one of America's most prestigious papers.

Autobiography/African-American Studies
0-679-74070-8

RACE MATTERS
by Cornel West

"Cornel West is one of the most authentic, brilliant, prophetic and healing voices in America today."   —Marian Wright Edelman

Bold in its thought and written with a redemptive passion grounded in the traditions of the African-American church, *Race Matters* is a work that ranges from the crisis in black leadership to the myths surrounding black sexuality, from affirmative action to black-Jewish relations.

African-American Studies/Current Affairs
0-679-74986-1

SELECTED POEMS
by Langston Hughes

The poems in this collection, chosen by Hughes himself shortly before his death in 1967, celebrate the experience of invisible men and women—portraying that experience in a voice that blended the spoken with the sung, that turned poetic lines into the phrases of jazz and blues. They spanned the range from the lyric to the polemic, ringing out "wonder and pain and terror . . . and the bone of life."

Poetry/Literature
0-394-40438-6

Available at your local bookstore, or call toll-free to order:
1-800-793-2665 (credit cards only).